ALTERNATIVE DELIVERY SYSTEMS

Edited by

Norbert Goldfield, MD
Medical Director
CIGNA Corporation
Hartford, Connecticut

Seth B. Goldsmith, ScD, JD
Professor
Program in Health Policy and Management
University of Massachusetts
School of Public Health
Amherst, Massachusetts

A collection of articles from
Journal of Ambulatory Care Management

AN ASPEN PUBLICATION®
Aspen Publishers, Inc.

1987

Rockville, Maryland
Royal Tunbridge Wells

Library of Congress Cataloging-in-Publication Data

Alternative delivery systems.

"An Aspen publication."
"A collection of articles from Journal of ambulatory care management."
Includes bibliographies and index.
1. Ambulatory medical care — Management. 2. Health maintenance organization — Administration. 3. Ambulatory medical care — United States — Management. 4. Health maintenance organizations — United States — Administration. I. Goldfield, Norbert. II. Goldsmith, Seth B. III. Journal of ambulatory care management. [DNLM: 1. Ambulatory Care — trends — United States — collected works. 2. Health Maintenance Organizations — United States — collected works. 3. Insurance, Health — trends — United States — collected works. W 275 AA1 A39]
RA411.A37 1986 362.1′2 86–14640
ISBN: 0–87189–615–X

Editorial Services: Marsha Davies

Library of Congress Catalog Card Number: 86–14640
ISBN: 0–87189–615–X

Printed in the United States of America

1 2 3 4 5

Table of Contents

Preface

The term alternative delivery system (ADS) is a misnomer. ADSs are not only becoming the mainstream, but traditional health insurance programs are building in "alternative" features into standard indemnity products. Rather than trumpeting the arrival of alternative health care delivery systems, the editors would like to highlight the manifold challenges ADSs face as they take over the traditional health insurance/delivery system.

- The most successful alternative delivery systems will be those that become "supermeds." By 1995, approximately 20 supermeds will control the majority of the health care system in the United States. Even though HUMANA lost $27,000,000 in its first quarter foray into the health insurance market, all successful health care players will need to provide traditional health insurance as an option. Conversely, indemnity providers are rapidly entering into the HMO/PPO/IPA field. Finally, many of the already large providers are rapidly expanding. In July 1986, Maxicare, Inc., one of the largest IPA providers in the country, acquired Health America, Inc.; itself a very large IPA deliverer.
- What is the balance between quality versus cost? Though health care researchers and physicians appreciate the lack of proven efficacy for many medical treatments, the perception appropriately persists that as one limits access, quality may suffer. Because of rapid expansion, for the next few years alternative delivery systems will focus on methods of containing costs through limits on access to the health care system (e.g., visits to subspecialists only through primary care gatekeepers, specific hospital contracts for inpatient care, etc.). However, as cost differentials begin to narrow between private health care networks, quality of care will become

increasingly important as a differentiating factor. Though health services researchers are more able to measure the quality of health care, it will become increasingly complex as the health care system moves into alternative delivery sites. For example, it is easier to measure the quality of care provided in a staff model HMO than that delivered in an IPA.

A minor, yet important, issue is that as quality becomes more important more privately held companies will emerge and attempt to market themselves as having the best quality of care measurement system. Unfortunately, many of these private concerns have not published any data to support their claim, and as a consequence, are relying on hype to achieve their marketing niche.

- Significant innovations will appear on the access to health care issue. For example, some supermeds are already offering health care as part of either flexible care or flexible benefits policies. In some parts of the country, individuals are able to join an HMO for their routine care, and, for an extra fee, can participate in a wrap-around option that permits them to go to a fee-for-service provider for unusual health care problems. Over and above the continuing efforts to more precisely measure quality, it is options such as these that will be touted as guaranteeing quality. Flexible benefits provide the ultimate choice for the individual as he or she is able to allocate, not only among health care choices, but to spread them throughout the employee benefit pie of vacation, day care, retirement, etc. Now that's an alternative delivery system!
- As the supermeds become more powerful, the traditional bulwark of the health care power pie—the medical profession—will continue to see its power ebb. Both the increasing physician surplus and the ability of the supermeds to control a large portion of the health care system will narrow the presence of the traditional fee-for-service sector. Even if the preponderance of patients will be served in an IPA situation in which the physician can see his patient in a private setting, increased use of utilization, cost, and quality controls will become ever more present. Though the medical profession will not be as preeminent as it has in the past, it is the editors' firm belief that active involvement of individual practitioners/medical profession and the successful management of the physician-executive relationship will provide a key to the success of health care delivery organizations.
- Though already discussed in general terms, access to care for the un/under insured continues to increase in importance. The gains that low income individuals made in the 1960s are slowly becoming eroded in the 1980s. Innovative approaches to health care for this

group of people are necessary. Simply spending money is not the answer. Studies such as the recently published work by John Ware in the *Lancet* indicating that low income individuals, corrected for health status, have poorer health status than middle income individuals, need to be followed up with studies designing interventions to raise the health status of low income individuals. The importance of health care to the poor and underinsured is not only an issue important in itself, but one which can threaten the continued privatization of health care services. Simply, if the supermeds are not willing to pick up the challenge, and provide the care or encourage the federal government to assume its appropriate responsibility, regulatory restrictions eventually will be placed on the supermeds. The choice is ours.

The essays in this book address many specific aspects of the previously listed trends in health care delivery. The essays fall into two categories: future directions in health care and how-to-achieve-it-models if that is the strategic direction for your business. Ambulatory care has come into its own as the critical–ever-expanding piece of the health care pie. We hope you find this collection useful in your ambulatory care endeavors.

Norbert Goldfield, MD
Seth B. Goldsmith, ScD, JD

Alternative delivery systems: health care on the move

Paul M. Ellwood, Jr., MD
President
Paul Ellwood & Associates
Consulting Director
InterStudy
Excelsior, Minnesota

OVER THE PAST 15 years, in attempting to stimulate market forces in the health industry, the author has coined a number of terms to describe competitive approaches to the delivery and financing of medical care—most notably, *health maintenance organization (HMO), preferred provider organization (PPO), and Medical Staff Hospital (MeSH) joint ventures.* The organizations that these terms describe are often referred to together as *alternative delivery systems (ADSs)* to distinguish them from the traditional ways of buying and selling medical care. Although the ADS label has stuck, it has now become a bit misleading: Alternative delivery systems are no longer alternative; they are fast becoming the mainstream.

InterStudy data show that total HMO enrollment in 480 plans hit 21.1 million as of December 1985. More than four million people joined health plans last year. The result was a 25.7% increase in HMO enrollment, which is an all-time record. If enrollment were to continue to grow at this rate per year throughout the next decade, by the mid-1990s HMO-type health plans would be providing medical care to more than 50% of the United States population. Although health care providers have been known to succumb to self-fulfilling prophecy, these numbers have a ring of inevitability about them, as confirmed by the actions of physicians.

Physicians have been increasingly drawn into HMOs. In 1985, the number of physicians participating in health plans exceeded 85,000—enough to serve about 30% of the United States population. This proportion will increase as health plans continue to attract physicians. The trend has become for HMOs to appeal particularly to solo and small-group, fee-for-service practitioners.

Another sign of the rapid proliferation of price—competitive health plans is the extraordinary competitive activity that has recently hit previously neglected cities—places that until very recently had high hospital use and little HMO activity. For example, in June 1985, only five HMOs were serving New York City; by the end of the year, twelve additional plans were either operational or planning to enter the market.

The impact of the rapid growth of alternative delivery systems will be profound. For physicians, the effect will be to accentuate the already existing oversupply. Projections of physician supply made by the Graduate Medical Education National Advisory Committee (GMENAC) in 1980 are turning out to be almost exactly on the mark. However, due to the growth of alternative delivery systems, the projections of the number of physicians actually needed are likely to turn out to be far too high. GMENAC relied on epidemiological models and could not have anticipated the extraordinary impact of health systems that allocate resources on the basis of market forces. It now looks as though by the year 2000 the physician force will be not only too large but also highly divided. One group of physicians—those affiliated with alternative delivery systems—will have somewhere between 800 and 1,000 patients each, whereas the other group of physicians—as many as 300,000—will be handling about 300 patients each. The same phenomenon will hit hospitals: Those tied into alternative delivery systems will thrive, whereas others will be left struggling to fill their beds or will be forced out of business.

The well-documented behavior pattern of physicians and hospitals with relatively few patients is to adopt a more intensive style of medical practice and to charge higher unit fees.

The impact of the rapid growth of alternative delivery systems will be profound. For physicians, the effect will be to accentuate the already existing oversupply.

"Have-not" physicians and hospitals thus become a liability to any health organization, employer, or insurer attempting to pay for them. The oversupply of physicians and beds, coupled with the inability to subsidize underutilized practitioners and half-empty hospitals, is likely to spell the end of "pure" conventional health insurance.

The revolutionary changes now underway in health care really have no stopping point: Virtually everyone who is insured will soon be drawn into some kind of price-competitive alternative delivery system—simply because no one will be able to afford the have-not physicians and hospitals. This point will likely be reached within the next 10 to 15 years.

That this is happening is clear in the emergence of what is now called "triple option" or "managed care" insurance products. These products make available to health care purchasers a package of HMO, PPO, and indemnity insurance for a single premium, which is experience rated and in some cases may even be guaranteed to increase no more than the Consumer Price Index for several years. Through managed care, the insurer is able to capture an entire account and to distribute risk by channelling the worst risks into the most managed options. One result is that the organizations serving whole accounts can grow at accelerated rates.

Within the next two decades health care delivery will be dominated by as few as eight to ten "SuperMeds"—huge national corporations that combine hospital, physician, and insurance services to provide price-competitive, comprehensive medical services. At the center of each of these SuperMeds will be a managed care system, acting to secure patients and to channel them to other components of the integrated system. SuperMeds will manage medical care by selecting the very best physicians, matching physicians to the population, and controlling health resources utilization; they will require as few as 1.9 hospital beds and 1.2 physicians for every 1,000 people for whose health they are responsible.

While in some ways the techniques for managing care resemble those of traditional group practices, some significant differences are emerging. The fledgling SuperMeds tend to disperse their physicians throughout the community; to link together independent physicians and get them to function as economic groups; to be flexible about payment arrangements, mixing prepayment, fee-for-service, and preferred provider insurance. They make extensive use of satellites—small, primary care groups of four or five physicians, easily accessible to residents and working people in a community. The extent to which the emerging systems will eventually rely on group practices or on individual physicians has not yet been decided: The trend is to use primary physicians as case managers and independent practice associations in addition to groups.

The huge care systems that are emerging have tremendous opportunities. As they become more and more the mainstream of medical care in the United States, they will have access to information on thousands of physicians diagnosing and treating millions of people. This information will provide them with unprecedented opportunities to develop superior systems of medical management and quality assurance. Once challenged on quality of care, they will soon be in the very best position to define quality and set the standards for the practice of medicine.

REFERENCE

U.S. Department of Health and Human Services. (1980). *Report to the Graduate Medical Education National Advisory Committee to the Secretary* (Vol 1, GMENAC summary report). Washington, D.C.: Government Printing Office.

Home health care: current trends and future opportunities

Connie Evashwick, ScD
President
CEA Consulting and Evaluation Associates
Los Angeles, California

THE HOME HEALTH field is burgeoning with activity.* From 1980 to 1984 the number of Medicare-certified home health agencies increased from 2,923 to 5,247 (*home health line,* 1985). The dollars spent on home health approximated $5.9 billion in 1982 and are projected to reach $18.2 billion in 1992 (Frost & Sullivan, 1983). Home infusion therapies of nutrition, antibiotic and chemotherapies have emerged as the latest applications of high technology in the home. Durable medical equipment (DME) supply to the home, formerly much ignored by health care providers, has come to the forefront of attention as an expanding and lucrative business.

In brief, the home health field is awhirl with growth, expansion, diversification, and innovation. To the administrator of an ambulatory health care

**The accelerating pace is evident: The statistics in this article that reflect 1984 data are already out of date. The basic trends continue and are moving in an exponential trajectory.*

service, this flurry of activity may be a complex bewilderment, yet one that may directly affect the operations of the freestanding or hospital-based ambulatory care program. Current issues and trends reveal implications and opportunities for administrators of ambulatory care services. Four basic services comprise the home care field (see Table 1).

MEDICARE-CERTIFIED HOME HEALTH AGENCIES

The most common type of home health agency is a Medicare-certified company that provides short-term, skilled services. Medicare has defined the required services to be skilled nursing, physical therapy, occupational therapy, speech therapy, medical social services, and home health aide care. Eligible patients are those who are being discharged from the hospital, are homebound, and require short-term nursing or physical therapy to enable them to regain independent functioning; services must be prescribed by a physician. Referrals typically come from hospital discharge planners or social workers. Care for an extended period of time or maintenance-level care, such as homemaker or personal care, is not included. Fifty to ninety percent of the clients of a typical Medicare-certified home health agency are over the age of 65. Nationally, the average patient receives 20 visits and stays in the program for 3 months.

Home health agencies bill Medicare, Medicaid, Workers' Compensation or private insurance directly on the patient's behalf. Medicare and most state programs reimburse on a cost basis, with set cost caps. Medicare-certified agencies also care for private pay and insurance patients, but such clients account for the vast majority of most agencies' business. In 1984, the national average cost of a home health visit ranged from $30 to $55, with rates as high as $65 to $100; a typical patient bill ranged from $460 to $1,500 (*home health line, 1984a*).

Medicare closely governs the operation of certified home health agencies. Staffing requirements are mandated, and the appropriateness of patient eligibility and visit norms are carefully scrutinized. The provision of other types of home care services or services provided by other disciplines is discouraged by the Medicare regulations and current reimbursement system.

The largest and oldest not-for-profit Medicare-certified home health agencies are the Visiting Nurses Associations (VNA). Until the late 1970s, the VNAs dominated the not-for-profit field. The largest national for-profit companies are Beverly Enterprises, Kelley Health Care Services, Personnel Pool of America, Upjohn Health Care Services, and Kimberly Home Health Care Inc. (*home health line, 1984c*). During the past few years, hospital-based home health agencies have mushroomed, and a variety of other organizations have entered the Medicare-certified home health arena. Beverly Enterprises and Hillhaven Home Care are among the fastest-growing proprietaries that have recently entered the Medicare field.

Table 1. Characteristics of four basic home care services

	Medicare certified home health agency	Private home care services	High technology home therapy	Durable medical equipment
Patients	Homebound; short-term with rehabilitation potential	Homebound patients requiring skilled or unskilled care	Parenteral, enteral, antibiotic, chemotherapy patients	Patients requiring short-term to indefinite use of equipment supplies at home
Services	Skilled nursing, skilled therapies, medical social work; home health aide	Skilled nursing, skilled therapies, medical social work, home health aide; unskilled homemaker, companion, live-in	Infusion therapies: parenteral, enteral, antibiotic, chemotherapy; supplies, mixing, home delivery, ongoing management; nursing follow-up	Durable medical equipment or supplies, general and oxygen; delivery and maintenance
Duration	Short-term (average 3 months); 1 hour per visit; 2–3 days per week;	Long-term or short-term; 4–24 hours per visit; 1–7 days per week	6 weeks to life-long	5 months per average rental
Charge	$35–$55 per visit; $1,200 per patient	$7–$35 per hour depending on skill-level	$1,300–$4,000 per nutrition patient per month. Varies for antibiotic and chemotherapy patients	$100 per month; $500 per patient rental period; rent or purchase option
Payment	Medicare; Medicaid; Workers' compensation; government contracts; other	Private insurance; patients and families; Workers' Compensation; other	Medicare; private insurance; other;	Medicare; Medicaid; Workers' Compensation; private insurance; patients and families
	Medicare pays first 20 visits of posthospital		Negotiated case-by-case	Covered 80%; patient pays 20% co-pay; recent change in Medicare to require purchase if <$120 or less costly to purchase than rent
Regulation/governance	Highly regulated by Medicare	Operates under business license		
Industry characteristics	Dominated by local not-for-profits, including VNAs and hospital-based agencies	Dominated by proprietaries and national chains	Fastest growing service; multiple components to coordinate; local and national companies	General/respiratory operations now merging; Local mom and pop businesses evolving into sophisticated national companies

PRIVATE HOME CARE SERVICES

Private home care services are less restricted by government-mandated services and by staffing and financial constraints. Rather, in most states, the services operate only under a business license.

Private home care agencies offer a wider range of services than their Medicare-certified counterparts. These include 24-hour nursing care, homemaker, live-in and companion, personal care, bathe and shave, as well as all of the skilled therapies. Clients are those who need extensive care, for example, several hours of care per day, daily care, or care over a prolonged or indefinite period of time.

Making valid market projections for private home care services is difficult. Because of the broader range of services, there are more potential clients. However, unlike the extensive data kept by Medicare, there is no national source of data on utilization. Referrals may come from physicians, hospitals, Medicare-certified home health agencies, other health care organizations, community agencies, and families and friends.

Private home care services are considerably less expensive per unit than those of Medicare-certified agencies because of the lower overhead. The average cost of a nursing visit is $25 to $30 per hour, compared to the $55 per visit for Medicare. Payment sources are primarily private individuals and families, Workers' Compensation, and private insurance companies.

The largest national private home care services are Upjohn Health Care Services, Kelley Health Care, Beverly Enterprises, Personnel Pool of America, Kimberly Home Health Care Inc., Quality Care, and Staff Builders Health Care Services (*Modern Healthcare,* 1984). Recently, many Medicare-certified agencies have started companion private home care services.

HIGH-TECHNOLOGY HOME THERAPY

High-technology home therapy is one of the most rapidly growing segments of the home health care field. A recent study by Rucker and Holmstedt (1984) projected an annual growth rate of 33% between 1984 and 1988, with the market growing from $277 million to reach $1 billion by 1988.

The four basic types of therapy are parenteral nutrition, enteral nutrition, antibiotic therapy, and chemotherapy. Parenteral and enteral nutrition therapy are for patients who have gastrointestinal and other conditions that prevent them from digesting nutrients normally. Nutrients are infused directly into the system. Antibiotic therapy and chemotherapy are for patients whose medication must be provided intravenously. To be appropriate for home infusion therapy, a patient must be in otherwise stable condition, have a home environment conducive to administration of the therapy, and themselves be able or have family who are able to administer the therapy.

The basic techniques for delivery of these therapies in the home have existed for a number of years. However, only with the growth of the senior population and the advent of hospital reimbursement, according to diagnostic related groups, (DRGs), have come the intense incentives to discharge patients rapidly and thus to make greater use of the home infusion therapy techniques. In brief, the growth in this market is driven more by environmental forces than by advancements in technology. Physician involvement and willingness to place patients in the home is critical. Educating physicians to understand and trust the high-technology home therapy program and developing patient protocols and regimens tailored to physicians' practices will determine the success and growth of these services.

Educating physicians to understand and trust the high-technology home therapy program and developing patient protocols and regimens tailored to physicians' practices will determine the success and growth of high-technology home therapy services.

Nationally, the number of persons at any given time receiving home infusion therapy is quite small. In 1981, 2,000 patients received home parenteral nutrition, and only1,000 received home enteral nutrition (*home health line,* 1983). The number of home parenteral patients is expected to increase to as many of 20,000 by 1990; the number of enteral patients is expected to increase even more dramatically—to as many as 50,000 in 1990 (HCFA Region V, 1983).

Antibiotic therapy and chemotherapy in the home are seen as having the greatest potential and likelihood of expansion in the future. Antibiotic therapy is projected to grow by as much as 80% during the next several years, with revenues reaching $350 million by 1988 (Rucker & Holmstedt, 1984). The potential patient base is much broader because persons with a wide range of illnesses may be prescribed antibiotic therapy, and progress in chemotherapy makes home care an increasing possibility for persons suffering from cancer.

The organization of a high-technology home therapy program is somewhat complex because several distinct services are required, and reimbursement is not uniform. The following are the basic components:

- select patients: four distinct patient populations; patients must have mental, functional, social, and environmental conditions conducive to following the home regimen;
- physician prescription;
- pharmaceuticals and preparation;
- ongoing delivery of supplies and equipment to the home;
- skilled nursing visits;
- emergency care;
- patient and family instruction;
- reimbursement of various components; and
- ongoing case management.

Some of those components apply to all types of home care. However, the applicability to high-technology home therapy is much more intensive. Moreover, the logistics of delivering these therapies in the home require extensive and continuing coordination of the various providers. For example, a high-technology home therapy program may involve a DME supply company, pharmacy, private or Medicare home health agency, hospice agency and hospital.

Although high-technology home therapy is expensive (e.g., $40,000 for a year-long parenteral nutrition patient), the cost is a fraction of providing comparable therapy in the hospital (e.g., $160,000 per year for the same patient). Moreover, patients are able to return to work or to their daily activities, receiving the therapy at night or during specific times of the day.

Typical charges range from $300 to $4,000 per month, with an average of $3,000 to $4,000 per month per parenteral nutrition patient, and $2,000 to $3,000 per month for an enteral nutrition patient (HCFA Region V, 1983). The charges for antibiotic therapy and chemotherapy vary considerably. Reimbursement is provided by most third-party insurers. However, payment is often negotiated on a case-by-case basis, and separate billing for each component may be necessary.

Several nationwide companies have organized comprehensive programs and are aggressively pursuing this growing market. The major national companies are Baxter Travenol, Hospital Pharmacies Incorporated (HPI), Home Health Care of America, American ContinueCare, and Abbott. In addition, numerous local companies are attempting to expand into this area.

High-technology home therapy companies are courting hospitals, home health agencies, physician groups, and ambulatory care centers as partners. The formal arrangements vary widely and capitalize on the strength of each party in the ability to offer the above components. Because of the relatively small number of patients, the complexity of the operations, the uncertainty of reimbursement, and the need to educate both providers and patients, collaboration tends to be more advantageous than establishing an independent program.

DURABLE MEDICAL EQUIPMENT

DME is defined by Medicare as "equipment that can withstand repeated use, is primarily and customarily used to serve a medical purpose, is generally not useful to a person in absence of an illness or injury, and is appropriate for use in the home." Typical examples of DME are hospital beds, wheelchairs, canes, crutches, and walkers. Oxygen therapy equipment and supplies and some of the equipment required for home infusion therapy are also classified as DME. Disposable supplies, such as bandages, are generally not included.

DME is usually prescribed by a physician. If the item is small, the patient may purchase it directly from a retail store. These range from medical supply companies to pharmacies to

Sears & Roebuck. If equipment is large, such as a bed, it must be obtained from a medical supply equipment company. Such companies deliver, maintain, and pick up DME at the patient's home. If a patient requires home health care, the home health agency may arrange for the equipment on the patient's behalf. Discharge planners and social workers from the hospital, staff of physicians' offices, or families may also contact the DME supply company directly to arrange delivery of the equipment to the patient's home.

DME may be rented or purchased, and until recently, 90% was rented. Medicare changed its regulations as of February 1, 1985. Currently, equipment costing less than $120 must be purchased. More expensive equipment must be purchased if its rental use over a prolonged period of time will cost more than purchase. The ratio of purchase to rental equipment is expected to change markedly, from 90:10 to perhaps as much as 60:40 (Abbey Medical, personal communication, May 14, 1985).

National DME companies estimate that approximately 6% of patients discharged from hospitals require some type of DME. Of patient orders, 36% are for patients being discharged from hospitals or nursing homes, 31% are for patients treated in physicians' offices, 23% are for walk-in patients, and the remaining 10% are from community and other sources (American Healthcare Systems, 1984). Respiratory therapy is a special segment of the DME market. Approximately half of DME use is for oxygen supplies and equipment.

DME charges average $100 per patient per month. The average duration for rental of equipment is five months. DME is paid for by Medicare, Medicaid, and other third-party insurers, provided it is prescribed by a physician and medical necessity is documented. Government, as well as some private insurance companies, have limitations on the types of equipment authorized as allowable expense. DME is usually covered by insurance for 80% of charges, with 20% paid by the client. Deductibles vary; under Medicare, there is a $75 deductible per year.

Patients are likely to pay directly for small items purchased from a rental store. However, if equipment is ordered for the patient through a home health agency or by a medical supply company, the home health agency or DME company usually bills the third-party payer on behalf of the patient. Often, these companies are willing to write off the patient's portion once the required "attempt to collect" has been made.

During the past several years, the DME supply field has changed drastically, from one of local, specialized "mom and pop" operations to one of growing national giants. Formerly, companies tended to concentrate in general DME or in oxygen equipment and supplies. Now, most companies are offering both. Currently, the largest DME companies are Abbey Medical, Foster Medical, Glasrock Medical Services, Healthdyne, National Medical

Home Care (. . . *home health line,* 1984 b). The largest of these has under 200 outlets, and none yet operates in all fifty states. However, acquisition, diversification, and expansion are rampant.

CURRENT TRENDS IN HOME CARE

Before examining the implications for ambulatory care service, a brief overview of trends in the home care field is essential.

- *Growth:* Primarily because of the pressures on hospitals to discharge patients early, home health is growing rapidly. New agencies are appearing, particularly those sponsored by hospitals. The portending growth of the senior population virtually assures high level of future demand.
- *Diversification and expansion:* As competition in the home care field increases and profit margins decrease, existing home care organizations are doing their best to expand their service packages and their geographic coverage in order to maintain or to capture new markets. Collaboration, joint ventures, and acquisitions abound. Formerly, all segments of the home care field were primarily local operations specializing in one aspect of home care. Nationwide companies and conglomerates offering the full range of services are now emerging.
- *Decreased profits:* Medicare is attempting to reduce its expenditures in all aspects of home care. Certified home health agencies, DME companies, and high-technology home therapy programs are facing changes in reimbursement that are likely to result in decreased revenues.
- *Changing regulations:* All home care organizations dealing with Medicare are confronted with a vast array of changes in policies, procedures, and reimbursement. On a number of issues, Medicare has not fully explicated the new regulations. The result is that the entire field is in a state of ongoing anticipation and constant change. Making financial and programmatic decisions about the future is thus difficult, and this makes negotiating partnership arrangements all the more complex.

The entire home health care field is in a state of ongoing anticipation and constant change. Making financial and programmatic decisions about the future is thus difficult, and this makes negotiating partnership arrangements all the more complex.

- *Collaboration with other health care providers:* To gain and secure access to a predictable or large patient base, home care providers are pursuing collaborative arrangements with hospitals, health maintenance organizations (HMOs), ambulatory care centers, or agencies in other segments of the home care business. Such arrangements are relatively new in the home health field, and thus the experience and operational models available as guides are scarce. Moreover, integrating services that have had nodding acquaintanceship but functioned quite independently is frought with all of the predictable problems of organizational change.

Implications for ambulatory care services

The evolution of the home health field presents considerable opportunity for ambulatory care services. The options for becoming involved are outlined below and summarized in Table 2. Each has different advantages in terms of attaining or maintaining market share, increasing revenue generation, maximizing use of available resources, or offering patients a comprehensive package of services. Organizational options are outlined below.

Starting your own service

Start-up of a new home care service costs $100 to $500,000—varying for each of the four services—and typically requires 18 months to break even. Such expenditures may be warranted if a sizable patient base is guaranteed. In rural communities where the service does not exist, start-up maybe the only option. Physician groups have started DME businesses in order to benefit from the tax advantages of owning capital equipment.

Purchase an existing service

Many small companies are considering sale. Buying an existing business eliminates start-up time, may add new patients to the ambulatory care service's market share, and includes staff with experience and expertise. The pitfalls are the usual problems inherent in organizational change.

Joint venturing

Many home companies are attempting to expand. They may be willing to contribute their expertise to a joint venture with an ambulatory care service which would contribute a patient base. After careful negotiation, respective roles for management and service activities might be split. Although the financial benefit would also be split, the combined efforts might produce a more lucrative venture than either would have individually.

Formally affiliating

A formal affiliation offers a way for the ambulatory care program to offer a service to its patients without any of the worries of financing or managing a new business. The affiliation agreement will typically delineate criteria and procedures for referral. This may enhance quality of care, streamline the referral process, and keep patients within the ambulatory care service system. A formal affiliation for a one- or two-year period may enable each party a chance to get to know each other's operations as a first step toward a closer legal and financial relationship.

Table 2. Goals

Arrangement	Generate revenue	Use fixed resources	Gain new market	Keep existing market	Enhance service to your patrons	Provide community service
Start own	+	Heavy start-up costs	+	+	+	Possibly
Purchase	+	Opportunity cost	+	+	+	
Joint venture	One half cost, one half revenue	Possibly	Possibly	+	+	Possibly
Contract with another agency to provide service (their name, they manage)				+	+	
Subcontract with another agency to provide service (your name; they manage)	+			+	+	Possibly
Subcontract with another agency to provide service (their name; you manage)	+	+	Possibly		Possibly	Possibly
Informal referral				+	+	

Contracting

The ambulatory care service could assume the financial risks and reap the benefits of offering a service to their patients, yet contract out for the management and day-to-day provision of care. The new HMO Medicare contracts offer opportunities for physician groups to assume responsibility for the home health and DME services, as well as for physician care. The ambulatory care service may commit to this, then subcontract with community agencies for the home care and DME portions.

Subcontracting as provider

This approach may enable the ambulatory care service to make better use of fixed resources and offer its patients certain services without assuming any of the financial risk. For example, DME companies must have respiratory therapists or trained nurses to teach patients the use of their equipment and to handle emergencies; high-technology home therapy programs need nurses to educate patients and to do home visits; private home care services occasionally need therapists but do not have temporary staff available. The ambulatory care program could offer these services on a contract basis. The ambulatory care service would receive additional revenues, and its patients would receive continuity of care, yet the service would have no financial risk.

Strengthening informal referral relationships

With the pressure for hospitals to discharge patients with acute conditions more quickly, the ambulatory care service may wish to strengthen its existing informal relationships with community home care programs. This would enable the ambulatory care service to remain more involved in the patient's progress and to enhance continuity of care from the perspective of the patient and family. The ambulatory care service is likely to provide the patient's ongoing care after the hospital and home-bound phase of illness. Thus knowing what has occurred in the home may enable the ambulatory care service to provide more effective and more efficient care. Inviting the local home health agency to place a liaison nurse in the ambulatory care center or sending a staff nurse to the home health agency's weekly case conference review are ways of increasing exchange of information and cooperation.

Each of the four home care services should be examined to determine how it can contribute to the ambulatory care service's market position and financial status. The financial and organizational arrangements of entering into a new service can be tailored to the particular needs of the ambulatory care service, and the arrangements can be different for each of the home care services.

Assessing the alternatives

Assuming that trends toward capitated financing and comprehensive service packages will continue, the ambulatory care service would be advised to move now in order to position itself for the future. To assess the potential of home care, and administrator of an ambulatory care center might consider the following options.

Clearly define goals

As noted above, different home care programs (as well as other diversification opportunities) can accomplish different objectives. The ambulatory care service must have its mission, long-range goals, and short-term objectives well defined. This then forms the basis for deciding which home care activities to consider in depth, and given a choice of arrangements, which option to select. Table 2 indicates how different arrangements can accomplish different objectives.

Project market demand

The projected use of each home care program should be estimated based on current patients and potential new patients. For DME and private home care, reliable data may not be available. Physicians, nurses, and social workers may need to keep records of referrals for a 3-month period. For the infusion therapies, specialist physicians may need to be polled to determine how many patients they might be willing to care for in the home if a carefully formulated home infusion therapy program were developed. Patients and families might be surveyed to ask if they have used home care or DME, or if they would look to the ambulatory care service for these services if available. Medicare HMOs represent an example of a potential new market. The ambulatory care service might be able to contract with the HMO to provide not only physician care, but also home health and DME as well.

Evaluate the competition

In many communities, home care agencies abound, and indeed, the field has become highly competitive. In urban areas, the yellow pages provide a startling revelation of the numerous private home care services, home health agencies, and DME suppliers. Before starting an entirely new program, an ambulatory care service must be certain that it has already captured or can capture a stable market large enough to make the program financially viable. Alternatively, the high competition may mean that an existing home health program would collaborate with the ambulatory care service to maximize benefits to both organizations. For an ambulatory care service that is part of a hospital or medical center, home care activities of other departments must be considered. The mental health center, for example, might already offer home care or have a contract with a community agency to do so. The local manifestations of the general trends in the home care field, as described above, should also be examined.

Assess community relations

In addition to objective analysis of competition and relative market share, community relations and existing referral patterns may affect a decision. For example, in a relatively small community where the VNA is widely recognized and supported as the predominant supplier of home health services, starting a new and competing organization might be far less successful than collaborating with the VNA. In several communities, medical centers have actually offered to or consummated purchase of the VNA.

Identify applicable regulations

In some states, home health services are regulated by state licensure and Certificate of Need (CON) requirements. The state of Florida, for example, has become infamous for CON restrictions on new Medicare home health agencies, which forced Johnson and Johnson to withdraw from the business. Medicare also has very strict regulations governing relationships between physicians and home care programs, constraints on referrals to any type of Medicare service, and so on. Federal, state, and local regulations governing new home care services should be identified.

Analyze financial feasibility

As with any new program being evaluated, a thorough financial analysis is critical. The profitability of home care, once fairly large, is being drastically reduced. Fine operating margins may not allow much room for error. Medicare programs, moreover, are still cost-reimbursed, and thus their major financial advantages are in offsetting fixed overhead. Also, the resources already available from the ambulatory care service should be examined to determine the marginal cost of entering a new business.

Secure physician support

The majority of home care services must be prescribed by a physician in order to be reimbursed by third-party payers. Thus the cooperation and support of the individual physicians is critical to the ultimate success of the program. If some of the physicians are already involved in other home care operations, they may either be dramatically opposed to or passive about the ambulatory care service starting a competing service or entering into a contract with a home care agency to which they do not wish to refer.

Examine internal resources

Staff and physical resources, as well as complementary programs, may influence the initiation of a home care service. The availability of time of administrative and clinical staff, the preferences and interest of leaders the existing operation of a related internal program or auxiliary service which may refer patients—all may affect a new home care service. In brief, the entry of an ambulatory care program into home care must represent an expansion which is consistent with the philosophical orientation and resource commitment of the total ambulatory care service to become sucessful; over the long term, the home care program must become an integral part of the total services offered through the ambulatory care service. Staff support and accompanying integrating mechanisms must be established.

Develop a marketing strategy

Most patients do not automatically think of their ambulatory care provider as also providing home health and DME. Thus, if the ambulatory care service does enter into home care in any way, it must conduct a marketing program in order to assure capturing the business. Staff time and budget must be allocated for this. The campaign should be conducted internally as well as with patients and families, insurance companies, the community, and any other potential referral source.

Anticipate interrelationships

Starting one of the basic home care services may be only a beginning. The future impact or potential of offering all four services should be anticipated as the program is structured and marketed.

• • •

Home health is one of the most rapidly growing areas of health care. From patient and provider perspectives, it can be a fine complement to ambulatory care. For the innovative ambulatory care service, the current climate of change and growth in home health represents an excellent opportunity for expansion.

The four basic home health services present an array of options. Each can be entered into separately or in concert with the others. A range of organizational options exist that can be selected to maximize the ambulatory care service's patient care, financial, legal, and market objectives. In examining the potential of home health, a vigorous approach is warranted. The strengths and detriments of each service and each arrangement should be assessed in relationship to the ambulatory care service's current and future environment.

REFERENCES

American Healthcare Systems. (1984, Fall). Internal document, Chicago.

Frost & Sullivan. (1983). *Home healthcare products and services market in the U.S.* New York: Frost & Sullivan.

Health Care Financing Administration Region 5. (1983). *Home parenteral and enteral nutrition support services* (Research Rep.), Chicago: HCFA Region.

. . . *home health line,* May 6, 1983, VIII, 86.

. . . *home health line,* May 28, 1984a, IX, 137.

. . . *home health line,* June 4, 1984b, IX, 146.

. . . *home health line,* October 29, 1984c, IX, 272.

. . . *home health line,* February 18, 1985, X, 51.

Modern Healthcare, May 1984, 170.

Rucker, B., & Holmstedt, K. (1984). *Home infusion therapy industry.* San Francisco: Hambrect & Quist.

Applied feasibility analysis for urgent care centers

Robert J. Parsons, PhD
Professor of Health Administration
Institute of Public Management and Health Administration
Brigham Young University
Provo, Utah
Senior Consultant
Brighton Consulting Group
Salt Lake City, Utah

William K. Willson, MHA
Consultant
Brighton Consulting Group
Salt Lake City, Utah

David F. Youkstetter, MA
Executive Vice President
Brighton Consulting Group
Salt Lake City, Utah

THE EVER-INCREASING competition in the health care industry is encouraging hospitals to provide services which have traditionally been inpatient but are now being provided in outpatient settings by other providers as well as by hospitals. These free-standing ambulatory or urgent care centers (UCCs) have created entirely new health care markets. Hospitals and physicians, in order to effectively compete in these markets, are having to learn about the characteristics of these services as well as the opportunities and risks inherent in developing UCCs.

To satisfy a growing demand for convenience medicine, these free-standing outpatient centers are growing rapidly. Originally UCCs were used as a substitute for the hospital emergency room, but as the demand increases, these centers are beginning to compete with the traditional physician's office as well (Friedman, 1982).

The author expresses appreciation to Rulon Stacey for his research assistance.

The success of the UCCs can be directly related to their intent to provide convenient access to quality medical care at a reasonable price. The public's growing insistence for this type of convenience medicine, combined with other economic and cultural factors, has influenced their growth (Cassak, 1982). These other factors include (1) the general migration of the U.S. population to the suburbs, (2) the dramatic increase in the number of physicians, (3) increased price sensitivity of purchasers, and (4) continued high inflation in the cost of medical services.

These influences are culminating in the emergence of a new balance between the private practice of medicine and the institutional practice of medicine. As both hospitals and physicians become more entrepreneurial in order to capture the growth in convenience medicine, their relationships are changing. Institutional loyalties of the past are giving way to joint-venture partnerships. The result is a very attractive forecast for urgent care centers.

Recently the literature has concentrated on growth, potential competitiveness, and the appropriateness of offering urgent care medical services. However, little data exist to help health care executives decide whether to enter the UCC market.

Entry into this market is further limited because the evolution of the convenience-medicine market is so unstable, and the low-market entry/exit barriers make finding a stable market niche very difficult. Latecomers to this market may find that, without enormous advertising capital expenditures, they too will have difficulty staying in the market.

It is estimated that 16% of the health care dollars is spent on outpatient services and that urgent care centers capture 25% of the outpatient services market (Boal, 1982). Those in the market competing for this 25% will find that, because of the possibility of large retail networks of outpatient centers, major corporations are investing in convenience medicine. These retailing networks will be able to generate referrals to either a hospital or to an HMO and thus create the economies of scale needed to maximize the benefits from television, newspaper, and radio advertising.

Hospitals, then, are facing increasing risks from new competition and from reimbursement pressures. If hospitals are to continue to grow and prosper, they must learn to innovate. Convenience medicine is one such innovation—one that will allow hospitals to grow in a market that is both cost conscious and consumer oriented. Much can be gained from identifying site selection criteria and assessing the urgent care center as a business venture.

SITE-SELECTION CRITERIA

To assist physicians and hospitals in evaluating proposed sites for urgent care centers, a number of site-selection criteria have been developed. These criteria have been reported in the literature as important environmental influences on a center's subsequent success, measured in terms of total patient visits.

The site-selection criteria are described in two groups. The first set of criteria focus exclusively on market size. The second set of criteria relate to market characteristics that influence the desirability of the site, irrespective of market size.

The overall rating of a site from these two sets of criteria does not necessarily mean an urgent care center should or should not be developed. Rather, it provides a method for assessing the likelihood of success from a narrow perspective—that of volume. Clearly, additional strategic consideratins are important and may often override the volume-oriented criteria. Following is a brief description of the overall market-size assessment method.

Market size assessment method

The overall estimate of market size for specific locations is a function of five steps:

1. The market area is defined. The primary market of an urgent care center typically accounts for approximately 80% of all center visits. Generally, this primary market consists of a two-mile radius around the center. Of course, this market definition varies with local traffic and trade patterns, geographic barriers, and so on.

2. An estimate is made of the total population within that market area. The primary care visit market potential is approximately 1.638 visits per person.

3. An estimate is made of an overall physician-visit use rate. The urgent care use rate is estimated to be between 200 and 270 visits per 1,000 population, where the population has convenient access to UCCs. This figure has been developed by national experts and urgent care developers based on survey results and has been verified by the experience of operating centers. Another way of stating this proposition is to say urgent care centers can generally be expected to garner between 12% and 16.5% of the total primary care visit market. Because approximately 80% of a center's volume is accounted for by residents in its primary market area, the market share range of 12% to 16.5% should be adjusted upward by 25% to establish a target market share value. The midpoint of the target range from 15% to 20.6% is approximately 18%.

4. The use rate is multiplied by the population size to yield an estimate of total market potential. The number of visits a center should reach to be financially successful is 30 visits per day. This represents approximately 11,000 visits per year. This target volume figure is used by an established urgent care developer and has been verified by several assistant administrators and center managers responsible for urgent care operations.

5. The overall market potential is expressed in terms of the market share required to reach the breakeven level.

The combination of an 18% target urgent care market share, an 11,000 visit target, and a 1.638 per capita primary care use rate requires that at least 38,000 people reside within the primary market for an urgent care center to appear feasible. The larger the population within the primary market area, the lower the necessary market share to reach breakeven. A site with a population of 50,000 within a two-mile radius would require a market share of only 13%, for example.

Step 1—define market area

Generally, the market area for an urgent care center is conservatively estimated to encompass a two-mile radius from the urgent care center. This market definition has been validated by results from patient origin studies performed by operating centers, the general literature, and market feasibility methodologies employed by urgent care center developers. The two-mile radius market area definition does not imply that the center will not provide services to residents outside of this geographic area. It simply is a reflection of the fact that urgent care is a convenience-oriented service. Therefore, the majority of visits are expected from residents within two miles of the center. The actual geographic area to be served by a particular center may be larger or smaller, depending on several major influences. Precise market definitions should be supported by explicit considerations of the following factors.

- The proximity of competitors—the two-mile radius definition assumes the nearest competitors are at least four miles away.
- Patterns of residential and commercial activity and significant geographic barriers should be considered—few markets are best defined simply by a circle with a two-mile radius.

Step 2—estimate population

The U.S. Census Bureau population estimates by census tract may be used to obtain an estimate of total population size within a two-mile radius. This information is also available by zip code from market research firms. Historical and projected population estimates provide a useful indication of population trends.

Step 3—estimate primary care physician visit rate

Because neither local nor state primary care office visit use rates are generally available, this estimate will need to be developed by adjusting national data to coincide with local conditions. That is, specific assumptions and parameters will need to be applied to national data to ascertain the primary care physician visit rate.

Step 4—assess total market potential

An estimate of the total number of primary care visits expected to be generated during the course of a year is simply the use rate estimate from Step 3 times the population estimate from Step 2.

Step 5—estimate market share required to reach breakeven point in the first year of operations

The estimated breakeven level of 11,000 patient visits per year is divided by the total market potential from Step 4. This market share then represents the degree of market penetration required to reach the breakeven level. The higher the required market share, the lower the likelihood of financial success. Consequently, those areas with a low required market share appear to hold the highest potential for success. If a specific center has a lower projected breakeven level than 11,000 visits per year (30/day), the specific reasons for this lower level should be explained and the target market share (18%) adjusted.

Market characteristics assessment method

The first five steps, then, assess market desirability solely from the perspective of market potential. Clearly, additional characteristics of the market should be taken into account. What follows is a description of these criteria, a rationale for their use, and an explanation of their target value. These criteria are to be used in conjunction with the estimate of required market penetration. In other words, an area that requires a comparatively high market share may still be deemed feasible if that area's characteristics match favorably with the target values.

Proximity of the proposed site to the nearest urgent care center is one of the most important environmental characteristics because nearby competitors decrease a center's ability to achieve a high market share.

Miles from nearest urgent care center

Proximity of the proposed site to the nearest urgent care center is one of the most important environmental characteristics because nearby competitors decrease a center's ability to achieve a high market share. A distance of four miles or greater was selected as the target value because the majority of a center's patients reside within a two-mile radius. A competing center four miles away, then, has a primary market without substantial overlap.

Miles from nearest emergency room

For reasons similar to those stated above, proximity of the proposed site to the nearest emergency room is another market characteristic of major importance. The target value of three miles or greater was selected because emergency departments are significant competition to urgent care centers. However, because emergency departments are not generally as convenience-market oriented as urgent care centers are, the target value is lower than that for urgent care centers.

Number of primary care physicians

The number of family practitioners, pediatricians, obstetricians and gynecologists (OB/GYNs), and general internal medicine physicians within a two-mile radius of the proposed site is another significant factor affecting competition. In fact, primary care physicians are generally viewed as the principal source of competition to urgent care centers. Therefore, the target value of 10 primary care physicians was selected because this represents approximately one-half the average of primary care physicians-to-population ratio, which serves as a conservative target value.

It is also important to avoid sites near areas with primary clinics or group practices. These may become direct competitors, too—if they aren't already.

Traffic volume per day at site

The average number of vehicles passing by a proposed site per day is also a significant characteristic when assessing the feasibility of an urgent care location. This figure assesses market potential in a different manner than total resident population. High traffic volume can somewhat offset low resident population. *Traffic on Highways* provides estimates on average traffic volume for specific areas. The target figure of 25,000 vehicles per day was selected because major arteries typically carry this much traffic.

Average household income

The average income per household is another market factor because of its influence on ability to pay and on use of convenience services. Although the evidence is mixed, some believe that there is a tendency for higher-income households to have a stronger convenience orientation—which is the market that urgent care is principally geared toward. There has been no solid evidence of this higher use rate of high-income families; however, collection problems may be reduced through careful site selection. Perhaps more important than income level is the stability of employment opportunities in particular areas. Smokestack industries, for example, are on the decline and thus may not provide a strong economic base for an urgent care center. The target amount selected for income was $20,000 or more.

Average age

Age is also a significant influence on the use of urgent care centers. Young families and singles comprise a major market segment for urgent care centers. These consumers are less likely to have an established relationship with a physician. A target average age of 35 years or younger was selected in light of a higher propensity for urgent care use by the younger population.

Percent of population over 65

The proportion of the population over 65 years of age is included as a criterion because the elderly are not generally high users of urgent care centers. The fact that they are more likely to have an existing physician–patient relationship and the fact that they have greater time flexibility explains their disinclination to use urgent care centers. The target proportion of 7.5% or less was selected because this average corresponds with the population average.

Average household size

Average household size was selected as a site-selection criterion because of the high use rate of families. The high incidence of minor childhood disease and the time scarcity of many families contribute to this high use rate. The target value of 3.0 or more persons per household was selected because the literature has shown that families with one or more children are high users of urgent care.

An application of these site-selection factors to five urgent care centers is presented in Table 1. Urgent care centers C and D have already reached break-even because of the low number of primary care physicians in the area and because they both meet 55% of the market characteristics.

DESIRABILITY AS A BUSINESS VENTURE

The determination of an urgent care center's desirability as a business venture is, in effect, a structural analysis of

Table 1. Evaluation of general site selection factors

		Name of urgent care center				
Criteria	**Target**	**A**	**B**	**C**	**D**	**E**
Market size						
Total population	>38,000	46,782	63,104	68,496	31,519	69,276
Primary care market potential	>61,940	76,255	102,860	111,648	51,376	112,920
Market share for break-even	<18%	14%	11%	10%	21%	10%
Market characteristics						
Miles from nearest UCC	>4.0	3	5	.5	6	3.5
Miles from nearest emergency dept.	>3.0	2	2	3	4	3
No. primary care MDs	<10	49	32	9	3	20
Traffic volume per day at site	>25,000	26,310	24,500	17,150	25,240	41,445
Average income	>$20,000	$23,838	$27,884	$21,154	$16,616	$15,761
Average housing value	>$60,000	$62,987	$76,553	$52,749	$43,375	$50,436
Average age	<35	31.2	29.9	21.0	27.5	29.7
Population over age 65	<7.5%	16.0%	10.0%	2.0%	9.6%	17.7%
Average household size	>3.0	2.23	2.61	3.67	2.41	1.98
Percent of target market characteristics met		44%	44%	55%	55%	22%

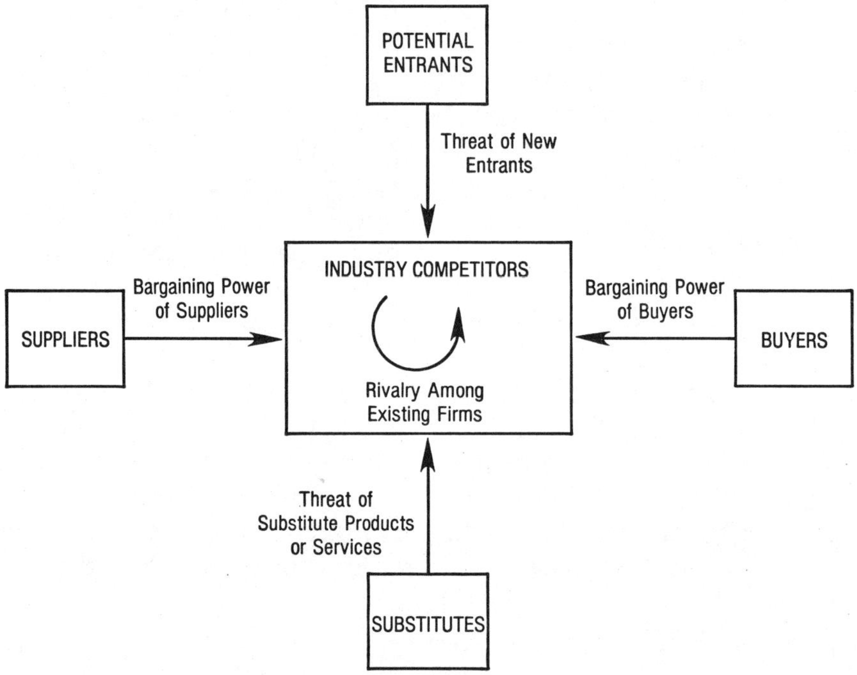

Figure 1. The five basic competitive forces that, collectively, determine the ultimate profit potential in the industry. Reprinted with permission of The Free Press, a Division of Macmillan, Inc. from *Competitive Strategy: Techniques for Analyzing Industries and Competitors* by Michael E. Porter. Copyright © 1980 by The Free Press.

the urgent care industry. This structural analysis, then, describes and predicts the intensity of competition in the urgent care industry. Industries that are intensely competitive are generally poor areas to invest in because returns are low and sporadic. Figure 1 shows the five basic competitive forces that, collectively, determine the ultimate profit potential in the industry. This section is organized around the following five competitive forces (Brighton Consulting Group, 1984):

- threat of new entrants;
- bargaining power of suppliers;
- threat of substitute products or services;
- bargaining power of buyers; and
- rivalry among existing firms.

Threat of new entrants

The stronger the threat of new entrants, the more competitive the industry and, therefore, the less desirable is additional investment. The principal influences on the strength of this threat to the urgent care market for hospitals or physicians include the following:

- economics of scale;
- perceived uniqueness of the product;
- capital requirements;

- switching costs;
- access to most favorable locations; and
- price levels.

The urgent care market is not characterized by significant economies of scale. Land, facility, equipment, supply, and personnel expenses cannot be substantially lowered through the establishment of multiple centers or larger centers. The major area of expenses that can be lowered is that of advertising. In fact, some industry observers believe that the economies of scale (and development of brand loyalty) in advertising will result in significant industry concentration through franchising. Generally, however, economies of scale are not believed to be significant and thus cannot be heavily relied on for protection of market position.

The urgent care centers are generally perceived by the public as undifferentiated. This is partly because of the novelty of this service and partly because convenience and price are the most important attributes from the consumer's perspective. Thus achieving a defensible market position on the basis of perceived uniqueness of the center by the public would be difficult. At this stage in the market, product differentiation is not high enough to serve as a significant barrier to entry into this market.

Capital requirements are fairly modest and capital availability is high. The capital requirements for an urgent care center average $350,000 to $450,000 if land, building, furniture, and equipment are leased. If they are purchased, the capital requirements are between $.50 and $.75 million. This level of investment does *not* serve as a major barrier to entry for physicians, hospitals, national chains, or entrepreneurs. There is currently high availability of venture capital for this endeavor.

Urgent care centers do not carry high "switching costs." That is, the consumer can change from one center to another without incurring significant additional expense or inconvenience. If, for example, all urgent care centers under one sponsor had coordinated medical records systems, consumers would face switching costs if they went to a competitor for care. In this example, the switching cost would be the consumers' time cost of repeating their medical history to the provider.

Access to favorable locations can serve as a barrier to entry. The major barrier to entry in the urgent care market is the limited availability of good locations. Developers can capitalize on their strategic locations by consciously networking their urgent care centers—that is, by clustering the centers so that areas between the centers could not provide the volume necessary to support a competitor. In general, a distance of four to four and one-half miles between centers creates a formidable entry barrier for that specific market.

The price levels of urgent care centers are high enough to attract additional competitors. Although average charges of UCCs are below those of emergency rooms, the charges are above those of private physicians. Thus physicians will likely be attracted into this market because of higher price levels. The price is also high enough that substantial profits are possible if high patient volume is achieved.

In summary, the UCC market is facing a significant threat of new entrants simply because there are few effective barriers to entry. This situation is worsened by the fact that there is already excess capacity in the market.

Bargaining power of suppliers

If a supplier of labor, equipment, or other necessities has substantial bargaining power, these suppliers can raise prices or reduce quality, thereby squeezing profitability out of an industry unable to recover cost increases in its price structure. Thus the more powerful the supplier, the less attractive the industry.

The urgent care market's major suppliers are physicians and other health care providers. Because of the current and projected increasing excess supply of health care providers, UCCs' major suppliers are without substantial market power. Therefore, suppliers do not pose a substantial competitive threat to urgent care centers.

Bargaining power of buyers

The bargaining power of a market's major buyers also influences its overall profitability. If the major buyers have substantial bargaining power, overall industry profitability is decreased. For the urgent care market, however, major buyers are generally comprised of individual consumers with little bargaining power. This has a positive influence on overall profit levels. Thus the small amount of bargaining power owned by urgent care buyers has the effect of reducing price sensitivity to some extent.

On the other hand, because urgent care is basically an undifferentiated product and because the buyer faces low switching costs, the market will still have some degree of price sensitivity. That is, price will not be the main focus of competition as long as it is within a reasonable competitive range. Because of the rapid growth of preferred provider organizations (PPOs), health maintenance organizations, (HMOs), and self-funded businesses, linkage with these major payers represents a significant market opportunity.

Pressure from substitute products

Strong pressure from substitute products can both reduce an industry's profit level and shorten the product life cycle. The urgent care market, in fact, faces its strongest competitive pressures from substitutes. The major substitutes for urgent care centers include primary care physician offices and emergency rooms.

Of all substitute products, primary care physicians pose the greatest threat to urgent care centers. The severity of this threat is a function of the number of primary care physicians, their projected growth rate, the type of conditions treated, and their relative ease in entering the urgent care market.

Not only does the size of the market served by primary care physicians in their private offices make them a formidable competitor, but the number of primary care physicians is projected to increase at a rapid rate through 1990. Thus the major substitute for urgent care—primary care physicians—is faced with a situation of physician oversupply where developing or maintaining a reasonable practice volume is becoming increasingly difficult. In response to this competitive market, primary care physicians are already expanding their office hours and days, actively marketing their services, and setting up their own urgent care centers (Brighton Consulting Group, 1984).

Private physicians can enter the urgent care market quite easily. If they extend their hours, advertise, and have a convenient location they find themselves providing a service not only comparable but possibly superior to urgent care centers. Their services may be superior to urgent care because they are more likely to provide the major component lacking in most UCCs—continuity of care. Consumers, in fact, list the lack of continuity as a major criticism of urgent care centers.

Emergency departments are also viewed as major competitors for the primary care market. Approximately 94% of total emergency department visits could be handled at a typical urgent care center. As emergency departments lose volume to urgent care centers, they will also become closer competitors by reducing waiting times, lowering prices, advertising, and other attempts at providing more convenient low-cost services. In fact, many emergency departments have indicated they are seriously considering or are already implementing such competitive tactics.

It is evident that physicians in private practice and emergency departments are intensifying competition for their share of the primary care market. The first stage of this competition is taking the form of convenience and of more competitive prices charged by emergency departments. In the near future, however, this form of competition is expected to shift emphasis to include continuity of care. The major strategic implication of this shift lies in the design of its physical facilities. Primary care centers, because they will house a broader representation of primary specialists, will need larger facilities. Flexibility and expandability, therefore, are important facility characteristics permitting a smooth transition from the current urgent care market to the future primary care market.

Flexibility and expandability are important facility characteristics permitting a smooth transition from the current urgent care market to the future primary care market.

Rivalry among existing firms

The intensity of the rivalry among existing firms is the final competitive force influencing the desirability of urgent care as a business venture. In this particular marketplace, the high strategic stakes of the various urgent care center sponsors provide the major influence on the intensity and form of competition between existing firms. Hospital ownership gives the urgent care market an intensity of competition unequaled in most other markets.

Unlike physician and entrepreneurial sponsors, hospitals enter the urgent care market with objectives in addition to profit maximization. For many hospitals, market security is a fundamental reason for involvement in the urgent care business. Hospitals view urgent care centers as a significant source of inpatient/outpatient ancillary and hospital medical staff referrals. This dual set of hospital objectives for urgent care centers results in a stronger commitment by the hospital to a particular market area including, perhaps, a tolerance for lower-earnings levels.

To illustrate the possible financial impact that an urgent care center might have on a sponsoring hospital, the following example is provided. Assume that an urgent care center operates at a break-even level of 11,000 visits per year and generates 20 inpatient admissions per 1,000 visits. This means that the urgent care center is responsible for 220 admissions. If the average charge per stay is approximately $2,400, additional revenue of $528,000 is generated for the hospital. If one-half of all costs are fixed, then the center makes a $264,000 contribution to overhead; a center that makes zero profit as a standalone business could actually be saving an operating margin if its support to the hospital is included. Although these figures may be optimistic, they do illustrate the high degree of support UCCs can provide their sponsoring hospitals. They also show why hospitals might be prone to stay in the UCC business when profit levels are too low to hold other sponsors' interest.

Another reason hospital sponsorship influences the intensity and form of competition is that the geographic market of interest is likely to be much narrower (the hospital's primary and secondary market area) than an entrepreneur who goes where opportunities lead.

• • •

Urgent care is not a promising standalone business venture. The market's substantial excess capacity, generally low-profit potential, high threat of new market entrants, high threat from substitute products or services, and probable intense rivalry among existing firms all point toward a highly competitive market with a low long-run profit potential. Other markets hold superior profit potential with lower risk.

If, on the other hand, urgent care center support to existing hospital operations are taken into account, urgent care is a viable business venture under the appropriate conditions. The center's ability to increase market security (referrals) and the ability to improve the marketability of health plans are strong strategic reasons for continued cautious investment. By taking advantage of the hospital's mar-

Table 2. Summary of strategic implications

Development concept	Strategic implication
The principal objective for hospital sponsorship of urgent care centers is market security.	Locate centers in underserved areas within hospital's market area (meet site selection criteria).
Urgent care center substitutes will respond to the convenience, cost-effectiveness needs of consumers.	Select sites and design facilities to inexpensive expansion and renovation of urgent care centers into primary care centers. Coordinate plans for urgent care with hospital emergency departments. Repackage emergency department services to make them more market sensitive when feasible.
Competition between physicians and hospitals for primary care will intensify.	Maximize joint-venture opportunities with medical staff. Avoid locations near group practices, clinics, and areas with significant numbers of medical staff offices.
The number of urgent care centers will increase, leading to intense competition between centers.	Raise barriers to entry: Overlap markets between same-sponors centers. Serve any remaining pockets of demand promptly—preempt competition. Be cautious in investing additional resources in new centers.
Urgent care is generally perceived as an undifferentiated commodity. Urgent care "chains and franchises" will dominate the market through marketing expertise and economies	Increase perceived differentiation of urgent care from the competition: Implement a coordinated, aggressive promotion campaign. Increase product standardization between centers. Integrate patient record system.

ket size and breadth, a defensible competitive niche can be established. This market position can be carved out through several specific strategies:

- Consciously raise entry barriers through strategic placement of any additional need centers.
- Increase customer switching costs by continued linkage of hospital payment plan benefits with the UCCs.
- Integrate patient record systems, which will also increase customer switching costs.
- Expand marketing efforts and emphasize a single UCC image.
- Take further advantage of economies of scale in marketing, and promote a UCC image that assists in the perception of uniqueness.
- Develop a product that can be differentiated and foster a consistency between urgent care centers.

- Explore means of establishing formal linkages with major payer groups.
- Engage in formal feasibility studies for those sites that substantially meet the site selection criteria.
- Design new facilities to be expandable and flexible, or commit to only short-term leases.

The strategic implications of an urgent care center as a business venture are summarized in Table 2.

REFERENCES

Brighton Consulting Group. (1984, October). *Survey of professional staff.* Salt Lake City: Brighton Consulting Group.

Boal, J. (1982, December). Health: A cure for the high cost of minor emergency health care. *Republic Scene,* pp. 8–12.

Cassak, D. (November 1982). The physician's office of tomorrow. *Surgical Business,* 18.

Friedman, E. (October 1982). Slicing the Pie Thinner. *Hospitals,* 56, 64.

Porter, M. E. (1980). *Competitive strategy: Techniques for analyzing industries and competitors.* New York: Macmillan, p. 4.

Utah Department of Transportation. (1983). *Report on the traffic on Utah highways.* Salt Lake City, Utah: Federal Highway Administration.

The national social health maintenance organization demonstration

Jay N. Greenberg, DSC
Walter N. Leutz, MSL, PhD
Ruby Abrahams, MSW
Health Policy Center
Brandeis University
Waltham, Massachusetts

IN THE SPRING of 1980 the Office of Research and Demonstrations, Health Care Financing Administration (HCFA), awarded a 3-year planning grant to the University Health Policy Consortium (UHPC) at Brandeis University to develop a prepaid, vertically integrated system of care for the elderly that has come to be known as the social/health maintenance organization (S/HMO).

Under this model, a single provider organization assumes responsibility for a full range of ambulatory, acute inpatient, rehabilitative, nursing home, home health, and personal care services under a prospectively determined fixed budget. Elderly persons who reside in the target marketing area are voluntarily enrolled through the marketing efforts of the S/HMO.

The major innovative features of the model are:

- comprehensive health and long-term care (LTC) benefits;

- consolidation of health and LTC under case management in one organized delivery system;
- financial risk for both medical care and LTC for the provider organization;
- voluntary enrollment of an elderly population that has a broad spectrum of care needs, from well to severely disabled;
- active participation of both Medicaid- and non-Medicaid-eligible Medicare enrollees;
- pooled private and public financing of health and LTC services; and
- extension of insurance principles to LTC.

In short, the S/HMO consolidates the system at all levels: provider, population, finance, and risk. Full consolidation gives the S/HMO the potential to be an extremely powerful intervention. The authors hypothesized that consolidation of services will make it possible to redefine and coordinate provider roles and relationships and to do so without some of the regulatory and reimbursement constraints that currently shape relationships. The membership concept gives providers authority to manage care of individuals across the full spectrum of services. The balanced membership has an important financial function in that it should create an insurance mechanism for LTC through the premium. The authors hypothesized that prepayment and funds pooling will remove financial barriers to innovation. Finally, giving financial risk to the S/HMO should make cost effectiveness an important criterion for decision making.

Four demonstration sites have spent the last 2 years planning their systems and negotiating contracts with HCFA and state Medicaid agencies. Site planning and development was financed by 18 foundations and the sponsoring organizations themselves. All four sites began marketing in early 1985. The demonstration will run for 42 months, although the "first year" of the project will actually be 18 months to allow sufficient experience for establishing second-year capitation rates.

The remainder of the discussion in this article details the decisions and arrangements that have been made in key areas of the program. The following topics covered are itemized below.

- *Organizational arrangements:* Who is sponsoring the S/HMOs, and where are they located?
- *Target population:* Whom will the S/HMO serve, and how will members be selected?
- *Benefits:* What services will be offered, and how fully will they be covered?
- *Financing:* How will individual and third party rates be calculated, and how much will the parties pay?
- *Quality assurance:* What measures of quality are appropriate, and how will standards be monitored?
- *Marketing:* How will the sponsors promote the S/HMO and what kind of product are they selling?
- *Risk sharing:* How risky is the S/HMO and how should financial

risk be allocated among the parties?

THE FOUR SITES: BASIC CHARACTERISTICS AND PROVIDER ARRANGEMENTS

The four organizations initiating sponsorship of the demonstration are:

- Metropolitan Jewish Geriatric Center (MJGC), Brooklyn, New York;
- Kaiser Permanente Medical Care Program, Portland, Oregon;
- Ebenezer Society, Minneapolis, Minnesota; and
- Senior Care Action Network (SCAN), Long Beach, California.

These providers were selected not only because each has a demonstrated capacity for providing high-quality services, but also because they represent a wide variety of organizational configurations and diverse experience in providing acute and chronic care to elderly populations. This diversity required each sponsor to take a different route to developing a fully integrated system. Appendix A presents a summary of the basic characteristics of each site and their respective provider arrangements.

MJGC owns two large nursing homes and operates a variety of community-based programs. It saw the S/HMO as a way to extend and consolidate its services to the elderly (Kodner, 1981). For medical services, MJGC created a new geriatric medical group in conjunction with Cornell University Medical College. Hospital services will be purchased from two community hospitals, and LTC will be obtained through MJGC. To pull the participants together, MJGC formed a closely controlled nonprofit corporation called Elderplan, Inc., which will be licensed in New York State as a health maintenance organization (HMO). Elderplan will make incentive payments to the medical group for meeting performance targets in the medical and hospital areas, but the two will also share risk for "bottom-line" (total system) profits and losses. Because MJGC's development effort has required the formation of several new entities, it has been expensive. However, the focus of all parties toward the S/HMO may make this a very powerful model.

Kaiser-Portland is a large established HMO that was an original site in the HMO Medicare demonstration (Galblum & Trieger, 1982; Greenlick, et al, 1983). Participation in both that demonstration and the S/HMO were motivated in part by the Kaiser system's large and growing elderly membership and the attractions of prepaid Medicare reimbursement. Given Kaiser's size and experience, it decided to develop the S/HMO's LTC services on its own rather than by taking on a formal partner. Issues of internal control are likely to be more difficult to work out at Kaiser than the structural issues. Because the S/HMO is a small, new program being grafted on to the large and established Kaiser system, it will not be possible to use direct incentive systems to motivate staff to cooperate with the S/HMO effort. In contrast to MJGC, the issue at Kaiser will be trying to obtain the attention of staff to convince them to change their behavior in line with S/HMO goals and practices.

Ebenezer Society is a comprehensive LTC provider with a range of services very similar to MJGC's. However, due to the Ebenezer's more limited corporate goals concerning expansion and to the already competitive HMO market in the Minneapolis-St. Paul area, Ebenezer was favorably disposed to follow UHPC's interest in the model of a long-term care agency affiliating with an existing HMO rather than starting its own. Its chosen partner was the Group Health Plan, Inc. (since renamed Group Health, Inc.), the largest and oldest HMO in the area. The partners solved incentive and service delivery issues early in the effort: Between themselves, they already controlled all the services required in the model, and they decided to share financial risk on the bottom line. That is, each would be reimbursed for its cost and then divide remaining profits or losses. More difficult to work out was finding a way to structure their relationship that allowed integration around S/HMO business but that still allowed each partner's other business to remain independent. The solution was a formal partnership with a series of written understandings concerning limits of liability and restraints on associated behavior.

SCAN is the third LTC sponsor, but this agency is very different from both MJGC and Ebenezer. It is a brokerage model case-management agency that provides no direct services of its own. Rather, it relies on an extensive network of referral relationships with existing community providers—both in the long-term and acute care sectors. Still, SCAN's corporate goal for the S/HMO was not unlike MJGC's, and it made the same key decision: Establishing a new HMO (SCAN Health Plan, Inc.) that would be closely controlled by the parent agency. However, due to its limited resource base and close working relationships with some large providers, SCAN decided to involve existing community providers much more closely in the S/HMO than did MJGC. SCAN will use a hospital-based individual practice association (IPA) at St. Mary's Center. Both of these partners (the hospital and the IPA) will be paid on a capitation basis with relatively strong risk-incentive provisions, especially in the case of the hospital. Whether these internal controls will be more or less effective than the total system performance rewards used at the other LTC sites will be an interesting question to follow in the demonstration.

Each of these sites faces a different set of opportunities and obstacles in development—both internal and external. These can only be highlighted here. Although Elderplan can draw on MJGC's chronic care experience, it faces the major tasks of building an HMO and a medical group from the ground up. Its major opportunity is a market that is large and basically untapped. Kaiser can rely on experience, image, and an established major market share. Its challenges are to learn the LTC business, to apply the learning to serving an aging membership, and to sell the community on its capacity to deliver LTC. Ebenezer and Group Health have strong suits in image and expertise in their respective areas. They face the external challenge of establishing a place in an extremely competitive HMO market that includes several senior plans, and the internal challenge of making the partnership work. SCAN's major problem is establishing some control over, and proper incentives within, a delivery system consisting of chronic care and medical services that are all contracted rather than closely controlled. Like Elderplan, it has an opportunity in a large, relatively untapped market.

Of course, other models for organizing S/HMOs are possible. A hospital-sponsored model is an obvious one, and in fact, the first S/HMO site designated was Mercy Hospital in Springfield, Massachusetts. Mercy withdrew early in the planning phase, however, when questions arose about financial feasibility, the size of its market, and support from physicians (Popko & Lasky, 1982). Currently, there are several hospitals around the country developing S/HMO-like systems. In some instances the hospital itself forms a wholly-owned subsidiary; in other cases the hospital is forming a joint venture with its medical staff.

TARGET POPULATION

An essential feature of the S/HMO model is that a balanced membership is enrolled. That is, the membership roughly reflects the local community population in terms of health status, especially chronic-impairment status. The demonstration places some additional requirements in the membership area in order to test the model's potential in the competitive open market. Sites will be enrolling members voluntarily through conventional marketing techniques, and both Medicare-only and Medicare–Medicaid elderly will be enrolled. Initial target membership is in the range of 4,000 within a year of the start of marketing.

An essential feature of the S/HMO model is that a balanced membership is enrolled. That is, the membership roughly reflects the local community population in terms of health status, especially chronic-impairment status.

The general rationales for the balanced membership have been mentioned already: the need to create an insurance mechanism through the premium, and the need to demonstrate how the care of the entire population can be managed. The overriding issue that is faced in actually obtaining the balanced population is selection bias, that is, how to attract and enroll a population that is neither "sicker" nor "healthier" than the desired population. Obviously, the potential for selection bias is enhanced by the open market model. If for the sake of argument the program was set up to serve the entire elderly population in a community, or if members were randomly assigned to the program and compelled to join, the potential for adverse selection would not arise except in a statistical sense.

One approach to avoiding unfavorable selection is found in the insurance industry where applicants are commonly screened for preexisting health conditions and excluded if such conditions are found. Screening is legitimate if premium assumptions are based on it, but as will be discussed below, this is not the case with the method of determining Medicare premiums. Medicare assumes that health status will be controlled by age and sex, and considers whether an individual is on welfare or resides in a nursing home. Screening on factors outside the formula "cheats the system."

The S/HMO demonstration was prohibited from using such "pure" health screens, but it has devised a "queuing" method, through which applicants are accepted or put on a waiting list according to their level of physical impairment. Two sites will begin enrollment using queuing, and the two others will use it if initial enrollment departs significantly from projections. Queuing is not health screening—a representative community sample of high-risk types will be allowed to join. In fact, the programs will be required to enroll their "fair share" of high-risk applicants. Thus the queuing mechanism should protect not only the S/HMO from adverse selection, but also the government from favorable selection. However, to the extent factors other than mental and physical functioning determine the need for LTC services and to the extent that these factors are not perfectly correlated with functional impairment, selection bias may still arise.

BENEFIT COVERAGE

The S/HMO model calls for a broad benefit package because one of its underlying assumptions is that substantial downward substitution of services is more likely when the financial incentives of prepaid capitation are combined with a vehicle to act on these incentives, namely, a wide array of lower-cost alternatives. In addition, market surveys suggest that potential enrollees prefer a wide array of home and community-based services.

Each site will provide all Medicare Part A and Part B services without the copayments and deductibles associated with these services (see Appendix B). In addition, acute care benefits include dentures, prescription drugs, optometry, audiometry, eyeglasses, hearing aids, preventive visits, and so on. Some of these will have copays as shown in Appendix B. All sites offer unlimited hospital days, and two sites have significantly extended "Medicare-type" skilled nursing facility (SNF) benefits.

The chronic care benefit package at each site includes case management, home nursing and therapies, personal care and homemaker services, adult day care, medical transportation, hospice and respite care, as well as chronic care in an SNF or intermediate care facility (ICF). Sites also include or will arrange for home-delivered meals, electronic response systems, chore and escort services, and other necessary transportation.

Although the service package is similar across sites, the depth and structural characteristics of the chronic care benefit varies substantially among the sites. The key structural features are summarized in Table 1. Elderplan is offering a gross benefit of $6,500 per year that is "interwined"; that is, it can be applied to either insitutional or non-institutional care or to some combination thereof. Coinsurance is $10 per visit for home and community-based services, up to a maximum of $100 per month, and 20% of costs for nursing home care, up to a maximum of $200 per month. The benefit is fully renewable in either setting for each new "benefit year." That is, the annual term of the benefit begins from the date on which the member first obtains an LTC plan, not from the date on which the member first joins the program.

The Elderplan benefit structure puts some specific constraints on resource allocation for case managers. Defining the benefit on the basis of a 12-month benefit period with monthly copay limits makes it possible, if not probable, that heavy utilizers (those needing more than five visits per week) will exceed the benefit well before the end of the contract year. Members will then need to go to self-pay or to Medicaid spend-down status until the benefit is renewable. The monthly copay limit will cause a somewhat faster use of benefits than an open-ended per visit or percentage charge and thus restrict the case manager's ability to stretch benefits across the full year through higher monthly cost sharing. These limits will impose pressure on case managers to find ways of monitoring and stretching available resources for members who do not easily qualify for spend-down eligibility. Finally, with the renewable nursing home benefit, the plan does not have any financial incentives for encouraging institutionalization of costly home care cases.

Similar to Elderplan, Seniors Plus limits the non-Medicaid chronic care benefit to $6,500 per year, with 20% copayment (see Table 1). There is no monthly benefit limit, so that as at Elderplan, the case managers will be under pressure to impose some limits in cases where the benefit is likely to expire before the contract year ends. Unlike Elderplan, there is no stated monthly limit on copays, so that Seniors Plus cannot pay more than 80% of chronic care costs at any time. This reduces the pressure on case managers somewhat compared with the Elderplan situation. Also, Seniors Plus uses the "contract year" rather than "benefit year," so that it would be possible for an enrollee to exceed the chronic care benefit within a 12-month period.

For SNF/ICF care, Seniors Plus imposes a lifetime limit of $8,000 (with 20% copay) for Medicare-only clients, which contrasts to Elderplan's renewable benefit. This lifetime limit could provide an incentive to encourage expensive chronic care clients to enter nursing homes. On the other hand, the requirement for admission review and ongoing review at regular intervals of

Table 1. Structure of long-term care benefits at the demonstration sites

Structural characteristic	Elderplan	Medicare partners	Medicare plus II	SCAN health plan
Annual benefit maximum (gross)				
Institutional	$6,500	$6,500	100 nursing home days	$7,500
Home and community based	$6,500	$6,500	$12,000	$7,500
Maximum possible total annual value	$6,500	$6,500	$12,000	$7,500
Renewability of institutional benefit	Fully renewable	$8,000 lifetime limit	Only for a new "spell of illness"	Fully renewable
Benefit period				
Institutional	By benefit year	By contract year	By contract year	By benefit year
Home and community based	By benefit year	By contract year	By month (1,000)	By benefit year
Cost sharing				
Institutional	20% of costs to maximum of $200 per month	20% of costs	10% of costs	15% copayment
Home and community	$10 per visit to maximum of $100 per month	20% of costs	10% of costs	$5 per visit to maximum of $100 per month

all S/HMO nursing home residents may work in the opposite direction in encouraging movement back to community services wherever possible.

Table 1 shows that Kaiser's Medicare Plus II has by far the deepest chronic care benefit of the four sites and that the benefit is structured differently. A $12,000 annual benefit is allocated to $1,000 monthly maximums for home and community-based services. Thus the resource coordinators do not need to worry about benefits lasting the whole year; they have more to offer than at other sites, and the small 10% copay reduces the impact of the member's resources on decision making. All of these factors decrease the likelihood of members' spending down in the community. Also, the monthly versus annual definition of benefits makes the benefit year/contract year distinction less important. Kaiser made the same choice as Seniors Plus in enhancing the value of home care by making its institutional

LTC benefit basically nonrenewable (and in Kaiser's case, considerably less valuable).

SCAN Health Plan's chronic care benefit is $7,500 per benefit year and is fully renewable in both institutional and noninstitutional settings. Coinsurance is 15% of costs for nursing home care and $5 per visit for home care (with a $100 per month coinsurance cap on home care). Thus the benefit structure constraints on providing chronic care are similar to constraints at Elderplan (see Table 1).

In summary, there are some important differences in the sites' chronic care benefits, and these differences reflect site-specific assumptions regarding demand, the impact of local competition on adverse selection, and the plan's ability to control the utilization of chronic care benefits. As will be discussed below, for Medicaid enrollees not eligible for Medicaid, all LTC benefits must be financed out of acute care savings and private premiums. Therefore, variations in LTC benefit packages also reflect different assumptions regarding expected acute care savings and the magnitude of the private premium.

In addition, given the limited resources available for chronic care services, all of the S/HMO sites are facing decisions concerning the most cost-effective targeting of these services. This involves development of criteria for decision making concerning both eligibility for the LTC benefit and service prescription for those deemed eligible. Eligibility criteria will be based on the existing preadmission screening formats developed by the state in which each site is located and will measure functional deficits, vulnerability for institutional placement, client's living situation, and unmet needs after all sources of informal care are taken into account. In addition to formal services, service prescription will include (to the fullest extent possible) encouragement and support of chronic care assistance that can be given by families, volunteers, and other informal caregivers. Decision criteria in these two areas will be further developed during the demonstration.

FINANCING AND REIMBURSEMENT

The S/HMO is financed by a pooling of public and private dollars. More specifically, for non-Medicaid eligibles, the S/HMO receives a monthly capitation payment or premium from Medicare and a monthly premium from the enrollees themselves. In addition, there are various copayments that the enrollee is required to pay for LTC services (see Table 1). For Medicaid eligibles, the S/HMO receives monthly

The S/HMO is financed by a pooling of public and private dollars. More specifically, for non-Medicaid eligibles, the S/HMO receives a monthly capitation payment or premium from Medicare and a monthly premium from the enrollees.

capitation payments from both Medicare and the state Medicaid program. At one site, Seniors Plus, the county will also provide financing for Title XX eligibles.

Translating this rather elegant concept into actual rates turned out to be a formidable task. First, the current methods that Medicare uses to reimburse HMOs has some perverse incentives built into it. Second, state Medicaid programs have little or no experience in setting capitation rates for elderly recipients. Finally, because funds are pooled, each payer was concerned about cost shifting. Presented below is a brief discussion of these issues, the methods adopted, and the resulting capitation rates. Space does not permit a complete discussion of these important issues. For a more complete treatment, the reader should refer to Leutz, et al, 1985 (especially chapter 6).

Medicare rate-setting

Both the concept and the basic elements of prospective, capitated Medicare reimbursement were established prior to the S/HMO demonstration (Kunkel & Powell, 1981; Trieger, Galblum, & Riley, 1981). The established methodology is called the adjusted average per capita costs (AAPCC). The concept of the AAPCC is to reimburse a program according to what it would have cost Medicare to serve the enrolled population in the fee-for-service sector. More specifically, it includes Medicare's share for Part A and B acute care services, that is, allowable costs less beneficiary payments for copays, deductibles, and expenses after benefits are exhausted. Medicare will pay the S/HMOs 100% of AAPCC.

The current AAPCC methodology begins with the estimate prepared for the Medicare trustees of Medicare's next year per national per capita costs. Second, the method estimates Medicare's per capita costs next year in the program's target county. This is called the area prevailing costs (APC) and is obtained by multiplying the national figure by a 5-year unweighted average of the ratio of national to county costs. Third, the formula estimates how expensive the enrolled population is relative to the county population according to a table of underwriting factors. The current underwriting factors (Table 2) are based on a statistical analysis of Medicare's fee-for-service costs in relation to beneficiary characteristics, as reported in the 1974–76 Current Medicare Surveys (Kunkel & Powell, 1981). The factors adjust reimbursement according to sex, age, whether a person is eligible for Medicaid, and whether a person resides in an LTC institution. The formula adjusts the APC by multiplying it by the ratio of the program membership's weighting of the underwriting factors to the county population's weighting. Thus if the members are more frequently in the high-cost cells than county residents, the AAPCC will be higher than the APC and vice versa. It is important to reiterate that these factors represent differentials in acute medical costs and to understand that Medicare payments

Table 2. AAPCC aged underwriting factors

Age/Sex	Institutional	Community welfare	Community nonwelfare
	Part A		
Male			
65–69	2.00	1.35	.70
70–74	2.25	1.65	.85
75–79	2.25	2.00	1.05
80–84	2.25	2.25	1.15
85 and over	2.25	2.30	1.20
Female			
65–69	1.70	.90	.60
70–74	1.90	1.15	.70
75–79	2.01	1.45	.85
80–84	2.00	1.70	1.05
85 and over	2.00	1.85	1.10
	Part B		
Male			
65–69	1.75	1.25	.85
70–74	1.80	1.45	1.00
75–79	1.80	1.55	1.10
80–84	1.80	1.60	1.10
85 and over	1.80	1.60	1.10
Female			
65–69	1.55	1.10	.70
70–74	1.60	1.15	.85
75–79	1.60	1.20	.95
80–84	1.60	1.20	.95
85 and over	1.60	1.20	.95

are meant to be sufficient to cover these acute costs rather than LTC costs. HCFA is currently reviewing alternatives to the current formula. It is not expected that the current S/HMO demonstration will be affected by any alteration in the formula, because negotiations have been conducted on the basis of the current formula. Future S/HMO sponsors should determine early which formula applies to them.

The current formula poses serious problems for the S/HMO as it is now being used to reimburse non-long-term-care programs. This problem relates to institutional underwriting factors, whereby reimbursement for an individual increases approximately twofold when the individual enters an LTC institution. Because a major goal of the S/HMO is to increase the proportion of seriously impaired individuals who can be maintained in community settings, a perverse incentive is created for the S/HMO: a seriously impaired individual who is maintained in the community is reimbursed at the low community-resident rate. Assuming for a moment that community-based and institutional benefits are about equal in value, and thus equal in cost to the plan, it would make financial sense for the S/HMO to encourage the individual member to enter an institution.

Because of this undesirable incentive, and because analyses of 1977 Current Medicare Survey data show that extremely impaired beneficiaries are just as costly to Medicare as nursing home residents (Gruenberg & Stuart, 1982), alternatives to the current AAPCC formula were explored. After the options were considered, a decision was made to ask for an alteration in the application of the current formula. Under this modification, S/HMO programs will be reimbursed according to the institutional underwriting factors for enrollees who are assessed to meet state certification requirements for placement in nursing homes but who remain in the community. This nursing home certifiable (NHC) formula will give S/HMOs incentives to maintain their impaired enrollees in community settings.

In order to incorporate a factor for NHC in the AAPCC, it was necessary to modify the current AAPCC underwriting factors for community residents. This is because the costs for the expensive NHC group are included in the costs for the community resident group in the calculation of the current AAPCC underwriting factors. The modification of the factors was calculated by Brandeis using the 1977 Current Medicare Survey. The Medicare costs for community beneficiaries who were in bed or at home most or all of the time due to a disability or who needed the help of another person in getting around in the community (about 5% of the community sample) were removed from the community group, and the factors were recalculated. The modified community factors displayed in Table 3 are on the average about 5% lower than the community factors in Table 2. This is consistent with the fact that the NHC beneficiaries who were removed are about twice as costly as the average. (Ninety-five percent of the community beneficiaries will be reimbursed at 95% of current AAPCC factors; 5% will be reimbursed at 200% of current factors: $.95 \times .95 + .05 \times 2 = 1$. The underwriting factors in Table 3 will be used to reimburse S/HMOs. (The institutional factors are the same as those shown in Table 2).

Medicaid rate-setting

The majority of the other third party payers—the four state Medicaid agencies—have little or no experience with prospective reimbursement mechanisms, and development has been different in each state. Only one of the Medicaid programs (California) has ever prepaid health costs for the elderly. Although California was able to establish separate rates according to Medicaid eligibility category and nursing home certifiability status, it did not have the data necessary to take a full rate-book approach. In Minnesota the site and state agreed in advance to

Table 3. NHC-revised underwriting factors for aged (based on AAPCC underwriting factors received November 1984)

Age/Sex	Institutional	Welfare	Nonwelfare
	Part A		
Male			
65–69	2.00	1.32	.67
70–74	2.25	1.61	.81
75–79	2.25	1.98	1.00
80–84	2.25	2.25	1.09
85 and over	2.25	2.31	1.13
Female			
65–69	1.70	.85	.58
70–74	1.90	1.07	.65
75–79	2.00	1.36	.77
80–84	2.00	1.64	.96
85 and over	2.00	1.81	.97
	Part B		
Male			
65–69	1.75	1.23	.83
70–74	1.80	1.43	.98
75–79	1.80	1.53	1.06
80–84	1.80	1.58	1.07
85 and over	1.80	1.58	1.07
Female			
65–69	1.55	1.07	.69
70–74	1.60	1.10	.82
75–79	1.60	1.12	.89
80–84	1.60	1.12	.89
85 and over	1.60	1.12	.89

base the premium on a rate-book type formula derived from state spending data. In New York the rates for separate service components are being negotiated by the site and the state. Points of reference are a limited set of Medicaid spending data and the site's initial finance estimates. In Oregon, the site used national data to devise Medicaid adjustments in its S/HMO community premium rate buildup. However, the state had difficulty determining the potential cost impact of the LTC part of the site's offer, and LTC benefits will be excluded pending a year-long study of Medicaid chronic care costs outside the S/HMO. Thus, to start out, only medical benefits will be included in the S/HMO for Medicaid enrollees in Oregon.

Private premiums

When discussing the private premiums, it is important to remember that the cost of LTC services must be covered entirely from acute care savings, private premiums, and copayments. The sites expect acute care savings to be somewhere between 20% and 30% of fee-for-service hospital costs. However, even then, levels of expected savings will cover only a fraction of the cost of LTC. The sites feared that a private premium high enough to cover the balance of expected costs of LTC would result in substantial adverse selection. Thus, in the demonstration, the approach to setting the private premiums was based more on marketing analyses than service cost calculations, and all sites decided to set private premiums marginally above the cost of private Medicare supplemental policies. As was discussed earlier, this resulted in a private LTC benefit that is below the level needed to insure for full LTC coverage.

Table 4 presents a summary of estimated monthly per member premiums by payer and by site. It should be remembered that both the Medicare and Medicaid rates are estimates based on expected enrollee characteristics.

QUALITY ASSURANCE (QA)

Basic approaches to QA in the S/HMO

Each S/HMO plan must assure that every provider included in the S/HMO system satisfies all federal and state requirements for certification and licensure and that all professionals practicing in the system meet professional and licensure standards. Each site must undertake ongoing activities that will ensure satisfactory performance by providers. With respect to licensure standards, all facilities providing basic and supplemental health services are required to be either (1) certified in accordance with Title XVIII

Table 4. Estimated 1985 monthly premiums by source by site

Site	Source			
	Private premium	Medicare	Medicaid	Other public payers
Kaiser	$47.00	$207.84*	$18.54**	No
Elderplan	$29.89	$274.51*	$340.00***	No
SCAN	$40.00	$288.53*	$91.44***	No
Seniors Plus	$29.50	$223.97*	$573.00***	Yes†

*Based on assumptions regarding enrollee distributions regarding age, sex, Medicaid status, nursing home residence, and impairment levels.

**Does not include cost of LTC. LTC will be purchased on a fee-for-service basis in the first year.

***Based on assumptions regarding proportions of enrollees who are nursing home certifiable or in nursing home residents and Medicaid eligibility category. For Seniors Plus, it is also based on assumptions regarding the age distribution of Medicaid enrollees.

†Maximum of $175,000 for first year will be available for Title XX eligible enrollees for chore and homemaker services.

of the Social Security Act or certified by the state where Title XIX SNFs are used; or (2) in the case of hospitals or accredited by the Joint Commission on Accreditation of Hospitals (JCAH). In addition, each site must describe its relationship with the local professional standards review organization (PSRO) or other federal QA entities in their local system. Finally, each site must have a system of medical records and records of LTC plans.

Mechanisms are being established at each site to undertake, on an ongoing basis, the following activities in both the medical and LTC components:

- peer review;
- utilization review;
- audits of medical care records and LTC plans; and
- a system to manage enrollee grievances.

QA committees are being established for both medical care and LTC. Provider performance in both areas will be reviewed, based on systematic data collection. Procedures are being established for taking remedial action when it is determined through peer review that inappropriate services have been provided or that services appropriate for the client have not been provided. Finally, accessibility as well as quality of care will be reviewed.

Site choices for QA of chronic care and client grievance procedures

Because HMOs and other prepaid providers have very little experience in the area of chronic care, the S/HMOs had to break much new ground. Each site's activities in the areas of chronic care quality assurance and client grievance procedures are outlined below. It is important to note that these are all planned activities. We fully expect that as the S/HMOs gain experience these procedures will be significantly modified.

At *Kaiser,* the development of QA programs for LTC will be ongoing during S/HMO operations. These programs will build on Kaiser's current system of quarterly auditing of home care patients. In addition, new methods of evaluating ambulatory care are being explored, such as computer-assisted chart abstracting systems that apply predetermined criteria to medical care data. Abstractors enter information about medical conditions, drugs, lab tests, and procedures prescribed by providers. The computer analyzes the chart information against the criteria and determines what further questions need to be asked. This system is currently being pilot tested and will be explored for its applicability to monitoring QA in LTC settings.

With regard to member grievances, Kaiser will follow its standard HMO member-satisfaction procedure. Information related to Kaiser services and procedures is provided to all new members, and each member is assigned to a health plan service representative. The service rep is responsible for orienting the member to the Kaiser system, for guiding and assisting the member to obtain appropriate services, and for receiving any member complaints. On receipt of a written complaint, the service rep determines the action required and responds to the client within 30 days. The written response contains the resolution of the complaint, the basis for the resolution, and notification that if not satisfied the member may request a review. The supervisor of member services provides this review. Regular, periodic reports of this operation are made to the management, medical chiefs, and hospital administration. It is important to note that at all S/HMO sites, members who are not satisfied with the internal solution of a grievance always have access to established Medicare grievance mechanisms.

At *Seniors Plus,* chronic care QA activities will be coordinated by a separate QA department, which has developed minimum standards for recordkeeping and other procedures, as well as protocols for treatment of chronic care clients. The QA department regularly audits nursing home client records, identifies problem areas, recommends strategies for correcting problems, and reports on resulting changes. The community service division has a 15-member advisory committee that includes clients, family members, professionals, and senior community residents whose responsibility is to conduct an annual review of all community programs. The review identifies issues, problem areas, and unmet needs, and makes recommendations for changes and future directions. In addition, a QA committee consisting of the director of the QA department (an RN), the director of rehabilitation (a physical therapist [PT]), an administrative staff person, and a medical advisor review clinical records quarterly on home care nursing clients and annually on all other clients. Case managers review all client records monthly to identify unmet needs, changes in client's situation, and to review the care process.

Seniors Plus grievance procedures are similar to those used at Kaiser. Formal complaints will be made to the member services director, who will (1) acknowledge receipt of the complaint within 5 days; (2) prepare a file investigating the complaint in relation to policy issues, decisions required, person responsible for the decision; and (3) collect information required to evaluate the complaint. This information will be forwarded to the appropriate decision maker, who will recommend a resolution to the member services director. The director will respond to the member within 30 days of the lodging of the complaint.

Elderplan will establish a case management systems review committee, consisting of Elderplan's general director, director of professional affairs, director of case management, the medical group medical director, a medical group primary care physician, and a physician extender. There is overlapping membership in the medical and long-term care QA committees, which reflects Elderplan's closely integrated system. The case management systems review committee will monitor both utilization and the quality of chronic care plans and services in terms of appropriateness, continuity, coordination, acceptance, and accessibility. Regularly scheduled case conferences will be held to discuss and analyze chronic care cases and the interventions used. This committee will be responsible for developing protocols and criteria for chronic care. It is recognized that this will require extensive developmental work because accepted specific standards for home care and downward substitutions are not currently available.

Like the other sites, Elderplan's grievance procedure uses the member representative as the receiver and coordinator of complaint action. Appeals can be made to Elderplan's general director, and/or to a grievance committee consisting of Elderplan's executive director, general director, director of professional affairs, and at least one Elderplan board member. Final appeal may be made to the state insurance department. The director of marketing will maintain a log of all formal grievances and complaints and their disposition, and prepare periodic summary reports.

Like Elderplan, *SCAN Health Plan* will establish a case management systems review committee to monitor the chronic care component and develop protocols and criteria for care in this area. Within the case management unit, a monthly random audit of client records by case management staff will be used to identify problems in recording or clinical treatment. This review follows a prescribed documented format that has been used by SCAN in the past. If standards have not been met, recommendations in writing are made to the case management supervisor, who will initiate corrective action and monitor as appropriate the client chart, client progress, or case management performance to ensure that the problem is rectified and does not recur.

SCAN Health Plan's grievance procedures are almost identical to Elderplan's. The member representative receives and coordinates complaint action, and the marketing director oversees the process. Appeal can be made to the SCAN administrator.

It must be reiterated that the above systems and procedures are only proposed and many have not yet been tested by experience.

MARKETING

Overview of approach taken

Although each site is taking a somewhat different approach to marketing, there are some striking similarities among their approaches. First, no site is placing much emphasis on mass media as a form of promotion. Instead, all of the sites will focus on individual and small-group contact. Second, each site is taking careful measures to make sure that a prospective enrollee fully understands the program prior to joining. The sites want to avoid possible complaints, disenrollment, and "bad press" associated with selling the elderly a product that they do not fully understand. Third, the basic message that each site is emphasizing in its various marketing campaigns is that of a program designed to specifically meet the care needs of the elderly–a program designed to keep people healthy and in their own homes. Fourth, each site will use somewhat different marketing strategies for Medicaid clients than they will for Medicare-only clients. Finally, each site's marketing plan has been approved by both HCFA and its respective state Medicaid agency.

Comparison of site marketing plans

Elderplan: Like the other S/HMO sites, Elderplan contrasts its basic approach to marketing to the mass media approaches used by most of the Medicare HMOs. Rather, the marketing effort will be locally oriented to groups and individuals. Resources to be used include:

- the influence of board members who represent important senior-citizen organizations;
- video and slide presentations to local groups;
- direct mailings using lists obtained from HCFA, the motor vehicles department, and other sources;
- health fairs and open houses; and
- ads in local newspapers.

The Medicaid marketing effort has been developed jointly with city and state agencies. The general approach will be (1) Medicaid will mail an announcement on the availability of Elderplan (including a special brochure), (2) Elderplan will train Medicaid caseworkers to present the program, and (3) the Elderplan marketing team will follow up on both efforts.

The intent for all segments of the population is to market in small groups and to establish personal contact with each enrollee. This will allow informed, nonpressured decisions to join and also allow early identification of impaired applicants. All applications will be initialed by a member services representative to certify that all program features have been explained. In these presentations as well as in mailings, Elderplan will distribute a basic brochure (laid out clearly with large type) on the decision process the elderly should follow in deciding to join. It will include questions and answers and be explicit on pluses and minuses. The marketing theme is "Elderplan takes the worry out of Medicare and adds health to your years." The emphasis will be on extra home support and prevention services, not nursing home benefits.

Medicare partners: To achieve its enrollment goals, Seniors Plus will orient its initial marketing efforts toward internal constituencies. Messages will include a mix of education, product information, and promotion. Media employed will include organizational newsletters, direct mail, endorsements by influential individuals, open meetings, and so on. Parallel to and supportive of the internal effort, there will be appeals to the general public through media advertising, a mailing to Medicare beneficiaries through the HCFA list, distribution of promotional materials through banks, and various attempts to attract media coverage of both the plan and the general needs and problems of the elderly concerning health and LTC.

Like Elderplan and other sites, Seniors Plus is preparing a short flyer and an informational brochure that explains the various features of the program and creates an image for the plan. An initial draft of the flyer to be mailed emphasizes the "90 years of combined experience" of the sponsors and the comprehensiveness of the coverage, and introduces the theme, "a health care plan so complete it follows you home." The brochure picks up the same themes and also highlights choice among a large number of Group Health, Inc. physicians, "taking the wait out of waiting rooms," and "encouraging healthy lifestyles"; it includes an endorsement from the powerful Metropolitan Senior Federation. The brochure seeks to put a positive face on the demonstration aspect of the program by pointing out that the comprehensive S/HMO benefits are available at only four sites around the country.

Marketing to the Medicaid segment of the market will be done in cooperation with the county welfare department. Details of the effort were still under negotiation as of this writing, but the intent is to have the Seniors Plus staff train the county staff to present the program as part of their normal, ongoing procedure. A separate informational brochure is being prepared, and it is hoped that mailings can be made and special meetings held where a slide tape or video presentation can be made to both new and current beneficiaries. The appeal will be based on quality and access as well as the availability of some additional waivered services not otherwise available in the state plan.

Medicare Plus II: Kaiser's marketing strategy for Medicare Plus II will emphasize the same themes and images as Plus I in selling the product, but it will use a very different approach in reaching the market. Whereas Medicare Plus I was promoted broadly with television, radio, and newspaper advertising, Plus II will be promoted through a direct-mail campaign supported by a community organization approach. The primary emphasis will be on reaching the non-Kaiser segment, but half the members are expected to come from conversions of current Kaiser seniors. Because of the already high penetration rate, site planners expect that they will have to reach virtually every eligible senior citizen in the county to meet their enrollment objectives. The primary mailing list will be the HCFA tape of Medicare beneficiaries (excluding current Kaiser members), supplemented by lists of seniors holding driver's licenses or bus passes. The 2,000 conversion members will be recruited through separate direct mail in specified geographic areas.

The Area Agency on Aging, the County/City Commission on Aging, and many senior-citizen groups have been supportive of the new program; the site has an advisory committee composed of these and other constituencies to advise on the marketing campaign and to provide liaison to community groups. Direct mail will be supported by group presentations and poster displays in the network of community groups and organizations.

The choice of the name "Medicare Plus II" is a reflection of Kaiser's choice to build on the name recognition and positive image of the prior demonstration in the community. The direct mail flyer that has been drafted also emphasizes the medical aspects of the program and downplays long-term care. The flyer announces "a bright idea in health care coverage from Kaiser-Permanente" under the image of an umbrella. The slogans are "Bigger Coverage—Better Protection—Greater Peace of Mind." The text starts with emphasis on comprehensive coverage of physician visits, hospital charges, lab tests, "and more." It continues with simplicity of paperwork, "no surprises" (no unplanned expenses), personal relationships with physicians, "and more." At the very end it announces "a new benefit that could help you stay in your home . . . if you become eligible for nursing home care." Thus Kaiser is not trying to develop an image as a long-term care provider, and its market entry strategy of internal development will hopefully not be a problem.

The marketing brochure is patterned very closely on the one produced for Plus I. It clearly explains benefits and repeatedly reviews the advantages and disadvantages of joining. The text seeks to emphasize the autonomy of each beneficiary by urging them to review the material carefully and asking in bold type, "Is this special program really for you?" Concerning the new "expanded care benefits" (i.e., long-term care), the brochure is very explicit about the advantages, range of services covered, and limitations. Again the emphasis is on services in the home, "where most people are happier, stay healthier, and fare better than they do in nursing homes." Family support is also mentioned, as is short-term nursing home care.

Kaiser expects to reach many Medicaid elderly through these efforts, but it is also working with state staff in designing a specific marketing and enrollment effort to take place in welfare offices. Details are not available as of this writing, but the plan is to have state caseworkers advise beneficiaries of the availability of the plan and hand out marketing materials. The caseworker will also handle enrollment.

SCAN Health Plan: The overall marketing strategy at SCAN is to create a positive image of the plan and to convince individuals to "pass the word" to others. The image sought is that of a high-quality retail merchant: SCAN wants to create the image of a "high-quality, up-market program that is unique and effective." The slogan being considered is "The SCAN Health Plan—A Better Way." The slogan is seen as simple for people to remember and repeat. It also invites comparisons to other plans—comparisons that SCAN feels it should win.

SCAN plans to use selected media as well as a coordinated direct mail and community organization approach to promote the plan. Using the HCFA tapes, mailings will be sequential by zip code area, supported by newspaper ads, targeted ads (e.g., billboards, buses, cabs), community presentations, teas, and media coverage. SCAN already has a half-hour radio program twice a month and can obtain time on cable TV.

The site is also considering a second-phase strategy to supplement the "pass the word" approach. The second phase would be based on approaches to the management of large housing complexes for the elderly and to large employers who offer good retirement benefits. The general goal in both cases would be to find ways to enroll concentrated blocks of members, perhaps at special rates.

PUBLIC PAYER RISK-SHARING

One of the most difficult and important development issues faced by this project in the early years of the program was public payer risk-sharing. Although all parties agreed that ultimately S/HMOs would be required to be at full financial risk (or find nongovernment entities to share the risk), Brandeis and the sites felt both the federal government and state governments should initially share financial risk with the sponsoring organizations. There are not only prudent management justifications for this position but important policy issues as well.

As a background to a consideration of the question of how much risk for the S/HMO entity, it is important to consider what types of risks providers face in the S/HMO. One half century ago Knight (1971) made the distinction between the concepts of *risk* and *uncertainty* in business ventures. The term *risk* can be applied to possible future events that can be predicted statistically, that is, the possible outcomes are known, and one can assign probabilities to each. In contrast, with *uncertainties* there is not enough information to assign probabilities to outcomes, and indeed the range of outcomes may not even be known. It is safe to say that at this point the S/HMO is full of uncertainties, including effectiveness in integrating the service system, appeal in the market, structure of new benefits, accuracy of cost estimates, aging of the membership, and adequacy of reimbursement arrangements with third parties.

Because of the magnitude of these risks and uncertainties in the demonstration, sponsors cannot be expected to have a great degree of control over these various systems or the overall financial outcomes, at least not in the beginning. Following the policy that financial responsibility should flow from control (Leighton, 1979; Zelten, 1981), because the S/HMO cannot expect to have a predictable level of control, it may be bad policy to put the S/HMO at full risk for service costs. Too much risk for providers would likely lead to extremely conservative, protective, and possibly dysfunctional behavior—certainly in the areas of cost estimates and benefit levels and possibly in caregiving decisions. Even with conservative strategies, the possibility of bankruptcy for sponsors could not be ruled out.

In recognition of these potential adverse effects of full risk, and because of the unavailability of conventional private reinsurance for this type of experimental program, Medicare and most Medicaid agencies agreed to "sharing" risk with the demonstration sites in the initial years of the project. That is, S/HMOs will still be put in the position of standing to earn or lose money for their efforts, but third parties will step in to limit losses (or gains) under conditions agreed on in advance. Such risk sharing should maintain efficiency incentives but at the same time protect against the dysfunctional effects of excessive risk. Prior to examining the potential and actual risk-sharing roles of the third parties, it is necessary to briefly review existing models for reinsurance and risk sharing.

HMOs commonly obtain reinsurance against potentially catastrophic cost overruns. The two most common models are "individual stop loss," through which the third party takes over responsibility for costs after an individual member's costs pass a set dollar threshold; and "aggregate stop loss," through which the third party takes responsibility for the costs of the entire membership after a set threshold is passed. Both individual and aggregate stop-loss coverage are usually obtained on an individual service, particularly hospitals (Miller, 1981). In HMOs these are typically reinsurance arrangements, that is, a premium is paid for the coverage. This is distinguished from risk sharing, where no premium is paid but where gains as well as losses can be shared. One important approach to risk sharing, at least in the literature (Leighton, 1979), is a risk-sharing "corridor." Through this mechanism, the provider and the third party can share set proportions of a particular risk over set ranges of loss (or gain) rather than simply handing the full risk from one to the other at the threshold.

All of these models and features are important precedents, but there are problems with using some of the predominant models in the S/HMO. Most importantly, the practice of insuring against costs only in a particular service area is problematic because of the substitutability of services within the consolidated system. If, for example, an S/HMO followed the common practice of insuring only against hospital costs, in the context of hospital cost overruns, it might be cheaper for the program to keep a patient in the hospital than it would to pay for more appropriate nursing home care (which was not protected by risk sharing). The same might be said for chronic nursing home care. Thus the S/HMO calls for risk-sharing models that not only protect against major costs such as hospital care but also are sensitive to the full range of service costs for which the program is responsible.

There is also, however, a second problem with insuring against particular areas of service costs that applies even if a range of cost areas are covered. Aggregate stop-loss arrangements (and to a lesser extent individual stop loss as well) rely on setting a threshold or performance goal as a trigger for coverage. This makes sense in an HMO (especially an experienced one) where performance standards have been established. The performance potential of the S/HMO has not been established, and setting a priori standards could easily distort outcomes. Performance targets for various service areas could acquire a life of their own, whether or not they represented the most efficient and effective mix of services for the membership. Thus risk-sharing arrangements that treat internal decisions neutrally are the most desirable. The arrangement that does this most effectively is aggregate stop-loss coverage on total plan losses and gains. This bottom-line risk sharing gives generalized incentives toward efficiency without specifying what efficiency means in each particular service area.

Bottom-line risk-sharing arrangements were recommended for the demonstration by Brandeis and they form the basic structure of risk sharing at most sites. Both Seniors Plus and Elderplan will begin operations sharing bottom-line risk in preset proportions with Medicare and Medicaid, with total loss (and gain) limits for the providers set at $250,000 and $150,000, respectively, in the first year. Seniors Plus also has a variety of risk-sharing corridors with Medicaid on LTC services. Kaiser and SCAN will begin risk sharing under selective approaches only. Kaiser will give risk on LTC gains and losses to Medicare but take full risk for acute care. SCAN has asked Medicare for individual stop-loss coverage on hospital costs and Medicaid for aggregate individual stop-loss as its primary risk protections. It has also, however, asked for a bottom-line arrangement, but at a much higher level than the other sites ($800,000).

Initial experience in the demonstration will shape the types and levels of risk sharing in the second year. The goal is to increase provider risk substantially in Year 2 and to go to full risk in Year 3. Full risk is an appropriate goal for the S/HMO, but it is a goal that must be approached with caution. Until a provider has proven its ability to control the service costs of the membership at a level consistent with both reimbursement levels and high-quality care, and until standards for quality and benefits are established, the strength of risk incentives should probably be limited to levels that can be absorbed without disaster.

• • •

It is important to be open about potential pitfalls of the S/HMO concept and to weigh these against advantages and opportunities. As the developers of the concept we must ask, "What happens if it really works?" An underlying assumption of the S/HMO is that the whole will be more powerful than the sum of its parts. This is a hopeful aphorism if one is taken with the myths of superheroes, but it is scary if one is reminded more of Dr. Frankenstein's monster. The key, of course is in the "creature's" brain—its motives, its knowledge, its compassion. The Frankenstein metaphor can be pushed quite far with the S/HMO. Do we as a society want to set the monster free and let providers decide who to serve with what benefits, or do we "keep the straps on" and require certain membership characteristics, benefits, and so on? Do we want to give the creature full power in the form of full risk, or do we "keep the electrodes on" and manage the flow of profits or losses? Do we want to let any provider sponsor a S/HMO, or do we screen prospective "brains," to exclude those with strictly profit-seeking motives, particular organizational affiliations, or questionable records with vulnerable populations (Greenlick, 1983). The metaphor is fanciful, but the concerns are real. These concerns are already being faced in the demonstration, and finding solutions will be critical if the model is to be more widely implemented. The benefits of learning about long-term care insurance will, it is hoped, be worth the potential dangers, and a demonstration setting allows good controls.

There are two other aspects of expanding insurance that are worth mentioning. First, Medicaid policymakers must decide how much and how quickly to turn over to an insurance mechanism Medicaid's current responsibility toward those who became poor because of high medical costs. States and general federal revenues currently support such spend-down cases, but their numbers should be reduced by the S/HMO and by other private long-term care insurance mechanisms. Should Medicaid somehow pay into such programs as a reward and an incentive for reducing spend-downs, or should it allow these costs to be shifted by only paying the costs of those who are already poor? "Privatizing" this spending too quickly will put a greater burden on new insurance, thus holding down benefits and inhibiting the programs' capacity to reduce spend-downs. By paying into such programs—at least at the start—the government could follow a well-established policy of encouraging private investment in a desired direction.

Second, there are other organizational configurations for S/HMOs that could be tested. There are no practical barriers to hospital or medical center sponsorship. Although hospitals should learn from Mercy Hospital's withdrawal from the demonstration, it should not be a deterrent. Links to other long-term care programs are also possible. For example, a relationship with a S/HMO could open a bigger market for a life care community by creating a noncampus model. Similarly, restriction of service to S/HMO delivery systems could be a way for private and public insurers to address the issue of moral hazard. This might open the way for insurance for community-based chronic care.

Finally, the central point made above must be reemphasized. The S/HMO's worth as a model and a demonstration will be measured in terms of how effectively it breaks down the "Catch-22" of long-term care. Health care providers think the place to break in first is to create standards and norms of chronic-care practice that yield cost-effective resource allocation decisions. The sites, the Brandeis Health Policy Center, the HCFA, and the foundation partners have made this the primary area of ongoing developmental research in the operations phase. As more is learned about managing services and members' needs, deeper chronic-care benefits must be tested.

REFERENCES

Galblum, J., & Trieger, S. (1982). Demonstrations of alternative delivery systems under Medicare and Medicaid. *Health Care Financing Review, 3*(3), 1–11.

Greenlick, M., Lamb, S., Carpenter, T., Fischer, T., Marks, S., & Cooper, W. (1983). A successful Medicare prospective payment demonstration, *Health Care Financing Review, 4*(4), 85–97.

Gruenberg, L., & Stuart, H. (1982). *A health status based AAPCC: The disability level approach.* Health Policy Center working paper. Waltham, MA: Brandeis University.

Knight, F. (1971). *Risk, Uncertainty and Profit.* University of Chicago Press: Chicago, IL.

Kodner, Dr. (1981). Who's S/HMO? *Home Health Care Services Quarterly, 2*(4), 57–68.

Kunkel, S., & Powell, C. (1981, June). The AAPCC under risk contracts with providers of health care. *Transactions, 33,* 57–66.

Leighton, R. (1979). Selective risk sharing: A new reimbursement alternative. In *Perspectives on Medicare Management.* Baltimore, MD: Health Care Financing Administration.

Leutz, W., Greenberg, J., Abrahams, R., Gruenberg, L., Diamond, L., & Prottas, J. (in press). *Issues, options and choices in creating Social/HMOs.* Lexington, MA: Lexington Books.

Miller, S.K. (1981). Reinsurance in an S/HMO Environment. Health Policy Center working paper. Brandeis University: Waltham, MA.

Popko, K., & Lasky, A. (1982, October). The Social/HMO: Is it feasible in a community hospital setting? *Hospital Progress, 63*(10), 50–53.

Trieger, S., Galblum, T., & Riley, G. (April 1981). *HMOs: Issues and alternatives for Medicare and Medicaid* (Publication No. 03107). Baltimore, MD: Health Care Financing Administration.

Zelten, R. (1981, Winter). Provider reimbursement alternatives and the placement of financial risk: A framework for analysis. *Topics in Health Care Financing,* 61–72.

Appendix A
Overview of S/HMO demonstration sites

Site sponsors	Type of sponsor	Relationships to partner(s)	Key opportunities	Key obstacles
Metropolitan Jewish Geriatric Center (MJGC) Brooklyn, NY (Elderplan, Inc.)	Comprehensive chronic care agency	Capitation contract and bottom-line risk sharing with small affiliated medical group Community hospital contracted on modified per diem basis	A large untapped market	Creating an HMO and medical group
Kaiser Permanente Medical Care Program Portland, OR (Medicare Plus II)	Large established HMO	No partners—S/HMO added to existing Kaiser system	Use experience and reputation	Creating LTC services
Ebenezer Society Minneapolis, MN (Seniors Plus)	Comprehensive chronic care agency	Partnership with large established HMO for all acute medical Bottom-line risk-sharing	Expertise and images of partners	Competitive HMO market
Senior Care Action Network (SCAN) Long Beach, CA	Case management/brokerage	Separate contracts with established medical group and medical center hospital Both on capitation/risk basis	Large untapped market	Management and incentives in the system

Source: Greenberg and Leutz, "The Social/Health Maintenance Organization and Its Role in Reforming the Long-Term Care System," in Feinstein, Gornick, Greenberg, *Long-Term Care Financing and Delivery Systems.* DHHS, HCFA, January 24, 1984 p. 59.

Appendix B

Social/HMO benefits package compared with Medicare Part A and Part B coverage

Benefits category	Medicare benefit	Social/HMO benefit
Institutional services		
Acute hospital	90 days each benefit period plus 60-day lifetime reserve $356 deductible per spell of illness on Part A benefits required Copays noted below are 1984 figures and assume deductible has been paid For each day between 61st and 90th day the beneficiary pays $89 For each reserve day, the payment is $178	Unlimited number of days for prescribed hospitalization at hospital approved by S/HMO Complete hospital services (inpatient and outpatient) including all physicians' and surgeons' services No deductibles, no charges
Psychiatric hospital	190 days lifetime Copayments same as inpatient hospital	190 day lifetime No copays, no charges
Skilled nursing facility care meeting Medicare criteria	After 3 consecutive days in hospital, transfer to SNF: first 20 days no charge; 21st thru 100th day, $44.50 per day.	No prior hospitalization requirement No deductibles, no charges Kaiser and SCAN, 100 days, Elderplan, 365 days Seniors Plus (unlimited days)
Skilled and intermediate nursing facility care of a custodial nature	Not covered	Covered up to limits of chronic care benefit Kaiser, 100 days, Elderplan and Seniors Plus, $6,500 SCAN, $7,500 Coinsurance and benefit periods vary (see Table 1)
Medical and related services		
Physician	Medicare pays 80% of allowable charges after $75 annual deductible on Part B benefits is paid Includes ambulatory (outpatient) surgery Physicals and preventive care not covered	Covers Medicare deductible and coinsurance Ambulatory surgery, routine physician exams, preventive care included Kaiser, $2 per visit Elderplan includes authorized house calls by physician or physician assistant
Nurse practitioner and Physician's assistant	80% of allowable charges when provided incident to physician services	Covered in full Kaiser, $2 per visit

Appendix B *(continued)*

Benefits category	Medicare benefit	Social/HMO benefit
Mental health outpatient visits	80% of physician charges up to $250 maximum (after $75 deductible) 80% of other professional charges	Kaiser, 6 visits per year to psychiatrist; no limit to other professionals Other sites, 20 visits per year Copay per visit: Kaiser, $2; Elderplan, $5; Medicare Plus, $10; SCAN, no charges
Foot care	Routine foot care services not covered except when performed as necessary part of a covered medical service Medicare pays 80% of allowable charges	Medically necessary podiatry: Kaiser, $2 copay; other sites, no charges Elderplan additionally provides routine foot care at $2 per visit
Blood work	First 3 pints not covered; then 80% of allowable	Covered in full
Medical equipment and supplies	80% of allowable charges on durable medical equipment, prosthetic devices, and supplies	Durable medical equipment, prosthetic devices and supplies covered in full when ordered and provided by plan
Lab and X-ray	Part B services—80% of allowable charges	Covered in full
Dentistry	80% of allowable charges *only* if it involves *surgery of the jaw,* setting fractures of the jaw and facial bones, treatment of oral infection, dental procedures that are integral part of medical procedures Routine dental services not covered	Medicare benefits covered in full, no charges All sites cover dentures under the chronic care benefit limits, with copays (Kaiser, 10%; Medicare Plus, 20%; Elderplan and SCAN, $50)—SCAN also covers routine care; Medicare Plus covers diagnostic and preventive care; Elderplan covers erupted tooth extractions and denture repair ($15 copay)
Outpatient physical therapy and speech pathology	Part B services—80% of allowable charges	Medicare outpatient physical therapy speech pathology services covered in full by sites No charges except Kaiser—$2 regular fee
Out-of-plan	Emergency and nonemergency services covered anywhere in the United States	Approved emergency services covered anywhere in the world Kaiser and SCAN, no charges Elderplan and Medicare Plus, 80% coverage of first $500 then same coverage as hospital and medical services described above

(continues)

Appendix B *(continued)*

Benefits category	Medicare benefit	Social/HMO benefit
Pharmacy	Not covered	Prescription drugs covered at all sites Copay range $1–$3.50
Optometry	Only covered if related to treatment of aphakia or if part of a covered medical service	Covered in full Kaiser, $2 copay Elderplan specifies one exam per year
Audiometry	Not covered	Covered in full Elderplan and Medicare Plus specify one exam per year Kaiser, $2 copay
Eyeglasses	Not covered (contact lenses for postcataract surgery patients: approximately 80%/20% per Part B	Covers one pair glasses in each 24-month period Kaiser and SCAN, no charge Elderplan, $10 copay; Medicare Plus, 50% copay
Hearing aids	Not covered	Covers one hearing aid in each 24-month period Kaiser, no charge Copays: Elderplan, $40; SCAN, $50; Medicare Plus, 50%
Home health and other community-based services		
Medicare home health care (includes visiting nurse; home health aide; occupational, speech, and physical therapies; and social work services)	100% of allowable costs, skilled care criteria and homebound	Medicare home health care covered in full Coverage expanded beyond skilled care and homebound criteria when approved for long-term care plan
In-home support (such as homemaker, personal health aide, medical transportation, medical day treatment, respite care; arranging and coordination of other services such as home-delivered meals, chore services, additional transportation, electronic monitoring)	Not covered	Covered with limits, copays, and renewability conditions as specified in Table 1 (varies by site)

(continues)

Appendix B *(continued)*

Benefits category	Medicare benefit	Social/HMO benefit
Hospice (includes home health care, inpatient treatment for acute and chronic symptom control, family respite, outpatient drugs, counseling and volunteer services for terminal cancer patients	5% copay or $5 per prescription for outpatient drugs, whichever is less 5% copay for inpatient respite costs, up to a maximum of $304 All other hospice services fully covered	Covered in full (no copays)

A phoenix rising: the municipal neighborhood family care center program is alive and well in New York City

Merle C. Cunningham, MD, MPH
Assistant Vice President for Ambulatory Care
New York City Health and Hospitals Corporation
Assistant Professor, Health Administration
Columbia University School of Public Health
New York, New York

RUMORS OF THE demise of the municipal Neighborhood Family Care Center (NFCC) Program in New York City are greatly exaggerated (Alford, 1975; Levin & Wolfson, 1984). Indeed, 10 years after the opening of the first NFCC, there are now 14 community-based health care centers operated by the New York City Health and Hospitals Corporation (HHC), which provide almost 650,000 visits annually to residents living in the service areas of the centers. This article reviews the history of the NFCC program from its genesis in the ideals of the Office of Economic Opportunity (OEO) Neighborhood Health Center in the 1960s, through a dormant period during the fiscal crisis in New York City in the mid-1970s, and into a recent period of revitalization, growth, and increased productivity in the 1980s.

The HHC was created in 1970 as a public benefit corporation to replace the former New York City Department of Hospitals. It currently operates 11 acute care hospitals, 4 long-term care facilities, and 14 community-based health centers—6 NFCCs and 8 satellite primary care sites. This system, the largest public multihospital system in the United States, provided more than 5.5 million ambulatory care visits in fiscal year 1984 (July 1983–June 1984). This represented almost half of the total workload of organized ambulatory care programs in New York City during that period. Figure 1 illustrates the distribution of that workload among the different service categories that constitute ambulatory care at HHC.

Of this total workload in fiscal 1984, 15% of the nonemergency health care visits (643,300) were provided at NFCCs and network satellites. These community-based programs all have their major emphasis on primary medical care: pediatrics, adult medicine, and women's health services (i.e., obstetrics/gynecology and family planning). The NFCCs also provide general dental services, limited mental health care services, and selected surgical, medical and pediatric subspecialty services. The distribution of this service load is depicted in Figure 2.

HISTORICAL BACKGROUND

In 1966, the Mayoral Commission on the Delivery of Personal Health Services (referred to as the Piel Commission) was appointed to make a thorough inquiry into the public sector health care system in New York City and to recommend specific measures

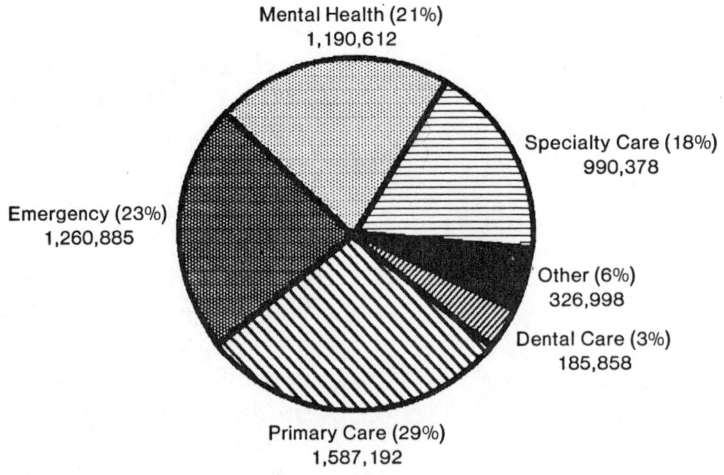

Figure 1. Distribution of ambulatory care visits by type of service in all facilities (N = 5,541,923 visits). Reprinted with permission of the HHC Office of Ambulatory Care Services.

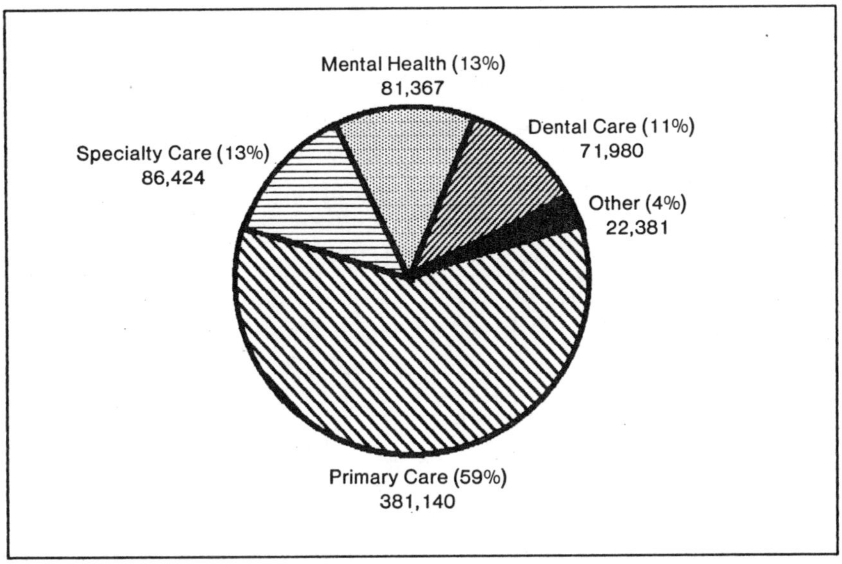

Figure 2. Distribution of ambulatory care visits by type of service in NFCCs (N = 643,292 visits). Reprinted with permission of the HHC Office of Ambulatory Care Services.

to strengthen and expand it. The report of that commission, *Comprehensive Community Health Services for New York City* (Commission on the Delivery of Personal Health Services, 1967), outlined an aggressive and innovative plan for a regional model of health care services delivery in New York City and recommended the creation of a new health services corporation with adequate authority and resources to design and implement that plan.

The regional planning model called for linking health service facilities in a borough by rational allocation of responsibility to form a comprehensive delivery system. According to the plan as displayed in Figure 3,

> Sites of primary care in each community are related to the community hospital. Each community hospital is tied, in turn, to the teaching hospital or medical school that serves as the regional medical center. The medical center in this model system also serves as a community hospital backing up the primary care facilities of its immediate community (Commission on the Delivery of Personal Health Services, 1967, p. 27).

The commission's report led to legislation in New York State that created the New York City Health and Hospitals Corporation in 1970, with an appropriate capital construction authority to begin the implementation of the plan. Three new acute care hospital facilities, each intended to replace one or more existing facilities, were designed, constructed, and eventually opened: North Central Bronx Hospital and Lincoln Medical and Mental Health Center in the Bronx, and Woodhull Medical and Mental Health Center in Brooklyn. Each facility was designed with an outpatient department (OPD) layout that resembled a medical group practice. There were two exam rooms and a consultation room for each provider. The size of each of these new OPDs was scaled down to handle a smaller workload based on the premise that a portion of the previous OPD workload would shift to newly constructed community-based primary care sites.

The NFCC program was designed in the early 1970s to provide these new sites of primary care in each community as outlined in the regional planning model. The NFCCs were patterned after the neighborhood health centers originally funded by the OEO in 1966 (Office of Economic Opportunity [OEO], 1968; Martin Luther King Fourth Annual Report, 1970; Stoecke and Candib, 1969). These large multispecialty group practice centers provided on-site primary medical care,

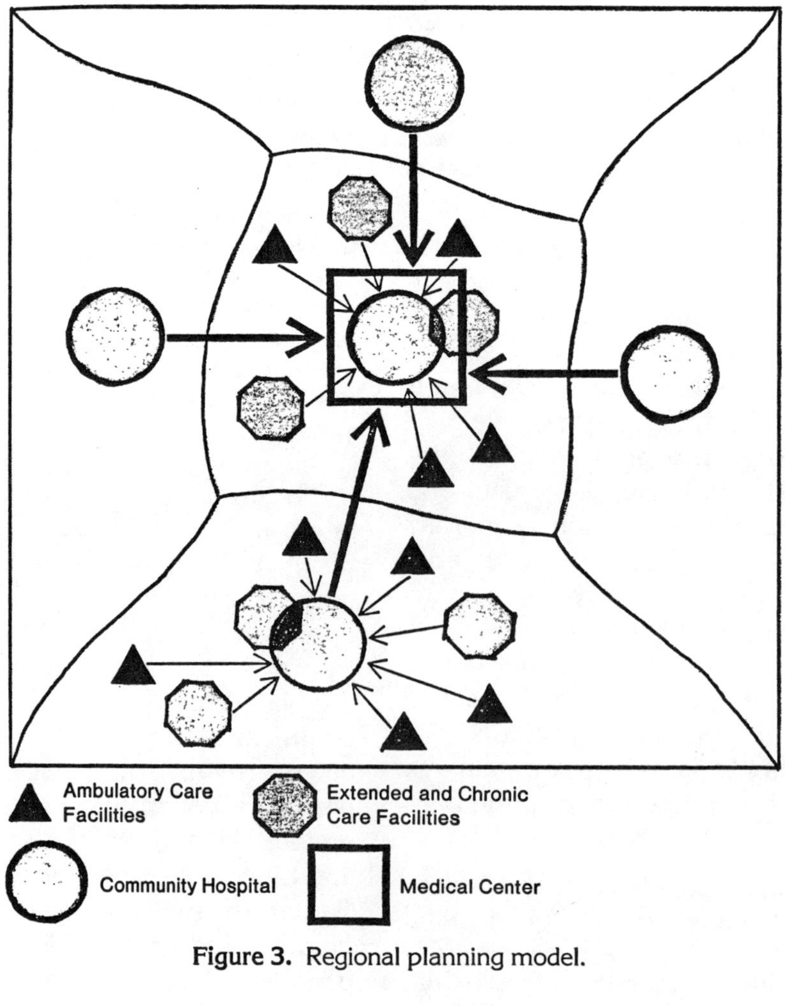

Figure 3. Regional planning model.

specialty care, and dental care as well as lab, X-ray, and pharmacy services. The HHC version, the NFCC, was designed to provide adequate space in each facility for a similar service program large enough to serve 55,000 patients who would generate approximately 160,000 annual visits at each site. Unlike the OEO-sponsored neighborhood health center, however, each NFCC was designed to also contain a substantial mental health component.

Unfortunately, the construction of seven NFCCs was nearing completion at the time of the fiscal crisis in New York City in the mid-1970s. The three NFCCs that were ready to be opened and staffed at that time were the converted outpatient departments of aged acute care hospitals that were eventually relocated (Morrisania NFCC), converted into a skilled nursing facility (Gouverneur NFCC), or closed (Sydenham NFCC). Two of the remaining 4 NFCCs (East New York NFCC and Belvis NFCC) were subsequently opened with partial staffing and resources provided to HHC by the U.S. Public Health Service through the National Health Service Corps and the Community Health Center Program, under federal Section 330 of the Public Health Act (Martin & Bohrer, 1980). The remaining two NFCCs were eventually sold (Soundview NFCC) or leased (Lower Washington Heights NFCC) to community organizations that independently obtained Section 330 community health center grants and now provide primary care services in those facilities.

In addition to these larger NFCCs, four smaller satellite primary care sites linked to NFCCs and backup hospitals had been established prior to 1982. The Harlem Primary Care Network received Section 330 funding in the late 1970s and established a network of three smaller satellite primary care sites in central Harlem in the service areas surrounding the Sydenham NFCC and Harlem Hospital. Another small primary care site (the Judson Center) had been opened in the lower east side of Manhattan as a satellite of the Gouverneur NFCC, with Bellevue as its backup hospital.

THE AMBULATORY CARE INITIATIVE

The HHC Ambulatory Care Initiative began in early 1982 with the establishment of a Corporate Office of Ambulatory Care Services charged with the task of critically analyzing the organization of existing community-based NFCCs, hospital-based outpatient departments (OPDs) and emergency services. In addition, it was asked to recommend and implement changes to improve or reconfigure service programs where needed.

Based on the subsequent Policy Statement on Ambulatory Care released in November 1982 by the corporate board of directors, HHC formally reestablished its commitment to provide quality personal health services to the communities served by HHC facilities. A broad set of goals, set forth in that policy statement, included:

- improving the accessibility and availability of needed outpatient services in appropriate community-based facilities as well as in hospital-based outpatient departments;
- developing a case-management approach for each patient with a specified primary care provider to supervise and coordinate care over time, through multiple levels of care (e.g., inpatient and outpatient) and among different subspecialty services as needed;
- providing a balance of primary care, specialty care, and emergency care at each facility and within each hospital service area as appropriate to meet the needs of the community; and
- assuring the efficiency and cost-effectiveness of each program through clear accountability of the medical and administrative leadership for the quality and quantity of services provided.

Several major functional components characterize the methodology designed to implement this initiative.

- *Needs assessment* refers to the development of a demographic and health status profile of (1) the "communities" in each hospital service area, and (2) the actual "users" of HHC services. These data permit an analysis of how well the programs at each network facility address the health needs of the at-risk populations in the program's service area and help guide the development of new programs and sites following a community-oriented primary care (COPC) methodology (Kark & Abramson, 1981; Nutting & Conner, 1984).
- Health care providers in charge of *diagnostic program management reviews* develop and apply an in-depth functional analysis of current ambulatory programs in each community-based and hospital-based facility. This serves as a baseline management review and helps identify priority areas for technical assistance or those areas in need of additional resources.
- Under the *"best model" work plan* each facility develops a work plan with a time-phased implementation schedule for its own "best model" program, consistent with the principles and expectations of the initiative.
- *Program monitoring and technical assistance* involve the corporate development and maintenance of (1) an ongoing monitoring methodology, and (2) a capacity to provide ongoing consultation and technical assistance to all HHC ambulatory care services programs.

As part of this initiative, extensive efforts have already led to the reconfiguration of most OPD clinics to primary care practices following the general principles of OPD conversion discussed elsewhere for public hospitals (Brown, 1968; San Augustin, Goldfrank, & Matz, 1976) and private, nonprofit hospitals (Block, 1980). This article, however, focuses only on the efforts and accomplishments of the ambulatory care initiative as they relate to the NFCC programs.

Diagnostic program management reviews

The NFCCs were the focus of the initial program management reviews. The methodology used for these reviews was modified from the original OEO Review Manual (Moorehead & Sparer, 1973) and the more recent BCHS Review Manual (Department of Health and Human Services, [DHHS], 1980), both of which were designed specifically for community health centers.

Between November of 1982 and June of 1983, review teams of 6 to 10 persons conducted 3-day on-site assessments of administrative, clinical, and financial management at each of the HHC community-based ambulatory care programs: the Morrisania and Belvis NFCCs in the Bronx (Lincoln Hospital backup), the Gouverneur NFCC (Bellevue Hospital backup), the Sydenham NFCC and the Harlem Primary Care Network (Harlem Hospital backup) in Manhattan, and the East New York NFCC in Brooklyn (Kings County Hospital backup). Each review generated a site visit report that became the basis for developing a best-model work plan by the local managers in consultation with an ongoing liaison person from the HHC Office of Ambulatory Care Services. Although some problems were local and specific to each facility, many findings identified generic problems across all corporate facilities. Action plans to correct local problems became the responsibility of the NFCC management team in conjunction with the executive director of the backup hospital. Action plans to analyze and correct corporate-wide system problems became the responsibility of the corporate office of ambulatory care in collaboration with the other appropriate corporate offices.

Each review generated a site visit report that became the basis for developing a best-model work plan by the local managers in consultation with an ongoing liaison person from the HHC Office of Ambulatory Care Services.

Program monitoring

A performance indicator reporting requirement (PIRR) was developed and implemented throughout all HHC facilities to enable each program manager and HHC central office to have a standardized set of reports with which to monitor performance trends over time. Patterned in concept after a similar federal reporting requirement (DHHS, 1982), these indicators were defined by work groups of facility managers and include parameters that represent useful information for administrative, clinical, and financial management of ambulatory care programs. The administrative indicators were implemented at the beginning of fiscal 1984 (July 1983) and are reported on a quarterly basis. The clinical indicators were implemented at the beginning of fiscal

1985 (July 1984) and are reported on a semiannual basis. The financial performance indicators were implemented at the beginning of fiscal 1986 (July 1985) and are also reported quarterly. Trend analysis reports are provided to each NFCC senior management team and backup hospital executive director and serve as a basis for periodic program monitoring at the local and corporate level. Selected highlights of these performance trends are presented in a later section of this article.

COMMUNITY-BASED NETWORK DEVELOPMENT

Efforts have been made to strengthen and develop organized systems of care within logical service areas. These efforts are reviewed briefly in terms of three different approaches—1) developing new sites; 2) expanding on-site specialty services; and 3) establishing hospital-based network liaison offices.

Site development

Seven new satellite primary care sites and one new NFCC have been designed and are now open or will be open by the end of calendar year 1985. These are presented briefly by borough.

Brooklyn (Kings County)

Woodhull Ambulatory Care Network

- The Maujer Street site opened in August 1982 in vacant space in the Williamsburg-Greenpoint District Health Center operated by the New York City Department of Health. Adolescent and adult services were provided as a satellite extension of the new Woodhull Hospital to complement the pediatric, women's health, dental, and mental health services already being provided at that facility. This became the first joint venture with the department of health.
- The Cumberland NFCC was designed and opened in July 1983 to serve the Fort Greene area as a replacement for the OPD services of the Cumberland Hospital, which closed that year. The new NFCC program provided a full range of family-oriented primary care medical and mental health services, including selected specialty services, as well as lab, X-ray and pharmacy services. In addition, a frequent shuttle service provided transportation for patients in need of additional diagnostic, ancillary, and subspecialty services at Woodhull, the backup hospital.
- The Greenpoint Health Center opened in September 1984 as a second joint venture with the New York City Department of Health, which closed a part-time child health station in the same neighborhood and assigned a pediatric nurse practitioner to become part of the primary care team at the new primary care center. The team provides care to all family members. In addition, limited lab and pharmacy services are available on-site. A similar shuttle service provides the vital transporta-

tion link to Woodhull as the backup hospital.

- The Bushwick site will open in the fall of 1985 in a comprehensive multiservice center owned and managed by yet another municipal agency, the New York City Human Resources Administration (HRA). This joint venture with HRA will also provide primary medical services for all family members. The new medical service will complement a mental health program currently offered in the same facility. In addition to limited lab and pharmacy services, this site will also be linked to Woodhull by shuttle service.

Coney Island Hospital Ambulatory Care Network

The Coney Island Community Health Center, partially supported by a Section 330 community health center grant, began providing family-oriented medical and dental health services in temporary facilities in November 1984 pending the completion of a new facility that was completed in August 1985. In addition, the medical staff provide family planning services in a nearby facility operated by the New York City HRA as another form of joint venture between the two agencies. Limited lab and pharmacy services are available at the new center, which is linked to Coney Island Hospital with a similar transportation system.

Queens (Queens County)

Queens Hospital Ambulatory Care Network

The South Jamaica Community Health Center, partially supported with a Section 330 community health center grant, is offering limited services at a temporary site pending the completion of its permanent location in another comprehensive multiservice center managed by HRA. On-site lab, pharmacy, and X-ray services will be available. Patients will be transported as needed to Queens Hospital for backup diagnostic and treatment services.

Manhattan (New York County)

Harlem Ambulatory Care Network

The Grant Houses site was added as a fourth primary care site in the Harlem Primary Care Network mentioned earlier. Limited lab and pharmacy services are available on-site. A van provides the needed transportation link with the referral backup services available at Harlem Hospital.

Bronx (Bronx County)

Lincoln Ambulatory Care Network

The Highbridge Center has been planned as a satellite of the Morrisania NFCC and will open in late 1985 to provide initial screening services in the Highbridge area of the Bronx. As demand increases, it will eventually provide a full range of primary medical care services to neighborhood families. Selected specialty services, lab, X-ray, and pharmacy services will be available at the Morrisania NFCC. More specialized backup services will be provided at Lincoln, the backup hospital.

On-site specialty services

Experience has shown that patients are more likely to identify with and commit themselves to ongoing care in a local primary care program that is able to provide a comprehensive service, including selected medical and surgical specialty care. When it is necessary to refer a patient to one or more specialty services at the backup hospital, there is a greater risk of losing that patient from comprehensive, continuous, preventive health care services.

To address this issue, an assessment was done of subspecialty utilization at all NFCCs to assure that the limited medical and surgical specialty services available on-site were appropriate. As a result of that assessment, selected subspecialty services were added or expanded at two NFCCs in fiscal 1984. Based on the frequency of off-site specialty referrals, four NFCCs have further documented the need for additional on-site services in the coming year.

Hospital-based network liaison offices

Prior to this initiative, the only hospital-based liaison office within the HHC system was at Bellevue Hospital and provided a linkage to the Gouverneur NFCC and its satellite, the Judson Center. Additional network liaison offices were funded in fiscal 1984 at two facilities (Harlem and Metropolitan) to help further strengthen the roles of these backup hospitals within their respective regional service networks. One additional hospital (Lincoln) received fiscal 1985 funds to establish a similar office to strengthen its linkages with the Belvis and Morrisania NFCCs.

At Harlem Hospital, a network referral system has been in place since 1983 to help shift the primary care workload away from the hospital's walk-in clinics and emergency service. Front desk clerks offer follow-up appointments at the Sydenham NFCC or at one of the four sites of the primary care network so that patients in need of ongoing care may receive it at the most convenient neighborhood location. This referral system is partly responsible for the increased utilization of the network sites during the past two years.

Similar network liaison offices with referral systems are being established in all other HHC hospitals that provide backup services to community-based primary care centers.

PROGRAM PERFORMANCE

Significant aspects of NFCC program performance include workload, efficiency, continuity of care, productivity, and quality of care.

Workload

The annual service volume in NFCCs is displayed in Figure 4, which shows the comparative sizes of the programs. Of the smaller satellite sites mentioned above, five were fully operational in fiscal 1984 and are represented here: the four sites of the Harlem Primary Care Network are included with the Sydenham NFCC, and the Judson Site is included with the Gouverneur NFCC. The size of the current workload ranges from 37,500 annual visits at Belvis NFCC to 219,400 annual visits at Gouverneur NFCC. The Belvis, East New York, and

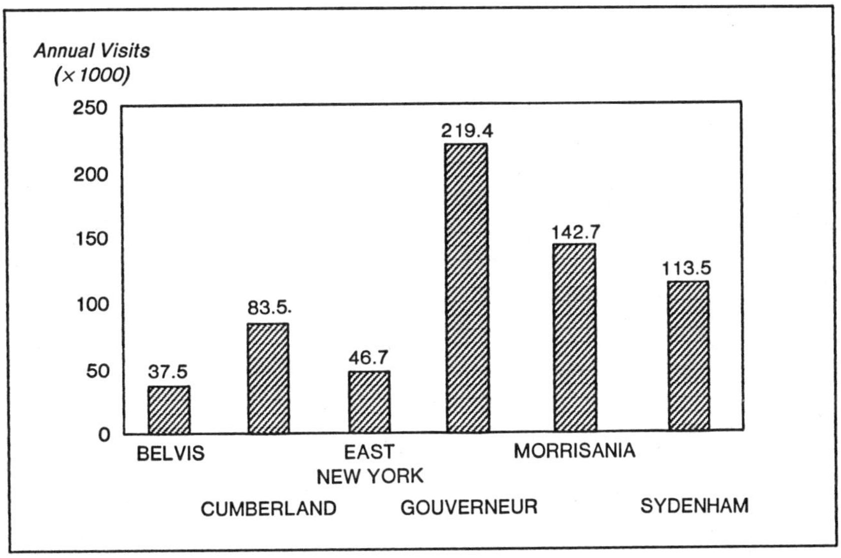

Figure 4. Annual NFCC workload by facility (N = 643,292 visits). Reprinted with permission of the HHC Office of Ambulatory Care Services.

Morrisania facilities were all designed and constructed with approximately the same square footage. All noted in Figure 4, the annual workload at the Belvis and the East New York facilities is far below that of Morrisania. Although utilization has increased at Belvis and East New York, the programs have still not yet been staffed to fully use the potential capacity of the buildings.

Efficiency

As an indicator of efficiency, each facility reports quarterly on the waiting time between the time of appointment and the time that the patient actually sees the provider. Appointment waiting times are plotted separately for each of the three primary care services: adult medicine, pediatrics, and women's health services—obstetrics and gynecology (OB/GYN). The performance trend over six quarterly reporting periods is displayed in Figure 5.

As shown, there has been a consistent improvement in average waiting time for all services—from about 50 to 60 minutes in the first quarter (Q1) of fiscal 1984 to 30 to 40 minutes in the second quarter (Q2) in fiscal 1985. A half-hour wait to see a primary care provider is reasonable and compares favorably with many private physician offices.

Continuity of care

As an indicator of continuity of care, each facility reports semiannually the proportion of visits within each primary care service to the same provider of record to whom the patient is assigned. This information comes from an audit of a sample of charts from patients who were active during the prior 6-month period. If the service is organized into teams (e.g., physician, nurse practitioner, midwife, etc.), a visit to any team member is counted as a visit to the same provider(s) of record. As seen in Figure 6, there has been a consistent improvement in continuity of care in all primary care services during these six reporting periods—from a low of around 70% of visits to the same provider during the first quarter (Q1) of fiscal 1984 up to 85 to 90% during the most recent period (Q2) in fiscal 1985. This indicator includes appointment visits as well as walk-in visits, most of which are referred to the assigned primary care provider if he or she is available. Again, this compares favorably with private physician group practices where patients may not always see their regular provider when they present for care without a prior appointment.

Productivity

On a quarterly basis, each facility computes productivity as the total number of primary care visits during the quarter divided by the full-time equivalent (FTE) provider staff. For the purposes of this computation, nurse practitioners, physician's assistants, and certified nurse midwives are considered equal to 0.5 FTE physician. The productivity trend over these six reporting periods is illustrated in Figure 7.

Although there is quarterly fluctuation, there has been a consistent increase in annual productivity from

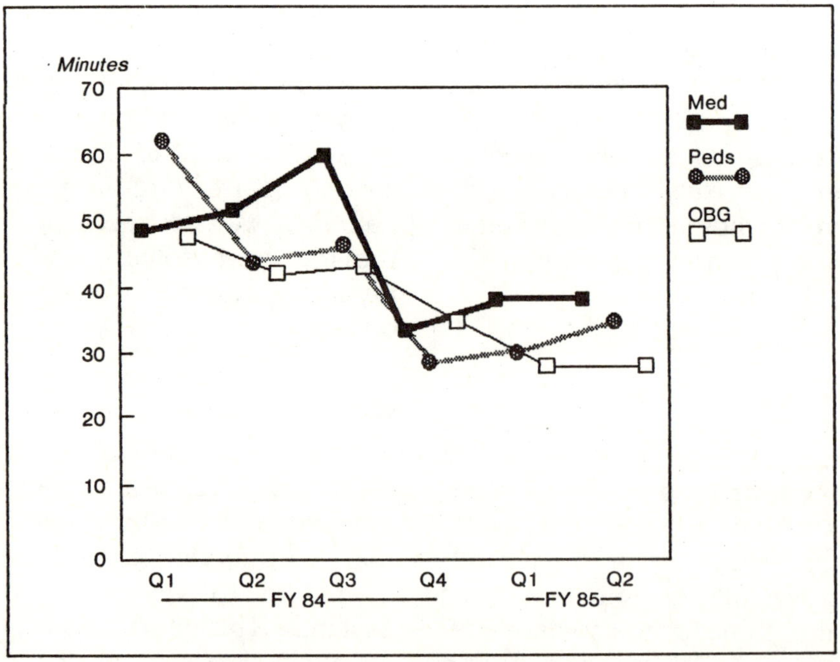

Figure 5. Efficiency indicator: appointment waiting time in NFCCs. Reprinted with permission of the HHC Office of Ambulatory Care Services.

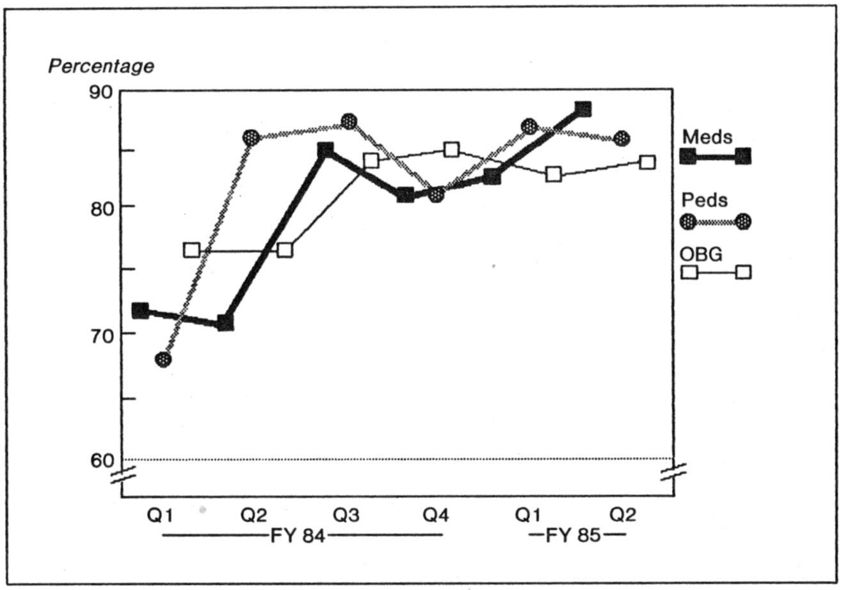

Figure 6. Continuity of care indicator: percentage of visits to same provider in NFCCs. Reprinted with permission of the HHC Office of Ambulatory Care Services.

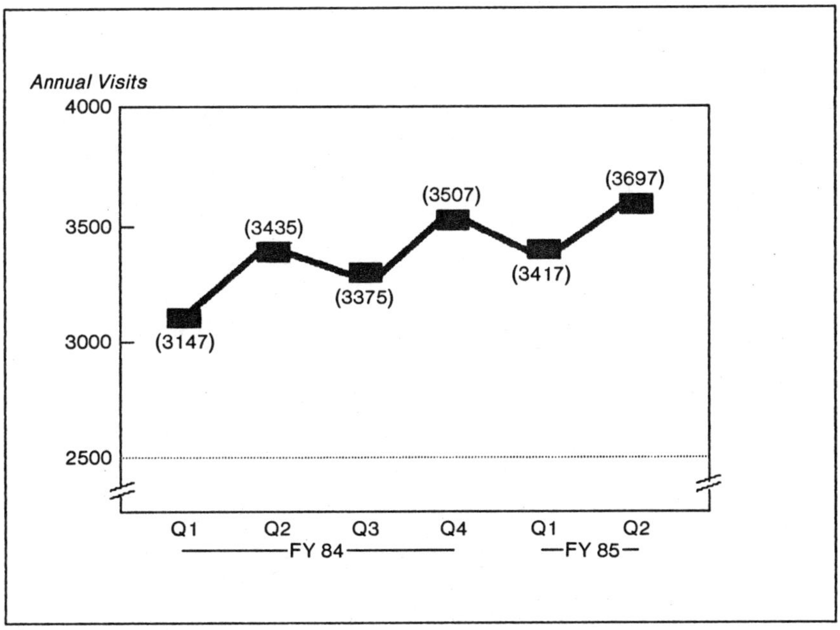

Figure 7. Productivity indicator: annual visits per provider in NFCCs. Reprinted with permission of the HHC Office of Ambulatory Care Services.

just over 3,100 annual visits per provider in the first quarter (Q1) of fiscal 1984 up to almost 3,700 annual visits per provider in the second quarter (Q2) of fiscal 1985. This improvement is partially explained on the basis of revised administrative and patient flow systems (i.e., improved medical records and a new automated booking system), increases in the number and quality of clerical and nursing support staff, and the replacement of part-time providers with full-time physicians who have completed primary care residency training programs in family medicine, pediatrics, or internal medicine.

Quality of care

As an indication of quality of care, each facility reports semiannually the results of chart audits within each primary care service. A sample of records is reviewed to determine the percentage of charts in compliance with selected parameters of care. This chart review is a basic component of the comprehensive quality assurance program for the overall facility.

The following clinical indicators were defined by an advisory group of medical directors from HHC facilities:

- percent of children age 2 immunized on schedule;
- percent of women age 35 to 60 with Pap smear result posted or documented in the medical record in the past 3 years;
- percent of men 40 or over with documented rectal exam and stool guaiac on the chart within the past year;
- percent of prenatal charts with weight, blood pressure, urinalysis, height of fundus and fetal heart rate documented at each prenatal visit; and
- percent of postpartum or postabortion adolescents (under 20 years) with documented family planning counseling on the chart.

These indicators, which focus on basic levels of health maintenance and disease prevention, were developed in fiscal 1984 and fully implemented in fiscal 1985. Therefore, no clinical performance trend data can be presented at this time. It is expected that by the end of 1985 a trend analysis of these clinical indicators will be available. This will assist local program managers and corporate staff in monitoring clinical performance.

FUTURE TRENDS

The NFCC program is, indeed, alive and well in New York City. Seven new satellite primary care centers and one new NFCC will be open by the end of 1985. Referral systems and formal linkages are being implemented by means of network liaison offices in six backup hospitals. Performance changes reveal improved efficiency, continuity of care, and productivity in the NFCC programs. Utilization of community-based sites continues to increase through efforts to shift an inappropriate primary care workload away from HHC's overloaded emergency services.

Although much has been accomplished, these efforts must be seen

> **Although much has been accomplished, these efforts must be seen within the larger framework of future trends in the U.S. health care industry from an organizational as well as a reimbursement and regulatory perspective.**

within the larger framework of future trends in the U.S. health care industry from an organizational as well as a reimbursement and regulatory perspective.

Organized systems of care

Although linkages among providers are improving, public funding for health services to the medically underserved remains limited and will most likely continue to decrease under the current federal administration.

In addition to HHC facilities and services in New York City, other providers who receive partial or full federal, state, or local public support include, but are not limited to:

- community health centers (medical and dental services) operated by local not-for-profit corporations partially supported with Section 330 grants;
- child health stations and pediatric treatment centers operated by the Bureau of Child Health of the New York City Department of Health;
- maternity and infant care programs (prenatal and family planning services) operated by the Medical and Health Research Association under contract with the New York City and New York State Departments of Health;
- school health programs operated by the Bureau of School Children's and Adolescent Health of the New York City Department of Health; and
- family planning programs operated by Planned Parenthood, by other licensed providers receiving partial support from Title X family planning grants, or by the HRA.

With shrinking resources and expanding need, it is imperative that these providers aggressively pursue all options aimed at collaboration and networking, both formal and informal, to assure the maximum use of these limited resources for the composite benefit of the medically underserved.

Reimbursement and regulatory environment

The ambulatory version of a DRG methodology is currently under development at Yale University (Fetter, 1980) and at Brandeis University (Lion, 1984) under grants from the Health Care Financing Administration (HCFA). An additional HCFA grant has recently been awarded to the New York State Office of Health Systems Management to develop its own version of a similar methodology.

Multiple public- and private-sector demonstrations are already at various stages of design and implementation in New York City, for example, the Metropolitan Hospital Health Plan, the South Queens Health Plan, the Bronx Health Plan, and the Bronx Perinatal Consortium. Each plan is based on some variation of the theme of modified or full capitation for a defined group of patients, some of which may be Medicaid recipients.

Heavy hospital length-of-stay penalties loom ahead from third party payers through new peer review organization (PRO) regulation. This may provide further financial incentives for hospitals to strengthen their linkages and backup support with community-based primary care programs in order to help reduce DRG-related length-of-stay through early discharge planning.

• • •

The potential for evolving a more rational system of primary, specialty, emergency, and inpatient care on a regional basis in New York City as outlined in 1967 by the Piel Commission Report may be greater now, in a time of financial austerity, than at any time in the past. The future survival of many community-based programs and some private, nonprofit hospitals may depend on networking and collaborative marketing through a "team" approach. Such an essential partnership among providers and community groups will facilitate the promotion of health in its fullest sense—the total physical, mental, and social well-being of the people. In that context, the NFCC program continues its rise from the ashes of the fiscal desert of the 1970s like the phoenix of Egyptian mythology to establish its solid position among other community-based programs that form the critical network of primary care services for the medically underserved in New York City.

REFERENCES

Alford, R. (1975). *Health care politics.* Chicago: University of Chicago Press, pp. 158–164.

Block, J. (1980). Hospital-sponsored primary care: The community hospital program of the Robert Wood Johnson Foundation. *Journal of Ambulatory Care Management, 3*(1), 1–14.

Brown, H. (January 1968). The delivery of personal health services and medical services for the poor: Concessions or prerogatives. *Milbank Memorial Fund Quarterly Supplement,* Part 2, 203–223.

Commission on the Delivery of Personal Health Services. (1967). *Comprehensive community health services for New York City.* Report of the Commission on the Delivery of Personal Health Services, p. 27.

Department of Health and Human Services. (May 1980). *Primary care effectiveness program review manual.* Rockville, MD: USPHS, HRA, BCHS.

Department of Health and Human Services. (January 1982). *Instruction manual for the BCHS common reporting requirement (BCRR).* Rockville, MD: USPHS, HSA, BCHS.

Fetter, R. (1980). *Ambulatory patient related groups.* Unpublished manuscript, Yale University.

Kark, S., & Abramson, J. (February, March 1981). Community focused health care. *Israel Journal of Medical Science, 17*(2–3), 65–70.

Levin, P., & Wolfson, J. (August 1984). Community-based ambulatory health services: The logic of the 1960's. *Journal of Ambulatory Care Management,* 7(3), 25–31.

Lion, J. (November 1984). Ambulatory visit groups: A prospective payment system for outpatient care. *Journal of Ambulatory Care Management,* 7(4), 30–45.

Martin, E., & Bohrer, R. (August 1980). The federal initiative in primary care. *Journal of Ambulatory Care Management, 3*(3), 33–45.

Martin Luther King Fourth Annual Report. (1970). Bronx, NY: Dr. Martin Luther King, Jr. Health Center.

Moorehead, M. A., & Sparer, G. (1973). *Ambulatory care health services review manual.* Evaluation

Unit, Department of Community Health, Albert Einstein College of Medicine, New York.
Nutting, P., & Conner, E. (April 1984). *Community oriented primary care: A practical assessment.* Washington, DC: National Institute of Medicine, National Academy Press.
Office of Economic Opportunity. (1968). *The comprehensive neighborhood health services program—Guidelines.* Washington, DC: OEO Office of Health Affairs.
San Augustin, M., Goldfrank, L., & Matz, R. (1976). Reorganization of ambulatory health care in an urban municipal hospital. *Archives of Internal Medicine, 136,* 1252–1266.
Stoeckle, J., & Candib, L. (June 1969). The neighborhood health center—Reform ideas of yesterday and today. *New England Journal of Medicine, 280*(25), 1385–1391.

Joint ventures in ambulatory care

Neal F. Bermas, PhD
Managing Partner
Bermas Associates
Pittsburgh, PA
Los Angeles, CA

THE HEALTH CARE industry today is recognizing that diversification is a survival strategy that must be given serious consideration. Many providers, however, are reluctant to explore businesses that are either unrelated to the delivery of traditional services or that conflict with the constituencies they are presently serving.

It is not surprising that ambulatory care projects are often among the first to be explored by providers confronted with increased competition for patients and with other pressures brought to bear as a result of Medicare's fixed-payment reimbursement system and other cost-cutting incentives. Ambulatory care minimizes reliance on traditional sources of revenue without straying too far from the provider's established area of expertise, namely, health care.

In addition to selecting ambulatory care as an appropriate option, providers are attempting to ensure successful diversification by pursuing ambulatory care projects on a joint-venture basis. A joint venture gives access to investment capital that might not otherwise be available from either debt or equity sources. Furthermore, the presence of a business partner minimizes risk by allowing a sharing of losses. While a provider who pursues joint ventures in ambulatory care will have to share profits and forfeit some managerial control, it is often the path of least resistance.

FACTORS DETERMINING PROJECT OUTCOMES

The trade-off between risk and control is clearly the basic issue to be addressed when assessing the financial, political, and managerial implications of joint ventures in ambulatory care. However, the many advantages and disadvantages of joint versus solo ventures cannot be reduced to a simple preference for more control and less risk (or vice versa). Many factors will contribute to determining the outcome of any given project. Some of those that should be examined when attempting to predict the ultimate profile of a joint venture in ambulatory care are noted below.

- Partners and their motivations: Potential partners may be health care providers or strictly business partners; partnerships may include physician group practices, individual physicians, hospitals, employer groups, or individual private investors.
- The nature of the partnership: The three basic models are (1) the contractual arrangement, in which no new legal entity is created; (2) the corporation, which is jointly owned by two or more investors; and (3) the limited partnership, which includes a general managing partner and a group of nonmanaging partners.
- Status as tax exempt or nonexempt: Any of the partners may find their tax status changed and their financial well-being affected as a result of the terms of the joint venture. One or more new entities may be formed, and it may or may not be advantageous to establish them as for-profit organizations.
- Relation of the ambulatory care unit to a hospital facility: Freestanding centers will of necessity be managed differently from hospital-based units and may be subject to legal constraints that have both managerial and financial implications.
- Nature of the service rendered: The possibilities include an array of physician specialties as well as a host of services such as a primary and emergency care, surgery, oncology, sports medicine, and so on. Any given service may result in more or less risk control for any given partner entity depending on current levels of demand in the marketplace and on the entity's expertise vis-à-vis that of its partner(s).

Before exploring specific ambulatory care projects, potential coventurers should give serious consideration to some general principles and characteristics that pertain to all joint ventures, whether in the provision of health care or of other products and services. First, a general understanding of the term *joint venture* is in order. Although it does not have an exact legal definition, Young & Bradford (1977) have suggested that it is an enterprise formed by two or more organizations or individuals, at least one of which is an entity already in operation as a going concern, for the purpose of conducting a new business. It thus includes associate equity owners who take an active role in the formation and operation—or formation or operation—of the business, in contrast to the simple role of passive investor.

Acknowledging this aspect of the coventurers as active partners is particularly important so that the going-concern partner understands that the new venture is a separate company and not a fully controlled subsidiary or division of its own operation. The joint venture should be viewed as autonomous and complete within itself. This attitude is more likely to develop if the agreement is structured so that the seeming "parent" is not granted an excessively large equity holding. In fact, no one venturer or investor should be permitted to dominate the business. Increasing the number of parties involved helps to obviate this problem but creates the knottier problem of complicating management and decision-making processes by virtue of a greater number of participants. However, persons or entities considering joint venturing may alleviate their fears that an untenable relationship could eventually develop. All parties concerned should devote time and effort to anticipating the requirements of a successful joint venture, recognizing that special problems may arise in addition to the usual ones encountered by any new business. The following elements have been suggested (Young & Bradford, 1977) for inclusion in a feasibility assessment:

- general statement of purpose and preliminary review of specific, tangible objectives;
- identification of factors that justify joint venturing, such as one's own shortcomings or the potential coventurer's strengths;
- description of assets available for contribution to the venture, including property, plant, equipment, and cash;
- market studies that include current demand and growth potential, competitor analysis, and pertinent demographics;
- pro forma financial statements that show a range of possibilities between a set of optimistic and pessimistic outcomes;
- organizational profile, including the number and types of employees needed, as well as a designation of responsibility and authority;
- analysis of legal issues likely to affect the formation and ongoing operation of the venture.

Some illustrations will demonstrate how joint venturing in ambulatory care may be financially and managerially preferable to going it alone. The following examples also suggest the wide array of structures available and the need to tailor each project to the environment in which it is being developed.

MEDICAL OFFICE BUILDINGS

One well-established form of joint venture involving hospitals and physicians or other investors is the medical office building (MOB), whereby facilities for physician practice offices are constructed in proximity to the hospital. The MOB offers the hospitals the ability to increase or maintain revenues by attracting physicians who will refer their patients to the hospital. In addition, the facility provides the hospitals with revenues from the physician-tenants to whom office space is leased. Physicians in return accrue the advantages of having their practices conveniently located to the hospital, perhaps under favorable rental terms if the hospital is concerned with attracting and keeping physicians in the neighborhood.

Additional financial benefits accrue to those physicians who become investors in an MOB project. As partners, physicians will share in the profits of the venture, and those profits may be allocated in one of several ways, depending on the legal nature of the partnership. The most important financial advantage, however, derives from the venture's ability to generate tax benefits that, although of no use to the typical not-for-profit hospital, can be passed along to the tax-paying physicians and other investors. Most notably, the laws concerning the accelerated depreciation of project costs allow investors to be favorably allocated the associated tax benefits. Furthermore, a heavily invested partner may reap additional tax benefits as a result of partnership losses (intentionally projected into the venture) considered in the calculation of personal income taxes.

Although joint MOB ventures have their overall advantages, the structuring of a mutually beneficial partnership is actually quite complicated and presents many potential pitfalls. One hypothetical arrangement that illustrates some of the complexities suggests that the hospital or its newly established not-for-profit affiliate construct the office building with funds from short-term, tax-exempt securities (Swett & Conley, 1984). The initiation of this process by a not-for-profit entity is important because a for-profit venture—such as a simple hospital–physician partnership—would not be permitted to finance itself with proceeds of tax-exempt debt, except for small-issue industrial development bonds (IDBs). As a second step in the process—and during construction—the funds obtained would be invested at higher-yielding taxable rates, allowing the hospital to realize investment income on the "spread." The completed MOB would subsequently be sold to a limited partnership consisting of the hospital and the physicians. The general partner in this arrangement would be a for-profit affiliate of the hospital, whereas physician investors would become limited partners. The for-profit affiliate would lease the MOB from the partnership, becoming the eventual owner in a sale-and-leaseback transaction, and would meanwhile sublease office space to individual physicians or physician groups. Fees for leases and subleases would be established such that income and tax benefits would accrue to the advantage of all parties concerned. Optimization of the total transaction might call for the eventual sale of the MOB back to the hospital, whereby the hospital could start the process over again with a new group of physician investors.

Whatever the contractual arrangements in establishing a joint MOB venture, a hospital must avoid generating substantial unrelated business income (UBI) that might jeopardize its tax-exempt status. Real estate development in itself is clearly not a charitable activity but may be judged as consistent with the hospital's tax-exempt purpose of expanding its patient base. However, because each joint venture is unique, the Internal Revenue Service (IRS) is likely to subject any such venture to careful scrutiny. This applies also to assuring that private partners such as physicians receive no inurement of benefits by reason of their association with a tax-exempt entity. For this reason, partnership agreements must be carefully worded. Referral of patients, one of the hospital's desired goals, must not be a condition for providing benefits to physicians nor raised as an issue during negotiations.

Management issues may arise when hospitals find that their medical staff members are also their MOB business partners. Although physicians will, of course, manage their own individual ambulatory care practices, management of the office building itself may be a source of disagreement. To the extent possible, all policies and procedures, as well as lines of authority and responsibility, should be established in writing and agreed to by all parties, just as legal and financial arrangements are contractually established.

To the extent possible, all policies and procedures, as well as lines of authority and responsibility, should be established in writing and agreed to by all parties, just as legal and financial arrangements are contractually established.

In addition, a hospital must not let its financial relationship with any physician or group of physicians influence the management of the hospital. Particularly with regard to issues affecting quality of care, a hospital must maintain the distance necessary to continue to review physicians objectively. This issue is avoided if the investment partners are persons other than local physicians or those who will actually use the facility. However, other conflict-of-interest issues could be raised if, for example, members of the hospital board or persons otherwise affiliated with the hospital are to become partners in the venture.

PRIMARY CARE CENTERS

Variations on the MOB venture are the assortment of primary care centers where care is provided at a relatively small neighborhood center during extended hours on a walk-in basis. A center may be established to treat minor emergencies as well as episodes of acute illness. Unlike the MOB arrangement, however, the partnership establishes a facility as a means for independent physicians to coordinate the provision of a health care service rather than simply as a building where physicians lease space to manage their individual practices. This implies the necessity for an organizational structure to manage the medical practice as well as the administrative aspects of the business partnership.

Agreeing on such a structure is difficult under any circumstances. The process is further complicated by state regulations that often restrict a business corporation in its ability to employ physicians to practice medicine on behalf of the corporation. Thus, if a facility is owned by some business entity not medically licensed (although made up of licensed hospital and physician investors), it must acknowledge that it advertises, collects fees, and so forth on behalf of the physicians practicing within the facility. The question of licensure itself is resolved in a dissimilar manner from state to state and further affects the managerial arrangements legally possible in any given area.

Another concern for hospitals seeking to collaborate in joint ventures in freestanding primary care centers is state Certificate-of-Need (CON) laws, which regulate the creation of health care facilities. A unit that is deemed an expansion of a hospital might be subject to CON regulation. A unit operated by some newly formed business entity such as a corporation or partnership involving hospitals, physicians, and others may not be subject to such regulation; if the facility itself is judged as a physician office building, regardless as to who owns it, CON requirements may not apply. Therefore, depending on who or what entity is considered, the owner and depending on the definition applied in identifying the facility by type, CON legislation may or may not have to be assessed. Recently, there has been some state legislative activity initiated in response to the rapid growth of freestanding primary care centers, and the tendency appears to be for greater state control with regard to both the development and operation of such centers (Punch, 1984).

Many of the issues already mentioned as applicable to formulating the optimal joint venture in MOBs are also relevant to joint ventures in primary care centers as well as in any other area of ambulatory care. These include the accrual of tax benefits to individual investors, the potential for enhanced hospital revenues (from the new business itself as well as from additional referrals), IRS scrutiny with regard to tax-exempt status, and so on.

AMBULATORY SURGERY CENTERS

As a response to the call for cost containment in the provision of medical care, ambulatory surgery centers have become an attractive joint-venture project. Technological advances and expanded third-party payment of outpatient surgery have further been enhanced by the feasibility of such projects. As with any diversification strategy, health care providers may proceed not only in response to these opportunities in the marketplace, but also to ward off threats. The so-called surgicenter market has been discovered by for-profit companies, some of which have plans to expand their networks of facilities nationwide. Facing this competition and also finding inpatient surgery a less profitable business to be in since the enactment of Medicare's prospective payment system, many hospitals see outpatient surgery as an appropriate solution. The decision to proceed on a joint-venture basis follows from the realization that potential competitors, namely physicians, can become collaborators and that it is possible for the hospital–physician relationship to generally become more productive.

For a hospital considering diversification and acknowledging the advantages of joint venturing, one further issue has financial implications that may motivate a hospital to opt for an ambulatory surgicenter over other projects. Under Medicare regulations, an ambulatory care center that engages primarily in surgical procedures might be eligible for reimbursement of its reasonable costs. This reimbursement level could be higher than that which a typical primary care center would receive by virtue of being reimbursed only for services rendered as Part B benefits. At the same time, a physician (or the hospital or its affiliate) who bills Medicare rather than patients will receive only the charges paid by the carrier, plus the beneficiary's deductibles and copayments—an amount that could fall short of the physician's "actual charges." Of course, none of these reimbursement issues is important if the relevant patient population is itself primarily not Medicare eligible.

SPECIALIZED SERVICES

General medicine and surgery are not the only forms of medical care appropriate for inclusion in a joint-venture strategy. An array of specialized diagnostic and treatment modalities that manage patients with renal disease, eating disorders, chemical dependencies, and so on are increasingly likely to be provided in an ambulatory setting because of the same financial incentives that make hospitals extend some of their general medical services to outpatient settings. One such specialized service that has caught the attention of hospitals and other investors for its potential to meet all criteria of a worthwhile joint-venture project is that made available through freestanding imaging centers that house computerized tomography (CT), ultrasound, and magnetic resonance scanners. At least one company, founded by a physician, has established itself as a national developer of these facilities and expects to be operating 100 of them within the next few years (Johnson, 1984).

The developer's plan accounts for many of the financial and managerial considerations that are relevant to joint ventures in medical office buildings and to primary care, and it proceeds in much the same way. The typical scheme calls for hospitals to serve as general partners and for physicians or other private investors to enter as limited partners. The project is attractive to hospitals because it allows them to cut their costs and to improve their relations with physicians. It also allows hospitals to provide an additional service that they may not be able to afford or get approved by state regulatory agencies if they were to attempt to set up such a service within the hospital. For investors, the usual tax advantages are possible if the transaction is properly structured. Finally, all parties gain from the revenues generated by the imaging center.

Managerial control of the imaging business is typically left to the designated partners or investors who determine what services will be offered and the rates to be charged. Physicians working within the facility maintain control of the medical aspects of the operation just as they would in any private practice setting where they pay rental fees to a hospital or its for-profit affiliate. In order to maintain this necessary distance between the managers of the business and the managers of the imaging practice, the partners may want to consider excluding radiologists from the investor group. This will also prevent conflict-of-interest claims that might otherwise arise when physician investors refer too many of their own patients to the imaging centers.

• • •

Health care providers are generally convinced of not only the feasibility of but also the necessity of diversifying into the provision of ambulatory care services. The decision to proceed on a joint-venture basis is warranted if financing will be facilitated, revenues enhanced, important relationships improved, and comprehensiveness and quality of care attained to a greater degree than would be possible under the terms of a solo venture. A realistic assessment of any proposed joint venture must also acknowledge the need to make trade-offs. Once the advantages are deemed to outweigh the disadvantages of joint venturing in general, potential coventurers should then be prepared to answer other more specific questions:

1. What ambulatory business should be entered?
2. Is there a suitable partner willing and able to collaborate?
3. What legal form should the venture take, given the nature of the service and the objectives of the investment partners?
4. Will it be advisable to engage the services of a third party to assist in the development of the venture?

Although competitive and other economic pressures may inject an urgency into this decision-making process, the many financial and managerial implications of joint ventures in ambulatory care should be carefully analyzed before contractual agreements are made or resources committed. For an inappropriate or poorly implemented diversification strategy may be more damaging than no diversification strategy at all.

REFERENCES

Johnson, D. (1984). Joint ventures. MRI paints bright picture for imaging center partnerships. *Modern Healthcare, 14*(6), 61–62, 68.

Punch, L. (1984). Emergi-centers fight state regs. *Modern Healthcare, 14*(6), 98–99.

Swett, T. F. & Conley, D. J. (1984). Joint ventures: The theory and practice. *Hospitals,58*(9), 95–96; 99–100.

Young, G. R. & Bradford, S. (1977). *Joint ventures: Planning and action.* New York: Financial Executives Research Foundation.

Survival strategies for HMOs

Eric N. Berkowitz, PhD
Professor of Marketing
School of Management
University of Massachusetts
Amherst, Massachusetts

THE COMPETITIVE environment of health maintenance organizations (HMOs) is increasing dramatically as rapid growth in membership attracts new plans. For existing organizations, the early strategies used to enroll members must be reexamined in the light of this competition. When health care providers effectively use marketing tactics, several alternative strategies for survival will present themselves.

There is little denial that in a dramatically brief time period a shift has occurred in the U.S. health care system—from a bed-driven perspective to one of ambulatory care. This change has resulted in a dramatic restructuring of organizations and the appearance of a multitude of new competitors in the marketplace. In all kinds of ambulatory care, from freestanding facilities, hospital-sponsored systems, and HMOs, there are increasing competitive pressures. Although the first half of this decade was marked by large-scale development of ambulatory care facilities, the second half of this decade may be categorized as the era of ambulatory care survival.

Between July 1982 and June 1983, 24 new HMOs were started nationwide, increasing the competition vying for the HMO participant ("Membership in HMOs," 1984). Specific attention is paid to HMOs and to alternative actions these organizations may pursue to maintain their position among more ambulatory care alternatives. These survival strategies are outlined with regard to the components of the marketing mix—distribution, pricing, service, and promotion.

NETWORKING—THE KEY TO DISTRIBUTION

Future survival for HMOs may well lie in the distribution element of the marketing mix, whereby market dominance could be achieved by networking. Networking can be explained in the context of levels and options. Networking occurs when providers in one geographic area join with those in another geographic area that offer similar services. Presently, HMOs offer coverage to subscribers who receive services outside the service area. Yet this service typically is only for emergency medical needs and is reimbursed at traditional indemnity plan levels. In a networked system, a subscriber would receive similar coverage outside the primary service area with little additional paperwork and at the usual copayment plan requirements.

A second network approach is for the HMO to work with other local providers who offer a different service. For example, an HMO might network with several area urgicenters to provide extended hour-coverage with no capital or personnel resource requirements for the organization.

A third network variation would involve linkages to major national referral centers. In this approach, an HMO would establish relationships with referral centers like Mayo, Baylor, Scripps, or Sloan-Kettering. Each facility would be contracted with to provide services in their respective areas of expertise. The networked HMO could then offer a subscriber access to the leading national health resources.

A large, networked HMO would be beneficial to both employers and employees. For many large corporations, employees are typically located at multiple cities around a state or the country. In this instance, a networked HMO may represent a cost-effective, viable option to offer employees. Control of employee health care costs can be more easily monitored with a centralized buying process at headquarters. Moreover, administrative costs can be dramatically reduced if one plan can be offered at all employee locations.

Employees also gain advantages from a large, networked system. Employees transferred between locations will be able to stay within the same health care system. Moreover, an HMO networked to well-known tertiary centers would dramatically reduce consumers' fears of constrained access in joining an HMO. Although referrals to the national networked centers would be highly restricted through protocols requiring physician referral, there would be a strong, positive halo effect of tying the HMO to the larger, nationally known health facility. The multistate network also has distinct consumer benefits in that such a network reduces consumer fears of no coverage when leaving the immediate service area. In the networked system, consumers could open the phone directory in the 100 major U.S. markets and see their health provider prominently listed.

These are early signs that networking has begun. Blue Cross presently offers their HMO in 21 states; Health America provides service to 18 states. Lacking in these systems is the ability of subscribers to receive care across state plans, but that difficulty could be overcome. Networking, a distribution strategy, may be a link to survival.

PRICING

A second element that contributes to survival strategies are alternative pricing programs. In the age of survival, as more competitors enter the market, price competition is difficult because of the existence of a number of alternative plans. Pricing the plan should be viewed with the loss-leader concept in mind.

Using this philosophy, the HMO should conduct marketing research for a target population to determine the appropriate copayment and monthly premium levels deemed most attractive. Trade-off analysis, such as conjoint analysis, can help determine which arrangement provides the most positive impression of a plan being viewed as the least costly, best coverage option (Green & Rao, 1971). For example, is it worthwhile to have a low monthly premium, yet several copayments for primary care visits, hospitalization, and so on? Or, would a plan be most positively valued with a higher monthly premium, but fewer copayments? In the survival stage, loss-leader pricing is important in recognizing that there are two aspects to price setting. Internal financial data based on utilization may set the price floor, but market expectations set the price ceiling. Sensitivity to the ceiling is critical in this phase of an HMO's existence.

Another valuable survival strategy is recognizing the role pricing may play in creating a barrier to entry into the market for other possible competitors (Porter, 1985). In this role, price is used to block new competitors. Typically, the HMO contract with the employer and subscriber is for a 1-year period, yet in the age of survival, several competitors have entered the market. In Honolulu, Minneapolis, Los Angeles, Chicago, Cincinnati, and Boston, there

Internal financial data based on utilization may set the price floor, but market expectations set the price ceiling. Sensitivity to the ceiling is critical in this phase of an HMO's existence.

are at least three competing HMOs. A barrier to entry could be developed through an extended pricing package. Existing HMOs using this method would offer contracts to employers who guarantee the price (or even discount it) if subscribers are offered 2-year contracts at a guaranteed rate. As later competitors enter the market, likely buyers who might switch plans have been insulated from such actions for an extended period of time.

SERVICE OPTIONS FOR SURVIVAL

The survival stage is the time for a reexamination of service offerings. New growth can be derived from capturing late joiners whose profile is similar to those of subscribers or by appealing to market segments that differ from existing subscribers geographically or demographically.

The late or potential subscribers are a group more critical or more skeptical about HMO advantages. For these consumers, the fear of restricted choice of physicians may be a salient factor in not enrolling. The survival strategy for this group involves reducing the perceived subscription barrier. To minimize this barrier, HMOs could use after-hour clinics or horizontally integrate with preferred provider organization (PPO) structure. The goal of both approaches is to encourage low-cost trial of the plan.

After-hour clinics open to both members and nonmembers of the plan could be established. Nonmembers who use the clinic would be billed for services at standard, market-rate charges. Records on nonmembers who use the system would include standard medical information and employee data. The HMO membership office would then integrate that consumer's name on a qualified prospect list; the list would be used for marketing during the company's reenrollment period. A month before the beginning of the reenrollment period, the department would send the consumer a letter recalling the visit and the fact that the HMO after-hours clinic was there to meet his or her needs. Moreover, the low cost of this service to HMO members should be highlighted along with a statement about the opportunity to become a member during the reenrollment period. An HMO brochure should accompany the letter.

Acting as a PPO or traditional insurance plan is a more difficult, but potentially more effective survival strategy. With this option, services of physicians who are not in the plan are offered at traditional coverage rates. Members who use HMO plan physicians are covered at the reduced copayment levels or at first-dollar coverage. The patient has the option of using physicians both inside and outside the HMO component. Incentives such as reduced health-club memberships, dental checkups, or reduced prescription costs might be offered as an incentive to switch. It is likely that during the year, trial might begin with primary care because of scheduling convenience. The enrollee would discover reasonable care at a substantially reduced cost. This low-cost, low-risk trial, if a positive experience, may result in having the consumer later using the plan specialists when needed, and eventually being a loyal HMO subscriber. Prudential, the nation's leading commercial group health insurance carrier, is preparing to market a program called the Prudential Health Care System. Beneficiaries will be provided incentives in the form of reduced copayments to use plan physicians, but they will not be locked into the system. ("Prudential to Offer," 1985).

In the marketing strategy to capture share, it is important to recognize that converting a "trier" to a subscriber is easier than getting the consumer who has no experience with the plan to become a subscriber. It is this premise that underlies both service survival strategies.

As noted, the other focus for additional growth is to attract new subscribers who are geographically or sociodemographically different from existing members. Because of this objective, multistate networking may have appeal. On a more limited basis, extension of service coverage to new local markets might also be an attractive alternative. Focusing on sociodemographically different markets has been the approach taken by Med Center HMO in Minneapolis and Choice Care in Cincinnati. Both organizations are aggressively pursuing enrollment programs to consumers over 65 years of age. This market segment was not the original target population for either plan, but now represents dramatic new growth opportunity.

PROMOTIONAL OPTIONS

The promotional element of the marketing mix also plays an important role in survival. In terms of advertising, the need is to highlight the selective, competitive advantages of the plan. In the early stages of any HMO's existence, a large portion of advertising copy is of a generic nature. The message describes the HMO concept and its general value to subscribers. In the later stage of survival with more competitors, advertising copy should shift away from generic, explanatory messages about HMOs. There are two reasons for this strategy—knowledge and emotion.

In terms of knowledge, it can be assumed that in the survival stage, all competing HMOs have contributed to the market's education of the generic concept of prepaid care. In terms of emotion, it is important to recognize in the survival stage that appeals to join an HMO are being made to late potential subscribers. Further highlighting of the HMO component as opposed to focusing on differential benefits may only serve to block comprehension of the message through prior misunderstandings or misperceptions formed by these consumers. Focusing instead on benefits of cost, coverage, or access as compared with competing health plans should not lend saliency to the HMO concept and prior biases. It just happens that the differential benefits addressed in the advertising are offered by an HMO.

Survival strategies should also change the focus of sales force efforts. Early HMO success is dependent on reaching a critical number of subscribers to whom overhead can be allocated. Most often, this is achieved by having the sales force direct their appeals to the largest employers. In the survival stage, sales force efforts should broaden to the small- to medium-size business. There is a greater likelihood that the small firm might offer only one HMO and thus there would be less competition for employees. Targeting smaller companies would increase the number of contacts, but also would result in shorter decision cycles from the employer because fewer people are usually involved. Moreover, for HMOs not part of a large multistate plan, the advantages held by large competitors would not be available to this segment of employers.

• • •

As more HMOs enter the market, competing plans must develop strategies for survival. These efforts must focus on creating barriers to entry for new competitors, and reducing barriers to entry for subscribers. Opportunities for new growth must be directed to expansion of the geographical or sociodemographical base of subscribers. In the face of increasing competitive pressures, the survival strategies for HMOs are dependent on creative use of the marketing mix elements—distribution, pricing, service, and promotion.

REFERENCES

Green, P. E., & Rao, V. R. (August 1971). Conjoint measurement for quantifying judgmental data. *Journal of Marketing Research 8,* 355–363.

Membership in HMOs is on the upswing. (July 1984). *Medical Economics,* p. 212.

Porter, M. (1985). *Competitive Advantage.* New York: Free Press.

Prudential to offer HMO/PPA plan. (April 1985). *Hospitals,* 26.

The development of urgent care centers

Robert J. Zasa, MSHA
President and
Chief Executive Officer
Ambulatory Services Development, Inc.
Glendale, California

DOC-IN-A-BOX, urgicenters, urgent care centers, minor emergency departments—these terms have filled health care literature for the last five years. What are these centers really? How does one develop them? What makes certain ones successful and other ones fail? This article answers these questions and outlines a successful development process for such a center.

URGENT CARE CENTERS: A PROFILE

Freestanding physician's office

An urgent care center is typically a freestanding physician's office that serves patients on a walk-in basis. Care is rendered for illnesses that are not life threatening. An urgent care center can take many forms. Many primary care physicians have extended their office hours instead of constructing any new space for urgent care services. The extended hours for this urgent care center model are usually from 8:00 A.M. to 10:00 P.M. on weekdays and services are rendered for approximately 10 to 16 hours on weekends. Many times the primary care physician who is on call for the group is the individual who covers the extended hours. Frequently, physicians' offices advertise the extended hours as an urgent care clinic or service. In addition, large multispecialty group practices have oftentimes dedicated space on their first floor for similar services. Sometimes, rotating specialists who are also on call serve these particular clinics as well as the primary care physicians. In some circumstances, the group hires physicians specifically to staff these centers and treats it as a separate cost department.

Hospital-sponsored urgent care centers

Another urgent care center form is that sponsored by hospitals. A national hospital company developed many of these in cities in which it has hospitals. The philosophy behind a hospital-sponsored urgent care center is to develop a primary care network in the community that increases the hospital's inpatient admissions. In addition, it allows the hospital's service area to be expanded. Hospitals have often hired physicians to staff these facilities. A more successful tactic has been to offer such facilities to existing primary care practices that have relationships with the hospital. These practices will add a physician themselves and staff these outlying clinics. This has served as a more successful model in retaining good physician relationships between existing groups and the hospital. Many hospitals that have developed urgent care centers have found that it takes approximately 60 patients on a daily basis to ensure the financial success of these centers. There are 2 to 3 patients per 100 visits admitted to the hospital for inpatient care.

Physician entrepreneur centers

Probably the most common model is a physician entrepreneur who alone develops one or several of these facilities. These facilities are typically between 2,000 and 3,500 square feet and offer basic X-ray, laboratory, and primary care walk-in services. In addition, it is common for an urgent care center to offer on-the-job injury services to the surrounding businesses and industries, hotels, restaurants, and office buildings. Some centers have expanded their services to include psychological counseling, thermography, pulmonary testing, periodic visits by rotating physician subspecialists, and preemployment physicals for insurance companies as well as for businesses.

Regardless of the model, there are many similarities to these centers. They are typically open between 10 and 16 hours per day, 7 days per week, including holidays. They offer laboratory, X-ray, and primary care services. They are commonly located in very visible, high-traffic areas. The daytime population that surrounds these centers is typically very high. Therefore, many of the facilities that have been put in bedroom communities have not done as well as those that are located closer to shopping areas, business office parks, and other areas that are highly populated during the day. A significant number of centers that have selected a bad location have failed. One large hospital system in the southeast developed an urgent care center in a suburban area where the population was growing rapidly. However, the actual location of the facility was off a main thoroughfare and hard to find. As a result, the urgent care center failed even though the daytime population of the area was large and increasing. Location is a key variable in development of a facility.

Development Steps For An Urgent Care Center

- Define purpose and goals of the center
- Determine competition
- Determine site and services
- Determine who is to medically staff the center
- Develop a capital budget and an operating budget
- Select architect and contractor (if building a freestanding facility)
- Select a director/coordinator for the project
- Develop operational systems for the center
- Define a marketing plan
- Ensure that all operational considerations are finalized prior to opening
- Develop and maintain tracking/evaluating system

DEVELOPMENT OF URGENT CARE CENTERS

The development approach should be simple and almost seems textbookish. However, many health care managers or physicians who have developed such centers have skipped very important steps along the way to ensuring that their center will be successful. The development process has also been complicated by bureaucracy. The development process should be a step-by-step, logical decision-making process. Writing down the process is an extremely important exercise. Listed in the box is a step-by-step process that has been found useful in developing successful centers. Regardless of the the urgent care center model, the development process is similar. All the steps should be followed to ensure a higher degree of success.

One of the major steps in developing such a facility is to clearly define why the facility is desired. From one physician's standpoint the urgent care center may be an excellent way to begin a new practice. The start-up costs of such a facility sometimes are less than buying into a very successful practice. However, the risk is very high as well. The risk is lowest for an existing group that can extend hours or dedicate part of the group's building to such a new service because it already has a patient base in place.

Many times existing groups provide

urgent care centers or extended hours as a retention strategy. As more physicians are graduating from medical schools and hospitals are becoming more aggressive, individual physicians and physician groups are employing strategies to retain the patients they currently serve as well as acquiring new patients. A large primary care group in Oregon has been very successful in using the urgent care/extended hours model to retain its patient base and to improve the services it currently delivers to existing patients. The physicians are building significant loyalty to the group by not having the patients go to the emergency department at the hospital, which is much more costly than being treated by the physician in the physician's office. This has also been a significant boon to the physicians' health maintenance organization (HMO) business because the cost of care is significantly reduced.

Hospitals have typically added urgent care centers to established primary care networks surrounding them. They have extended their service area, and as a result, increased admissions. A negative example of the implementation of this strategy involves a large hospital in Texas that developed approximately 12 urgent care centers in the surrounding community and hired physicians for each of the facilities. These physicians competed with all of the hospital's primary care physicians, who were responsible for a large number of admissions. The hospital did not extend an invitation to the existing primary care physicians in the community to use the centers under either contractual arrangements or otherwise. As a result, within six months of the opening of these facilities, the primary care physicians in the city boycotted the hospital and drove its admissions to a very low point. This low census continued for approximately a month until the hospital announced that it would sell the urgent care centers to primary care physicians. Several HMOs are also interested in purchasing these centers now to expand their network. In summary, the hospital failed to clearly define why it was going into the urgent care business and the ramifications of doing so.

Establish objectives

It is essential that an organization write a clear definition of why it wishes to develop a surgical center and what goals are to be accomplished by developing such a facility. The criteria on which the goals are based can be used later in evaluating the success of the center. Success of such centers is not always measured merely in financial terms. Several hospitals and groups that have developed centers but have not documented their expectations later found that there was a significant amount of finger pointing when the facility was not as successful as all had hoped it would be. Also, the lack of stated goals made the decision whether to continue the service very difficult.

These goals have typically been stated in terms of expected visits on a daily basis, number of new patients to be served over a period of time, admissions to the hospital, additional revenue to the organization, income to an individual physician (for physician-owned facilities), expansion of service area (particularly important to HMOs, large group practices, and hospitals that are networking in the community), profits, and the ability to enter into new businesses to serve new populations, such as patients from business and industry. Some hospital-sponsored centers have been located next to airports, seaports, and other heavily industrialized areas. Thus, the hospital may be able to tap this new market that it has not been serving in the past. Using the urgent care center as an entrée, more organizations have broadened their service base to gain a foothold and new clients. They have then bundled together additional services for these new clients.

Identify the competition

The second step in developing such a facility is to be aware of the competition and its location. This is one of the most important planning steps in the process. Competition should not be viewed as just another urgent care center that may be located within the same service area. Competition should be interpreted broadly to include any service within a 20-minute drive of the proposed location that will compete in any way with the services that the new urgent care center will offer. Competition may include hospital emergency departments; extended hours by existing physicians' offices; infirmaries contained within a large business or industry; other clinics in the area that may call themselves industrial medicine clinics or occupational medicine clinics that also provide similar services; contracts that businesses have with mobile primary care screening units; and occupational medicine companies. In one circumstance, an urgent care center was developed in proximity to several large businesses. After the center opened, administrators found that these large businesses, although having a large daytime population, had already contracted for services at a much cheaper rate with a mobile occupational health services company. This significantly reduced the expected visits to the urgent care center.

These instances are not exhausted. However, they illustrate that any kind of competition to the services of the urgent care center must be identified. Medicare cost reports that list what new services the hospitals will consider offering in the following year

Competition should be interpreted broadly to include any service within a 20-minute drive of the proposed location that will compete in any way with the services that the urgent care center will offer.

are a common way of finding out what competition is on the horizon. Discussion with specialists and other primary care physicians can reveal referral patterns of potential competitors. A physician who successfully developed four urgent care centers in a southeastern city spent six months discussing with specialists—each located within a 15-minute drive of his proposed sites—the plans to develop the centers. Not only did he acquire knowledge about where the competition would be, but he also developed superb relationships with these specialists, which allowed his urgent care patients to receive referral care much more quickly. This service in turn prompted his patients to report favorably to their neighbors and friends about the urgent care centers, encouraging more business for the centers.

In addition to identifying the competitors, there are specific things one needs to know in order to compete successfully. What services do the competitors offer? What hours of operation do the competitors have? What network or organizational ties do the competitors have that would prevent the urgent care center from gaining market share? Most urgent care centers will grow at the expense of their competition due to the proliferation of physicians currently in practice and hospital and HMO aggressiveness in offering similar services. These facts point out the imperativeness of knowing the competition. Not knowing the competition is one of the major failures of most urgent care centers.

Determine the site

After identifying the competition, the third step is to determine the site for the urgent care center. In developing a center, the old real estate adage, "location, location, location," is definitely a major key to success. Many organizations have followed the location selection practices of the food franchises as well as local banks. These organizations do a considerable amount of research on traffic patterns within the community. The large hamburger chains look for daytime traffic of 60 thousand people per day passing by a targeted site during business hours. Daytime population is key. Demographics regarding this as well as traffic studies can be obtained from the local chamber of commerce, the city economic development council, and other public resources within the community. It is extremely important that the facility also be located on the appropriate side of the street. One urgent care center developed by a hospital was made a very attractive offer on property on one side of a major thoroughfare. Traffic studies verified that there was significant traffic on this road during the day. Another plot of land was available directly across the street. Access to both parcels of land was similar. However, in looking at the data more specifically, it was found that during the daytime operation of the urgent care center, the eastern property was more attractive—there was more traffic on that side of the road during the hours of operation. The other side of the road, although heavily traveled, experienced traffic between 4:00 P.M. and 6:00 P.M. when individuals were leaving the city to go home. These were obviously not optimal times to serve that particular public. The site selection was based on these facts.

Buy versus lease

One other consideration in selecting a site is whether to build or lease. Many urgent care centers have been placed in shopping center strips. Other centers have been allowed to lease space in medical office buildings that are close to hospitals in order to directly compete with the hospitals' emergency departments. Some centers have built on a freestanding site very close to a shopping area or densely populated area. Construction costs of a freestanding facility are substantial. There is also a significant risk in building a facility due to its single-purpose use.

It is very hard to convert an urgent care center to another use. Many centers have found a good location to lease in initial years. Frequently a first right of refusal on contiguous space is negotiated in such a lease. Long-term leases can be particularly beneficial because the owner of the building shares the risk with the urgent care center and is more apt to help with appropriate signs and tenant improvement allowances. Long-term leases (5 years) are only recommended when there is great confidence in the site location.

Although sophisticated direct mail campaigns and radio and newspaper advertising are prevalent, market research has always shown that the location of a facility is its biggest marketing asset. The services delivered are important, but no matter how good the service, a bad location is certain to have a negative effect on the center. It is helpful to display a prominent outside sign advertising the center, because the most common way for people to find urgent care centers is by driving past the facility and seeing a sign. Nevertheless, a poor location is extremely difficult to overcome. A large hospital developed a center approximately 50 yards off a main thoroughfare. A billboard was used to advertise the location. The passing motorists' psychological barrier at leaving the main road and driving even 50 yards was never overcome by the facility, and it was finally moved to a better location.

Another consideration with respect to location is how consumers deal with cross streets and other natural traffic patterns. In northern California, there is one major thoroughfare that separates two medical communities. Two urgent care centers were developed, one above the major thoroughfare and one south of it. The consumers traveling south of the major thoroughfare felt they were entering into an area of lesser socio–economic status. Consequently, the urgent care center north of the major thoroughfare thrived whereas the area to the south failed, even though the care was equally good in both facilities.

Staff considerations

The next major consideration is staffing the center. What type of physician and under what type of agreement will the physician practice in the facility? What hours of operation will the facility have that will also dictate the amount of staffing required? The personality of the physician and the ability of the center to deliver care are both important.

The urgent care center delivers episodic care for the patient who typically sees the physician only one time. It is of particular importance in the current medical–legal climate that the physician establish a rapport with the patient during this care even though the care is not for life-threatening complications. This rapport decreases the possibility of lawsuits that tend to occur more often as a result of the episodic care rendered in an urgent care center.

The personality of the physician becomes a major marketing factor for the facility. The most successful urgent care centers have had the physicians vested in the facility in some manner. Many urgent care centers have experienced a high turnover of physicians because the physicians have had no interest in the facility other than receipt of a nominal salary. "You get what you pay for" is very true with urgent care centers. If the physician feels vested in the facility in some manner it becomes "his or her practice" and "his or her patients," and there is a significant difference in the operation of the centers, use of supplies, the way the physician presents himself or herself to the patients, and the attitude of the staff.

OPERATIONALIZATION OF URGENT CARE CENTERS

These major planning factors settled, the developer of the urgent care center can now begin the operational phase of the development.

Budgeting and pricing

Budgets and capital requirements need to be determined. These costs include equipment, staffing, and the working capital necessary to support the facility for the first year. These need to be written down and compared with conservative estimates of patient flow. Costs of an urgent care center vary not only by site but also by regions of the country. A wide range to consider is between $300,000 and $800,000. Costs will be higher for developing the freestanding center.

Many facilities equip themselves with good, refurbished equipment that will help reduce the costs significantly. Medical supply costs can be contained by joining large group purchasing consortia available on a local basis. Finally, staffing of the facility can vary greatly. Many times centers employ individuals who are both registered X-ray technicians and certified laboratory technicians in order to have the individuals serve multiple uses. In these facilities most people are totally cross trained so that the staffing can be held to a minimum. This is particularly important in the first year of operation. A part-time employee pool to cover the center during peak times is recommended. This

An urgent care center should be budgeted to spend a significant amount of money for marketing, particularly if it is a freestanding facility.

pool can be increased as the business develops. The major expenses of such a center are the salaries and supplies as well as the physicians' salary or financial arrangements.

Pricing is important as well. A competition analyst should reveal what the rates are within the community for comparable services. Businesses sometimes supply urgent care center physicians with retainers in order to provide a budgeted on-the-job injury service to that company. A final key budget consideration is that of marketing. Urgent care centers have typically spent a significant amount of funds the first year in developing a presence in the community. Billboard, radio, newspaper, and direct mail campaigns are common. These campaigns can run between $30,000 and $50,000 or more per year. A significant amount of free publicity can be gained by having free clinics as well as other types of screening programs in the facility open to the public. However, an urgent care center, particularly if it is a freestanding facility, should be budgeted to spend a significant amount of money for marketing.

Selecting a contractor

If the facility will be freestanding, a contractor and architect need to be selected and an appropriate floorplan layout determined. The Medical Group Management Association in Denver, Colorado, and the National Association of Ambulatory Care, in Dallas, Texas, have material on urgent care centers. Much of this contains sample marketing material as well as layouts of such facilities. Depending on the clientele that one expects to serve, the space (particularly if leased) and the types of services offered will dictate the configuration. Contractors will bid on the project. A good rule of thumb is to assess what the costs of a typical physician's office are in the community to determine the cost per square foot of such a center. A firm timetable should be set as to the time of developing working drawings with the architect and planning construction with the contractor. A guaranteed maximum price, including all of the items required in the building, should be negotiated. Construction contracts can have penalty clauses if the contractors are late and bonus clauses if they are early that are based on a dollar amount per day. This provides the contractor with an incentive to complete the project in the appropriate time and at the satisfaction of the owner. It is desirable, although not necessary, in urgent care centers to have the patients that are discharged leave from a different entrance than those who are coming in for care. This is particularly true if both industrial medicine and primary care for families will be performed in the urgent care center. Some urgent care centers have separate waiting rooms to serve these two very distinct consumers. There seems to be two major traffic-flow patterns in most urgent care centers. The first is similar to an emergency department where curtained partitions are used. The other common model is individual examination rooms such as the kind available in a typical physician's office.

Selecting a project coordinator

The next developmental consideration is to select a director to coordinate the project. Often this is the physician-owner or an assistant administrator of a health care organization. This individual should be given the written goals of the project as well as responsibility to develop a budget and timetable under which the project should be completed. The director should also be responsible for the following: developing a simplified medical record system, salary scale and staffing pattern; selecting a telephone system; determining how laundry and linen are to be handled (many centers have a washing machine for towels and linens, which helps to significantly reduce the linen expense); ensuring that appropriate general, property, and professional liability insurances are obtained; developing a preventive maintenance program for all equipment and for the building; arranging for adequate housekeeping services; developing a personnel manual and benefit package; selecting a computer—essential not only for billing but also for marketing purposes; developing the forms and the patient flow systems that will be reviewed by the physicians and nurses; and making sure all the appropriate equipment is selected and delivered on time. The director is also typically involved with the marketing effort. He or she should develop all the business office systems for accounts payable and accounts receivable, and insurance filing.

Marketing

The marketing effort for an urgent care center is critical. It is important that a center attain a presence in the community. This is particularly true if it is a freestanding center. As stated earlier, a prominent sign outside is a major consideration. It should be clear and lit on both sides at night in order to be seen during all hours. Second, a temporary office and telephone number should be developed before completion of the building. This will help the facility gain a presence in the market prior to opening. Such an office is necessary for preopening marketing, carrying out developmental activities, interviewing vendors, and temporarily housing staff.

The director should be responsible for developing a marketing plan and a budget. Oftentimes a local public relations and advertising firm is contracted for a set fee to develop a preopening and grand opening campaign. The cost can range from \$3,000 to \$5,000. This flat fee will cover the public relations firm's time but not any media costs that will be incurred. The media mix will vary by community.

Direct sales are also very important. There will be a considerable number of one-on-one visits that the physician and/or the director will make prior to the opening of the facility. Although time-consuming, one-on-one sales to groups that can use the center can help reduce the number of media dollars that are spent in promoting an urgent care center. Various consumers should be visited, such as HMOs, preferred provider organizations (PPOs), businesses in the surrounding area, schools, city hall, and any other large organization the center feels it will serve. The director should coordinate the sales effort. Industrial medicine will be a service, so relationships with plant nurses at various industries are essential. A hotline telephone number to the urgent care center is often set up to allow these plant nurses to gain direct access to a physician or a nurse for assistance with on-the-job injuries. Frequently, urgent care centers complete workmen's compensation insurance forms as a service to these industries. The pre-opening marketing activities will include these arrangements.

The computer system should be programmed to track where the patient came from based on zip code, where the patient was employed, who the patient's primary care physician is, and what specialist the patient was sent to for referral. This will be useful information that can be reviewed on a monthly basis in order to determine where the patients are coming from and to increase visits from those areas. A physician-owned urgent care center in Alabama routinely sends a letter to all the referring physicians at the end of the year indicating how many patients the urgent care center has referred to them. This has engendered intense loyalty between the center and the referring physicians. The physicians feel strongly about the urgent care center and have encouraged many patients to use it. Brochures about urgent care centers are commonly found in the specialists' offices. The relationships with the subspecialties are particularly important.

Brochures and other printed information that highlight the cost-effectiveness of an urgent care center should be developed. These materials will be used for marketing the center. Tours can be set up for various groups if the urgent care center is a unique service in the area and warrants such attention. Contracts are sometimes negotiated between employers and urgent care center to take care of their patients on a daily basis. It is often hard to compete with the advertising budgets of large hospitals for such a small facility. It is therefore essential that the marketing effort be a coordinated one making best use of available dollars and time.

Upon the grand opening of the center, a radio station will sometimes set up a remote broadcast from the center. The promotion of the center is usually accompanied by an open-house event with promotional giveaways. Again, this is particularly common with free-standing centers. Medical groups that have extended their hours typically send notices to all of their patients, either through their newsletter or to accompany their bill. They have also gone back into the files and sent notices to all old patients, notifying them that they are expanding their services. In short, there needs to be a significant marketing campaign near the opening of the center to make sure that the opening is acknowledged. It is also important that this be sustained throughout the first year. The facility will soon be forgotten if it does not have subsequent marketing campaigns to sustain public awareness of its presence. Significant dollars should be allowed for this effort. All promotional material should include a map, a telephone number, and the hours of operation of the facility. It is important to communicate this information clearly to the public. Distribution of this literature in as many places in the community as possible is desirable.

TRACKING AND PLANNING FOR CONTINUED DEVELOPMENT

There are two final steps in the development process. First, the final operational review of the facility should be a painstaking check to ensure that all the details have been finalized prior to patients entering the facility. A checklist should include making sure the staff is aware of the paper flow and patient flow procedures, and the manner in which the patients will be treated. All supplies, equipment, forms, and the computer and business office systems should be reviewed to ensure that everything is in place. This final check is extremely important because many details are often omitted. Without checking, the operator of the urgent care center runs the risk of having something go wrong during the first few patient visits.

After the opening, there should be a daily and weekly meeting with the staff to work out any operational problems that have been experienced within the first weeks. Such meetings have proved helpful in correcting minor problems and making sure that the corrections are well communicated to the staff. Each staff member who may have worked in the health care field for a number of years will have different habits, will be familiar with different systems, and will need to be oriented to the new center's team practices.

Finally, to ensure that the developmental steps have been successful and to measure goal achievement, a tracking/evaluating system needs to be established. Computer data, combined with the original goals of the center, should be periodically reviewed. The information from the computer will assist the director and/or the physicians to redirect their efforts toward promoting the center and achieving their goals. Without this tracking system the facility cannot be evaluated objectively.

The task of developing an urgent care center can be a risky yet rewarding experience. If realistic expectations are set and proper steps are taken, the original goals can be accomplished. The effort is a significant one, and before the process begins planners must realize it will take a considerable amount of time and energy. Those who are committed to this effort can succeed.

The second generation of selective contracting: another look at PPOs

Joan B. Trauner, PhD
Director
National Health Care Group
Coopers and Lybrand
San Francisco, California

Assistant Adjunct Professor of Health Policy
Institute for Health Policy Studies
University of California
San Francisco, California

SINCE THE beginning of the 1980s, the health services literature has been replete with discussions about the pros and cons of selective contracting in conjunction with the redesign of indemnity/service benefits. The new delivery systems that have subsequently emerged all share one common characteristic: they have been organized and marketed on the basis of their potential for management of health care costs. All segments of the health care industry (insurance carriers, third party administrators and consultants, investor-owned and nonprofit multiinstitutional chains, individual hospitals and physician groups, and health care purchasers [primarily employers and unions]), have become involved to some degree in selective contracting. For these new systems, the purchaser of group benefits, that is, the individual employer or union, is ultimately responsible for design of the basic health benefits package and for creating incentives to use the selected panel of hospitals and health professionals. These new delivery systems are often grouped under a catchall classification and are popularly referred to as preferred provider organizations (PPOs).

The plans that initially emerged in the marketplace—to be referred to hereafter as the first generation of PPOs—have done little to alter traditional practice patterns, particularly for ambulatory services. More recently, a second generation of contracting has emerged, in which health care payers seek to limit their financial risk through new types of benefit packages and/or financial arrangements with health care providers. The first section of this article will describe the changes that are occurring as the second generation of plans appear in the marketplace; the second section presents a checklist of items to be considered before entering into one of the new forms of PPO agreements.

For the first generation of plans, most organizers of PPOs focused their energies initially on the contracting process, attempting to select cost-efficient hospitals and/or to negotiate discounted rates. For professional services, the emphasis was on securing adequate physician representation for both primary care and specialty services. Practice patterns have been restructured only to the extent that PPO arrangements have involved implementation of utilization controls and/or restrictions on referrals to nonparticipating providers.

IMPACT ON MEDICAL PRACTICE PATTERNS

According to a recent survey of 134 operational PPOs, there was almost no evidence of risk-sharing arrangements other than the use of diagnosis-based prospective payment to hospitals (Rice, deLissovoy, Gabel, and Ermann, in press). The vast majority of plans paid for hospital services based on per diem rates (40%) or discounted charges (36%); only 15% routinely paid hospitals using a case mix or diagnosis-based reimbursement definition, while another 8% used the latter method occasionally. To pay physicians, almost 70% of the plans used a fee schedule, with 20% discounting usual charges and 9% paying usual or prevailing fees. Few plans have implemented any type of gatekeeper system where primary care physicians direct all patient care. Of special importance, the same study found that most employer groups, when implementing PPO programs, were using positive incentives in the form of lower coinsurance and/or lower deductibles rather than increasing costs for nonusers of the PPO panel. About one-quarter of the respondents had also introduced extra benefits, such as well-baby care, to provide an added inducement to use contracting providers. Thus, the first generation of PPOs has taken a relatively benign approach to restructuring medical practice patterns. Those utilization controls that are in place generally extend only to inpatient hospital services, typically through the implementation of (a) preadmission review of hospital admissions, (b) concurrent review of hospital stays, (c) mandatory second surgical opinion programs, and (d) retrospective review of hospital stays and billing procedures. Profiling of physician practice patterns has been initiated at some PPOs, but usually the emphasis has been on uncovering outlier behavior. In most cases, physicians participating in PPO arrangements have received little or no timely information from payers about their relative performance, either as individuals, or compared to colleagues if they contract through a particular hospital-based group or multispecialty clinic.

There are indications that "business as usual" may not be long lived. Based on informal interviews with over 30 administrators of PPOs in California, Minnesota, and Florida, it appears that health benefit packages are being redesigned to include one or more of the following: (a) the underwriting of benefits with guaranteed premiums for extended periods of time; (b) an increased use of negative incentives, such as increased copayments and deductibles, that financially "lock in" patients to contracting providers; (c) the use of gatekeeper systems to control access to specialty services; (d) creation of "carve outs" for specific medical/dental services; and (e) elimination of coverage for care provided by nonpanel providers. To the extent that the second generation of health plans limit access of subscribers to contracting providers through financial incentives and restrictions on health plan coverage, the distinction between PPOs and prepaid plans or health maintenance organizations (HMOs) becomes increasingly blurred. Each of these five trends is reviewed below, followed by a discussion of factors to be considered in negotiating a PPO contract.

Guaranteed rates

Traditionally, health care underwriters have compensated for underwriting losses through retrospective or prospective adjustment of premiums in experience-rated groups. More recently, in an attempt to expand their market and, in the case of plans sponsored by multiinstitutional hospital chains, to promote use of their affiliated facilities, a number of plan underwriters have begun to guarantee premium rates for extended periods of time without any provision for subsequent adjustment of rates. For example, the approach pioneered by Humana, Inc., for its Care Plus program involves establishing an initial premium based on group experience and demographics and then adjusting the rate according to the consumer price index. In the case of Care Plus, for a given employer group to be eligible for guaranteed rates, 75% of hospital admissions must be in Humana-affiliated facilities. Guaranteed rates are also being introduced by other multiinstitutional hospital chains, by Blue Cross/Blue Shield plans, and by joint ventures between commercial insurance carriers and provider groups. To the extent that guaranteed rates are predicated on use of contracting facilities and/or professionals, they provide an incentive for employers and unions to redesign benefit packages to promote their use. Thus, with the use of guaranteed rates, employers and unions may be less hesitant to increase copayments and deductibles to channel patients to contracting providers.

Negative incentives

As described above, the first generation of PPOs often offered improved benefits for care by panel providers. When negative incentives are implemented, out-of-pocket costs can increase significantly when care is rendered outside the provider panel (Trauner, 1983). For example, assuming a preexisting indemnity package with a 20% coinsurance rate and a $100 deductible per individual, a plan with negative incentives may increase the copayment rate to 30% or 40% and the deductible to $200; furthermore, payment of usual and customary fees to physicians may be eliminated, with payment thereafter based on discounted charges negotiated with panel providers. As a result, patients who use nonpanel providers may end up with effective copayment rates far greater than the specified rates. The net effect of any implementation of negative incentives is to "lock-in" subscribers to contracting providers, particularly for high-cost ambulatory and hospital-based care.

Gatekeeper systems

To protect their market share, some HMOs have begun to develop separate PPO programs. Many of these PPO plans rely on gatekeeper systems in which primary care physicians control access to specialists and hospital services. Under these programs—and to a lesser extent, under new PPO programs being organized by employers, health insurers, and third party administrators—the primary care physician becomes responsible for managing all health care services delivered to an individual or to a family unit. (Some plans allow each individual family member to sign up with a separate contracting primary care provider, and others require registration of the entire family with one provider.) Some plans define primary care providers as family/general practitioners and pediatricians, and others extend the list to include internists and obstetricians/gynecologists.

Some plans define primary care providers as family/general practitioners and pediatricians, and others extend the list to include internists and obstetricians/gynecologists.

The use of gatekeeper systems facilitates development of risk-sharing arrangements with primary providers. These arrangements may exist in the form of (a) targeted utilization rates, (b) capitated payments to providers on the basis of the number of patients under their care, and (c) creation of risk pools for specialty services and/or hospital care. Targeted utilization rates consist of specifying standards—after age, sex, and case mix adjustments—for use of specific services, such as the number of inpatient days per 1,000 patients, surgical services per 1,000 patients, and office ancillary (laboratory and X-ray) services per 1,000 patients.* Groups of primary care physicians may receive bonus payments if they meet utilization standards, and/or penalties may be instituted if standards are not met. Capitated payments consist of a flat rate of reimbursement per subscriber/per month or per family unit/per month, regardless of the use of health services. Additionally, under some capitated programs, risk pools are created to cover the cost of specialty services and/or hospital care. To the extent that there are funds left in the risk pool, they will accrue, in part or in whole, to the benefit of the primary care provider; conversely, any deficits in the risk pools may result in a withhold from the primary care physician's capitated income. (In some capitated systems, there is an automatic withhold from capitated income to offset any potential deficits in specialty/hospital risk pools.) Thus, the net effect of a gatekeeper system is to create economic incentives for treating physicians to control use of high-cost specialty and ancillary services and to provide care in the most cost-effective location.

A modified form of gatekeeper system involves the creation of global fees for specific conditions or procedures. In this case, the "primary" physician may be the surgeon or obstetrician directly responsible for the case. For example, in the PPO arrangement between Hewlett Packard and El Camino Hospital, in Mountain View, California, and its preferred physician group, a global fee is predetermined for two surgical procedures (herniorrhaphy and cholecystectomy), and all charges for hospital, medical, and ancillary services are debited against this sum. When treatment is concluded and charges are totaled, including charges from the treating surgeon, if there is a debit in the account, then the surgeon's fee may be reduced by as much as 25%; conversely, if there is a credit, the fee may be increased by as much as 25%. Thus, the gatekeeper approach creates new incentives for physicians to provide care in a more cost-effective manner.

Carve outs

The PPO market is also witnessing the development of "carve outs" for specific categories of service, such as mental health, substance abuse, vision care, and dental services. Under typical "carve out" arrangements, plan subscribers are required to obtain some or all services from contracting providers. For example, under a mental health plan, a group of providers may contract to provide care on a capitated basis (a) all outpatient counseling and therapy, (b) outpatient care plus preadmission hospital review/concurrent review, and/or (c) all inpatient and outpatient services. In some "carve outs," plan subscribers retain the right to see noncontracting providers, but at re-

**The terminology used to track HMO utilization is typically inpatient days per 1,000* members, *surgical services per 1,000* members, *etc. However, to the extent that enrollees in a PPO retain coverage for care by noncontracting providers, then the use of the term "members" is inappropriate. In such a case, the PPO does not constitute a closed delivery system, and the targeted utilization rates will not ordinarily be applicable for plan eligibles who receive all or most of their care from noncontracting providers.*

duced levels of coverage; in others, all care must be rendered by contracting providers. To the extent that subscribers are "locked in" to contracting providers, implementation of risk-sharing arrangements becomes possible.

Exclusive provider organizations

Some employers have begun to offer benefit packages where their employees are required to obtain all their health care (except emergency services) from contracting providers. The distinction between these arrangements, often called exclusive provider organizations (EPOs), and preferred provider organizations rests solely on the design of the underlying benefit package; the same set of hospitals and professionals can be used to market both preferred and exclusive provider arrangements.

Because of their "lock-in" provisions, EPOs have many of the attributes of HMOs from an underwriting standpoint; subscribers lack freedom of choice in selection of providers outside the designated panel, so risk-sharing arrangements with providers, including the use of capitated payments, can be implemented. Early entrants into the development of exclusive provider arrangements include (a) HMOs, operating through separate legal subsidiaries, (b) multiinstitutional, investor-owned hospital chains, and (c) multispecialty group practices. More recently, a number of insurance carriers and Blue Cross/Blue Shield plans have begun to develop EPO arrangements, largely to overcome the restrictions inherent in marketing HMO benefits (the lack of flexibility in benefit design and premium pricing for HMOs due to mandatory benefit packages and, for federally qualified plans, limitations on use of copayments and requirements for community rating).

The net effect of the changes described above is to move PPOs more in the direction of "managed" health systems. In time, it is possible that the arbitrary distinctions now used to describe PPOs, EPOs, and HMOs will become meaningless. In the interim, however, providers are faced with the problem of evaluating highly disparate PPO / EPO contracts, with payment rates, requirements for utilization review, and provider networks varying contract by contract. Because there are numerous contracting guides, published by local and state medical associations and by specialty societies, the next section focuses on those factors that are unique to risk sharing and the second generation of PPO contracting (American Society of Internal Medicine, 1983; California Medical Association, 1985).

EVALUATION OF PPO/EPO CONTRACTS

Actuarial analysis of risk-sharing arrangements

Until recently, most insurance carriers, third party administrators (TPAs), and employers who self-administer their health benefits, did not collect sufficiently detailed information on case mix and patient demographics to develop risk-sharing arrangements. Although aggregate data have been available in some communities and/or states on average hospital costs per day and per admission, and Medicare data can provide guidelines on length of stay for a given diagnosis, this information has not been sufficiently detailed to allow most carriers/TPAs to determine optimal utilization rates for their enrollee base, with appropriate age/sex/case mix adjustments. As a result, for the second generation of selective contracting, the implementation of targeted utilization rates and/or capitated programs has involved some guesswork on the part of plan sponsors. In some cases, the quoted rates are derived from statistics available for existing HMOs, in others from the performance of specific employer group(s) for which a detailed analysis of claims has been conducted.

Thus, in assessing a proposed PPO/EPO contract for which risk sharing is proposed, the provider should seek information on how the targeted utilization rates and/or capitated payments were calculated. If possible, data should be obtained according to age and sex categories. Information on which employer groups have signed up for the program or will be solicited for participation should also be sought. If large employers in the local community with multiple-option health benefits programs are included, the provider should ask for enrollment statistics for those groups, and specifically question the plan sponsor about problems of adverse selection (i.e., a concentration of high utilizers and/or older employees in the basic indemnity plan offered by the employer). Provider groups should also examine the characteristics of their own existing patient base; if detailed cost and utilization data are available and a capitated rate is proposed, it may be worthwhile to consult an actuary to develop projections for comparison with the rates offered by the PPO.

Analysis of proposed preferred provider network

In most cases, a PPO will negotiate agreements simultaneously with a series of providers on a local or regional basis; as a result, it is often impossible to determine in advance of signing a contract the names of other participating providers. If an exclusive provider arrangement is proposed and all referrals must be made within the "preferred" panel, the provider should sign a contract only if there is adequate coverage of tertiary and specialty services, and of ancillary, home health, and pharmacy services. The reputation of the other providers and their geographic accessibility is also important. In signing a contract for an exclusive provider arrangement, a provider may wish to retain the right to withdraw from a contract within a set number of days after obtaining the full list of participating providers.

Recordkeeping and provider feedback

When a gatekeeper system is implemented with any type of risk-withhold, timely information on costs of specialty and hospital care is required. Will the gatekeeper be required to review all claims before submitting them to a carrier/TPA for payment? If the claims go directly to a carrier/TPA, how often will the gatekeeper receive feedback about referral and hospital costs? Will the gatekeeper be required to have centralized recordkeeping and/or to keep track of all patient encounters, including referrals? Evaluation of any gatekeeping program requires an assessment of administrative capabilities and costs by the participating provider. In particular, the provider will need to determine if the current billing system is adequate to handle increased volume and to provide necessary management reports.

Liability for emergency services and care outside the service area

For risk-sharing arrangements, contract terms should delineate how provider payment will be affected by use of emergency services, within and outside the service area, and for urgent care services outside the service area. If the risk-sharing account of a contracting provider will be debited for incurred charges, is there a maximum amount of liability? Will the provider be required to monitor out-of-area and emergency care and to arrange for transfer of patients to contracting facilities?

For risk-sharing arrangements, contract terms should delineate how provider payment will be affected by use of emergency services, within and outside the service area, and for urgent care services outside the service area.

Limited financial liability for catastrophic illness

Does the plan limit the liability of the provider for high-cost illness? For example, in calculating performance under targeted utilization rates, are outlier cases eliminated from the analysis? For risk-sharing pools and capitated programs, is there a stop-loss after which incurred charges are no longer debited to the provider account? For capitated programs, is aggregate stop-loss available to limit exposure across a provider's PPO/EPO patient base?

Patient education

What educational materials will a PPO/EPO provide its enrollees to inform them about restrictions on use of health benefits outside the provider panel? If a patient fails to use contracting providers, what is the financial impact on the contracting provider? Can a provider request that a patient who fails to adhere to PPO/EPO procedures be removed from his or her panel?

Contract renegotiation/termination

Many original PPO contracts require provider participation for a 1-year period, with 30 to 90 days advance notice for termination of the contract. In some cases, the contract is automatically renewed, without renegotiation of rates, unless a written request is forwarded to the plan sponsor within a specific time. For second generation plans, provisions for automatic contract renewal, at preexisting rates, should be eliminated. Instead, a process for renegotiation of rates and contract terms should be specified; in particular, prior to initiating the renegotiation process, provision should be made for adequate disclosure of cost and utilization data for participating PPO/EPO accounts.

• • •

The preceding listing of factors to be evaluated prior to signing a PPO/EPO contract is not exhaustive; rather it is designed to show the complexity of new risk-sharing arrangements and the need for obtaining professional advice before participating in these programs. As case management, both financial and medical, replaces the uncoordinated delivery of health services in the fee-for-service system, health care providers will need greater administrative and ancillary support services to function efficiently. The provider who becomes involved in the second generation of selective contracting is, in effect, embarking on a new mode of health care delivery, one that may bear increasing resemblance to practice patterns under prepaid systems.

REFERENCES

American Society of Internal Medicine. (1983). *The PPO Perspective* (Publication No. 357-25M). Washington, DC: Author.

California Medical Association. (1985). *Revised physician's contracting handbook.* San Francisco, CA: Author.

Rice, T., deLissovoy, G., Gabel, J., & Ermann, D. (in press). The state of PPOs: Results from a national survey. *Health Affairs.*

Trauner, J. (1983). *Preferred provider organizations: The California experiment.* San Francisco: University of California, Institute for Health Policy Studies.

Who's got the money? Who's got the patients?—the administrator's response to PPOs and self-funding

Jay Wolfson, DrPH
Associate Professor
College of Public Health
University of South Florida
Visiting Fulbright Professor
University of Tokyo Medical School
National Institute of Public Health
Tokyo, Japan

Peter J. Levin, ScD
Dean
College of Public Health
University of South Florida
Tampa, Florida

MARKET SHARE fever has permeated the health care arena. Each player in the health care system has either demanded, or has developed responses to the demands of others for cost control. An abundance of special deals are being offered by providers and third parties. At the same time, group purchasers in the private and public sectors are trying out their newly found wisdom and market strength to influence the organization and delivery of health care services. They have joined coalitions, required comparative cost and utilization data from third parties, hospitals, and physician groups, and conducted direct negotiations with individual providers.

In the midst of these new marketplace activities, PPOs have emerged as the dominant rubric for a range of products, organizations, and arrangements. These have been developed, marketed, and solicited by hospitals, ambulatory care centers, group practices, medical societies, insurance companies, third parties, labor unions, government agencies, business coalitions, and Wall Street investors. There are examples of each of these players buying and selling PPOs—which testifies to the flexibility of the product, and to the validity of the comment, "When you've seen one PPO, you've seen one PPO!" (Sunshine, 1983).

How should hospital administrators respond to the advent of PPOs, the demands of group purchasers, the activities of competitors, and the implications and opportunities created by self-funding?

This article offers a general discussion of issues that should be of particular concern to administrators of health care services—especially ambulatory care programs—in their efforts to respond rationally to PPOs. These issues include cost sharing effects on receivables and revenues; "discounting" and thereby possibly undercutting oneself; the separate ambulatory care market; new financial players in health care; and self-funding.

COST SHARING: THE MOVING FORCE BEHIND PPOs

One of the common features among all PPOs is the use of cost sharing as an incentive or disincentive to utilization. There are a number of generic models of PPOs, and each incorporates various uses of cost sharing at the deductible and/or the copayment level (Trauner, 1983; Wolfson & Levin, 1985).

Cost sharing has several purposes. It is intended to (a) more actively involve the patient in the care process through financial awareness, (b) reduce the financial burden on the insurance risk pool, and (c) when used in PPOs, act as an explicit motivator for the use of certain service providers.

Although the effect of cost sharing on use of services has been hotly debated for years (Newhouse et al, 1981; Wolfson, 1982), the impact of cost sharing on service providers has only begun to attract attention.

The principal effect of any increase in cost sharing on a provider is that the provider must resort to collecting a larger amount from the service user rather than from the third party. There is evidence to suggest that the collection of increased cost-sharing dollars requires very aggressive collection systems, and that receivables can be adversely affected (Wolfson, 1983).

Suppose that Provider A has a service market that consists of patients who are members of various third party schemes. Some of these patients, who have traditionally used this provider, become eligible for PPO participation through their own group plan. Because of negotiations made by the third party representing these patients, a facility other than Provider A is selected as the closest "preferred provider." Under the provisions of the PPO, patients who seek care from Provider A (excluding cases of emergency) will be penalized by having to pay 50% of the reasonable and customary costs, rather than the usual 20%.

If PPO patients continue to seek care at Provider A, the provider may face the problem of dramatically reduced reimbursement from the patients' third party. Because of the financial disincentive, when PPO patients stop using Provider A, service volume and revenue may be reduced.

Antitrust suits will, no doubt, continue to play in the courts on this issue, but in the foreseeable future, increased cost sharing to discourage use of certain providers will be a reality in the marketplace.

A nonpreferred provider may have to deal with unexpected effects on receivables and revenues because of the cost-sharing feature of PPOs. If a considerable percentage of PPO patients use a facility that is not a PPO participant, there may be three immediate results: (a) the need to develop a very effective patient billing and collection system, (b) a decrease in the use of services, and (c) a reduction in revenues. These are fundamental revenue issues. The first addresses receivables management, whereas the second is concerned with strategic planning, product development and marketing activities, and the third with basic financial stability.

To make up for reduced receivables from those third parties that sponsor PPOs, nonparticipating providers will have to develop the ability to collect a larger amount from the PPO patient, either at the time of service or as soon as possible thereafter. This means that administrators and financial officers will have to put on the hat of the bill collector—an unpleasant thought when seeking to attract patients in a competitive marketplace.

Throughout the 1970s and into the early 1980s, one of the advantages of third party involvement has been the softening of the collection function in health care through a reimbursement system that was based either on usual and customary fees, or fee schedules that were more or less uniform across third parties. Assignment of benefits created a convenient mechanism for further obscuring the financial component of the provider–patient relationship.

Many ambulatory care systems that have depended on larger out-of-pocket payments from patients in the past may actually have an advantage over some inpatient organizations because of traditionally lower or restricted insurance coverage for noninpatient services. For this reason, the financial management systems of ambulatory care services may already be prepared to bill individual patients and follow up effectively on uncollected amounts.

Nonetheless, administrators should be sensitive to the impact of the ramifications of cost sharing on both receivables and revenues. An aggressive receivables management system requires an accounts aging capability, clear policies about patient payment, billing periods, and appropriate, aggressive interventions (stern letters reminding patients, telephone calls, collection agency involvement, and legal recourse).

The effectiveness of any billing and collections system has to be weighed against the possibly negative consequences of collections policies that are too aggressive. The relationship between collection practices, revenues,

The effectiveness of any billing and collections system has to be weighed against the possibly negative consequences of collections policies that are too aggressive.

and service volume is suggested in Figure 1.

Revenue and volume can be affected by payment and collection policies. A strict collection policy (D-1) would act to deter certain users from seeking care (Q-1) and would ostensibly guarantee a higher level of collection. A very permissive or lenient collection policy (D-2) would encourage higher volume (Q-2), but would not help to increase the PPO's ability to collect these charges. In fact, total revenue may remain constant (revenue at Q-1 and Q-2 are equal) while volume may increase; this reduces net income. The obvious trade off here is in realized revenue per unit of volume.

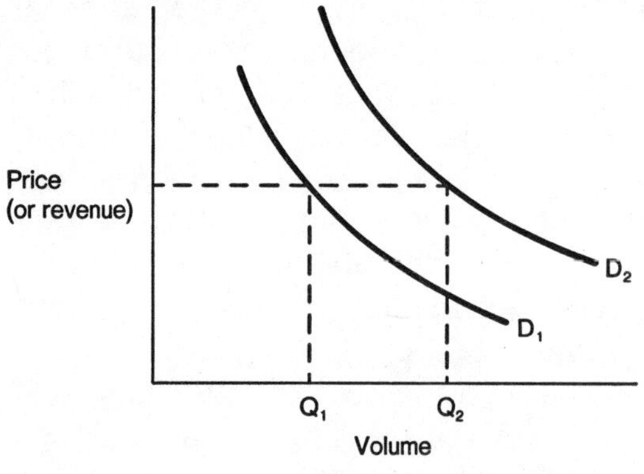

Figure 1. Collections practices, revenues, and volume. 1 = strict collection; 2 = permissive collection.

If collection practices are very lenient, it is possible to face the problem of a high level of receivables and a large volume. Traditionally public sector and nonprofit ambulatory care programs avoided aggressive collection policies. Thus the consumer population came to expect that they would not be given a difficult time about paying. Many municipal and state ambulatory care systems have faced the dilemma of serving their mission to the community versus surviving. In the case of a large, five-clinic, multiservice family planning system, management policy was to avoid formal notices, and to avoid mentioning past due amounts when patients in arrears came in for services. No amount of volume can make up for an inability to collect revenues.

On the other hand, collection policies that are too strict may have the effect of discouraging certain patients from seeking care. Depending on the economic and social conditions of a provider's service market and the strength of the provider's reputation in the community, a strict policy can have different effects. If service volume is reduced to only those who can afford to pay the out-of-pocket amounts, then total volume and revenue may drop substantially.

In the case of PPOs, much will depend on a thorough market analysis of all insurance products and PPO arrangements affecting a particular service area. From a strategic planning perspective, this is a vital place to start. The provisions of PPOs will differ, and in order to prepare for and/or respond to the effects that one PPO might have on the revenues and patients of another, administrators will have to keep well informed about the different products that are being marketed in the service area.

If a provider participates, or is contemplating participation in a PPO, the cost-sharing and receivables management issue is only the beginning.

DISCOUNTING: UNDERCUTTING YOUR OWN COSTS?

PPOs are often characterized as offering a form of "discounted health care" to select service populations based on a set of understandings. Generally, there are four sets of provisions that may be included in the understandings between provider and purchaser in a PPO situation.

The purchaser agrees to encourage its beneficiary population to seek care at the preferred provider. This is done through cost-sharing incentives. In exchange, the provider agrees to "discount" rates to contracted purchasers or to beneficiaries. Often, the purchaser also agrees to expedite reimbursement to aid the cash flow needs of the provider. A final component present in many PPO relationships is the agreement by the provider to offer some form of utilization review to the purchaser or the purchaser's third party, and/or to offer special services such as health education and promotion to the purchaser's beneficiaries (Wolfson & Levin, 1985, p. 123).

The problem for many providers is that they may not know much about the real costs of their own operations, and may face the dilemma of offering prices or terms that undercut their real costs. This may be especially true in the case of "specialty PPO" situations, such as those involving dental care or eye care.

Product-line analysis is a managerial accounting technique that provides information on the actual costs and profit margins associated with each kind of product that is sold by an organization. In health care, there are wide variations in the profit margins and volume/profit relationships across health service products offered by a provider. Some services, treatments, and programs are clearly more profitable than others; often, these are known to the administrator. However, all too often, the reasons for the profitability of certain services are not well understood—especially the cost–volume relationship.

In the case of some PPO arrangements, a provider may contract to offer either a full range of "standard" health care services or a limited range of services. In either case, the provider must be in a position to know which products are "loss leaders," designed to serve as entrées to the use of other services; which products are clearly profitable, though perhaps only within certain margins of volume; and which products are definitely "dogs."

The techniques for doing this involve the analysis of fixed and variable costs for each line of health care product based on direct and indirect cost classifications, and the calculation of profitability margins within various volume ranges, given a series of assumptions about revenue sources and collectability rates. This kind of information can be used by management to adjust costs, where possible, and to more accurately price products and project the effects of variations in utilization and revenue sources.

Table 1 is an example of a simple product-line analysis of several health care services that require the determination of fixed costs (those that remain constant regardless of volume) and variable costs (those that can change with volume). This determination is made for each service and the total institution or cost center. The contribution margin represents the revenue from sales less the variable expenses, or the profits rendered by the sale of each product beyond the point at which fixed costs have been met.

In scenario 1, sales mix for a known period of time is analyzed using three products as examples: surgery 1, procedure 2, and consult 3. The table displays the volume revenues, cost per unit, and the profit margin for each product along with summaries in the total column.

Scenario 2 shows the effects of subtle changes in the volume of some services on total profit. These changes may occur as a consequence of a formal management policy or a shift in demand, which may be brought about by alterations in reimbursement policy or by demographic or morbidity changes.

In a competitive arena, where bailout money is not easily available if an organization faces deficits, the ambulatory care administrator has to be especially sensitive to the relationship between the price of health care products and real costs. In the PPO market, never-ending "cost-plus" reimbursement from a third party is a dream. Administrators will have to know their products in order to negotiate competitive prices without undercutting their own costs. The vital elements in this process are basic cost accounting practices; accurate, historical, updata-

Table 1. Product-line analysis

	Scenario 1			
	Surgery 1	**Procedure 2**	**Consult 3**	**Total profit**
Volume	10	20	150	
Revenue/unit	$2,000	$500	$25	
Cost/unit	$1,400	$100	$ 5	
Contribution margin	$ 600	$400	$20	
Profit	$6,000	$8,000	$3,000	$17,000
		Scenario 2		
Volume	5	30	250	Total profit
Profit	$3,000	$12,000	$5,000	$20,000

ble financial reporting systems; and reasonably detailed data about utilization patterns and local market conditions.

AMBULATORY CARE: A SEPARATE AND DESIRABLE PRODUCT

Not long ago, insurance reimbursement for a variety of procedures and treatments was usually limited to services provided on an inpatient basis. The world has changed. The avoidance of inpatient hospitalization is now one of the objects of cost containment efforts. A variety of third party incentives have been injected into the health care system to reduce hospitalization or to limit lengths of stay. Second surgical opinion, preadmission testing, preadmission authorization, and financial incentives for ambulatory surgery have become increasingly popular and overdue features of health benefit plans.

PPO contracts frequently include cost-sharing incentives to use ambulatory rather than hospital outpatient services. In response to these PPO provisions and the outpatient incentives that are now being designed into non-PPO reimbursement plans, the ambulatory care marketplace has mushroomed. Every kind of provider has recognized the advantages of expanding or developing ambulatory delivery systems.

Not-for-profit and investor owned hospital organizations have expanded their outpatient departments, and now own and operate primary care clinics, surgicenters, and even HMOs that may be physically and geographically separate from their hospitals. In great part, this activity follows the model proposed by Goldsmith for vertically integrating hospital organizations to increase market share and cash flow (Goldsmith, 1982). Changes in the capital market and tax provisions have encouraged hospitals to seek joint venture agreements with medical staff for the construction of separate facilities and spin-off corporations. Medical societies are forming individual practice associations (IPAs) and other arrangements to offer ambulatory care services in order to compete with local HMOs and hospital clinics; group practices have blossomed into a wide range of configurations, in many cases exerting strong influence on local and even regional health care patterns and economics.

Many providers have capitalized on particular segments of the ambulatory care market. For example, industrial health clinics are evolving into much more than treatment sites for work-related accidents (though the worker's compensation treatment market has also expanded). A broadly defined industrial health center can include health risk appraisals, special programs in diet and nutrition, smoking cessation and physical fitness, along with the more traditional treatment of industrial accidents and preemployment physicals. Such services may be especially attractive to potential group purchasers if they are marketed as part of a preferred provider system within a health promotion context.

These services, as well as the broad range of ambulatory surgery and medical treatment activities, are not tied to the inpatient process. In summation, ambulatory care has come into its own as a legitimate, autonomous form of health care delivery, with its own market. PPOs may offer a timely opportunity to capitalize on this market opportunity, provided the technical management of the PPO arrangement is administratively and financially sophisticated.

SELF-FUNDING: NEW FINANCIAL PLAYERS IN HEALTH CARE

PPOs, by definition, cause providers to interact with a new group of purchasers, such as individual companies or coalitions of business organizations. There are new players in the game, and the rules have also changed (Wolfson & Levin, 1985). These players are a primary source of patients—employees and dependents—and they are becoming increasingly well informed about purchasing health benefits as products. In addition, some vital changes have taken place within the health financing arena itself, introducing several new services and organizations that seek to control the flow of money to providers.

Self-funding, third party administration, and self-administration of health benefits now must be understood and addressed by the effective ambulatory care administrator.

Self-funding, third party administration, and self-administration of health benefits now must be understood and addressed by the effective ambulatory care administrator.

Self-funding of health benefits has become the most popular method to pay for health benefits. Employee benefit trusts, or special interest-earning accounts dedicated to health benefit expenses, have become a dominant method of financing health benefits. Employers deposit money in these funds and then arrange to draw against them as health expenses are incurred. Administrative services organizations (ASOs) or third party administrators (TPAs) are contracted to pay health claims from these funds. By using a tax-exempt 501–C–9, an employee benefit trust fund, or other financial vehicles, it has become possible for employers to gain some advantages in the use of these monies. Self-funding avoids the payment of state premium taxes—required when insurance is purchased, sets more identifiable limits on administrative costs of plan management, and affords the employer the present value of the money—previously given entirely to insurance companies as money in their bank.

Self-funding usually involves a contract with a third party administrator (TPA) or an administrative services organization (ASO) contract with an insurance carrier. The role of the fiscal intermediary in self-funding is to process claims and arrange for bills to be paid out of the benefit trust or another account. The insurance function, *per se,* is eliminated, though employers usually purchase various forms of stop-loss coverage to protect themselves against excess risk. Some employers may even encourage their employees to purchase supplemental coverage.

The self-funding marketplace has become important because it has introduced the TPA as an autonomous agent of the employer. The TPA is not involved in the sale of insurance products, and has as its sole function the effective review of claims and the control of costs. Insurance companies and Blue plans were very aware of the impact of TPAs on the market, and early developed their ASO product to perform essentially the same function.

Claims management is one of the key functions of TPAs and ASOs, and it has become the dominant product that they aggressively market in the nation's leading business and insurance journals. It is through the claim management process that cost containment can best be exercised on behalf of the group purchaser. Consequently, some TPAs and ASOs have developed rather sophisticated, computerized protocol systems for reviewing and paying health benefit claims to providers.

In addition to this claim management function, however, and as part of their explicit cost-control mission, TPAs and ASOs can become very active in the marketing and negotiation of PPOs. As the representative of large employers and other groups, it is natural for the third party to see the opportunity to act as a broker for services and to use the PPO as a vehicle for securing better prices.

Third parties, therefore, are currently engaged in at least two levels of PPO activity: as organizers and as customers. In some cases, a third party will form a PPO by soliciting provider participants from service areas. This solicitation may be based on detailed price and service data already available in the reimbursement files of the third party, or it may be based on market surveys and direct contact with potential providers. The third party will act as a health care manager and play a key role in the organization and delivery of care by exerting influence though reimbursement policy.

The second form of PPO activity among third parties involves them as customers. This is a particularly important opportunity for health care providers. In this case, providers approach third parties with PPO products, and the providers act as the managers of the PPO, whereas the third party continues to act principally as the fiscal agent for employers and groups.

Traditional insurance plans are also involved in PPOs; but the role of third parties vis-à-vis self-funding, and the increased activity among business organizations as purchasers of health products, has forced significant changes in the health care arena. The ambulatory care administrator must be knowledgeable about these changes and capitalize on them for the benefit of his organization. For instance, there is no reason why ambulatory care organizations cannot make agreements with TPAs to offer products jointly. Hospitals are just beginning to realize that they are often the largest employer in town and have their own leverage.

Much of the new computer hardware and software that has been developed for the third party claims management has found its way into the hands of other organizations. In addition to self-funding, a number of business organizations have decided to become directly involved in the processing and payment of health benefit claims. To do this, they have often expanded their personnel and payroll departments, added a few computer work stations, and become their own third party. A multitude of systems for claims management and utilization review have exploded in the marketplace, filling the pages of insurance and personnel journals. Many of these packages reimburse based on a constantly updatable, reasonable, and customary charge basis. Some provide protocols for flagging claim items and problem providers. A few even offer analytic reporting capabilities that can help administrators to better understand the dynamics of utilization and cost trends in an employee population. A hospital personnel department with a minicomputer, the right software, a means of handling excess risk, and some creativity can soon become someone's partner in an ASO arrangement or PPO.

• • •

To respond adequately to PPOs and the potential of self-funding, administrators will have to become familiar with the new and expanded roles of employers, business coalitions, privately sponsored professional review organizations, and the myriad of third parties. These new players know they have acquired greater control over the flow of health care dollars and patients. The ambulatory care administrator must pay close attention to the flow of these dollars and patient sources. In response to the changing market, administrators will have to be well-informed and very creative in financial management and patient cost-effective care. They are no longer just managers of a facility or type of service. They are responsible for selling, providing, and encouraging high quality health services through the management of the largely, as yet, unmanaged ambulatory care component.

The resourcefulness of health care administrators will be challenged by PPOs and self-funding. In addition to keeping abreast of the market, and exercising more effective financial control, health care providers must address another issue: quality.

As the rate of health costs levels off, and as price variability among providers becomes minimal, the quality of these health services will become more important. Third parties, business organizations, and patients will want to know why, given similar prices for the same health care product, one PPO,

HMO, or provider is "better" than another. This may not only become a basis for negotiation, but also one for reimbursement.

To answer these quality questions, clinical data and carefully constructed screenings, coupled with patient-satisfaction data will have to be used in a creative, though objective, fashion. The administrator's response to changes in the health care arena has only begun.

REFERENCES

Sunshine, J. (1983). *PPOs—their growth and implications.* Paper presented at the 111th Annual Meeting of the American Public Health Association, Dallas, TX.

Wolfson, J., & Levin, P.J. (1985). *Managing employee health benefits: A guide to cost control.* Homewood, IL: Dow Jones-Irwin, pp. 122–127.

Trauner, J. B. (1983). *Preferred provider organizations: The California experience.* San Francisco: University of California Press.

Newhouse, J. P., Manning, W. G., Norris, L. L., Orr, R., Duan, N., Keeler, E. B., Leibowitz, A., Marquis, M. S., Phelps, C., E., and Brook, R. H. (1981). Some interim results from a controlled trial of cost sharing in health insurance. *New England Journal of Medicine, 305* (25), 1501–1507.

Wolfson, J., Kapadia, A., Decker, M., Sear, A., and Roht, L. (December 1982). Effects of cost-sharing on users of a state's health service program. *Medical Care, 20,* 1178–1187.

Wolfson, J. (February 1983). Cost sharing effects on providers. *Hospitals, 57,* 47.

Goldsmith, J. (1982). *Can hospitals survive?* Homewood, IL: Dow Jones-Irwin.

Some notes on the development of an IPA model HMO

S. Alan Savitz, MD
Corporate IPA Medical Director
IPA Development

Paul R. Roberts, MPH
Senior Vice President
IPA Development
CIGNA Healthplans of California, Inc.
Glendale, California

THIS IS A TIME when large numbers of national networks of health maintenance organizations (HMOs) are quickly forming. The parent corporations—usually with substantial financial resources—have been the large insurance companies, large HMOs, (like Kaiser-Permanente and the for-profits) and the large for-profit hospital chains. In choosing models for HMO implementation, rapid expansion has favored the selection of individual practice association (IPA) development.

One factor, the escalating cost of land and facilities, is making the development of staff and group practice model HMOs prohibitively expensive. In addition, success in marketing a staff or group model plan can lead

---

The authors acknowledge technical assistance received from Carole Blackburn in the preparation of this article.

The opinions and conclusions expressed herein are those of the authors and are not those of the CIGNA Corporation, its affiliates or subsidiaries.

quickly to service capacity problems. Moreover, higher start-up costs and clustering of resources make it difficult for the staff model to cover wide geographic areas. Alternatively, a network of hospitals and existing physician offices provides an IPA with a less costly yet more accessible health care system for a large geographic area. Another reason for the explosive interest in IPAs[1] relates to consumer preferences and market acceptability. There is a large segment of the population that is not interested in securing health care services in a clinic atmosphere, which many people perceive to exist in a staff or group model HMO. Finally, patients must change physicians to join a staff model.

With only an estimated 6% of the population enrolled in HMOs nationwide, it would be difficult to argue that group practice prepayment has now gained wider acceptance than the traditional fee-for-service delivery mode. However, it appears that there is a high appeal and potential enrollment for an organization that combines the cost containment and comprehensive benefit nature of an HMO with the traditional private practice concept reflected by the local physician's office. It now seems possible, with the use of sophisticated computer information systems, to monitor the care provided by individual physicians so that cost-effective utilization patterns can be as satisfactory in an IPA model HMO as they are in a staff or group model HMO.[2]

IPAs, generally unlike their more centralized counterparts, can work as well in rural as in urban environments. An economic element appeals to physicians: These open panel IPA alternatives present a method for physicians to preserve and protect the private practice of fee-for-service medicine, while affording them an opportunity to compete with organized delivery systems. With all the changes noted in the health care delivery system in recent years, groups of independent physicians and hospitals are pursuing the sponsorship of developing IPAs. Because many of the concepts inherent in this approach are not well understood, it is the purpose of this article to clarify the salient features associated with such developments.

IPA FRAMEWORK

An IPA is a specific type of HMO. Figure 1 depicts the three major HMO alternative organizational configurations. The HMO is a legal entity that provides or arranges for the provision of basic and supplemental health services to its members for a fixed fee. An IPA means a partnership, association, or corporation that delivers or arranges for the delivery of health services and that has entered into written service agreements or arrangements with health professionals. These individuals provide their professional services in accordance with an agreed on compensation arrangement. It is necessary to focus on some of the principal aspects associated with the development of an IPA providing alternative approaches

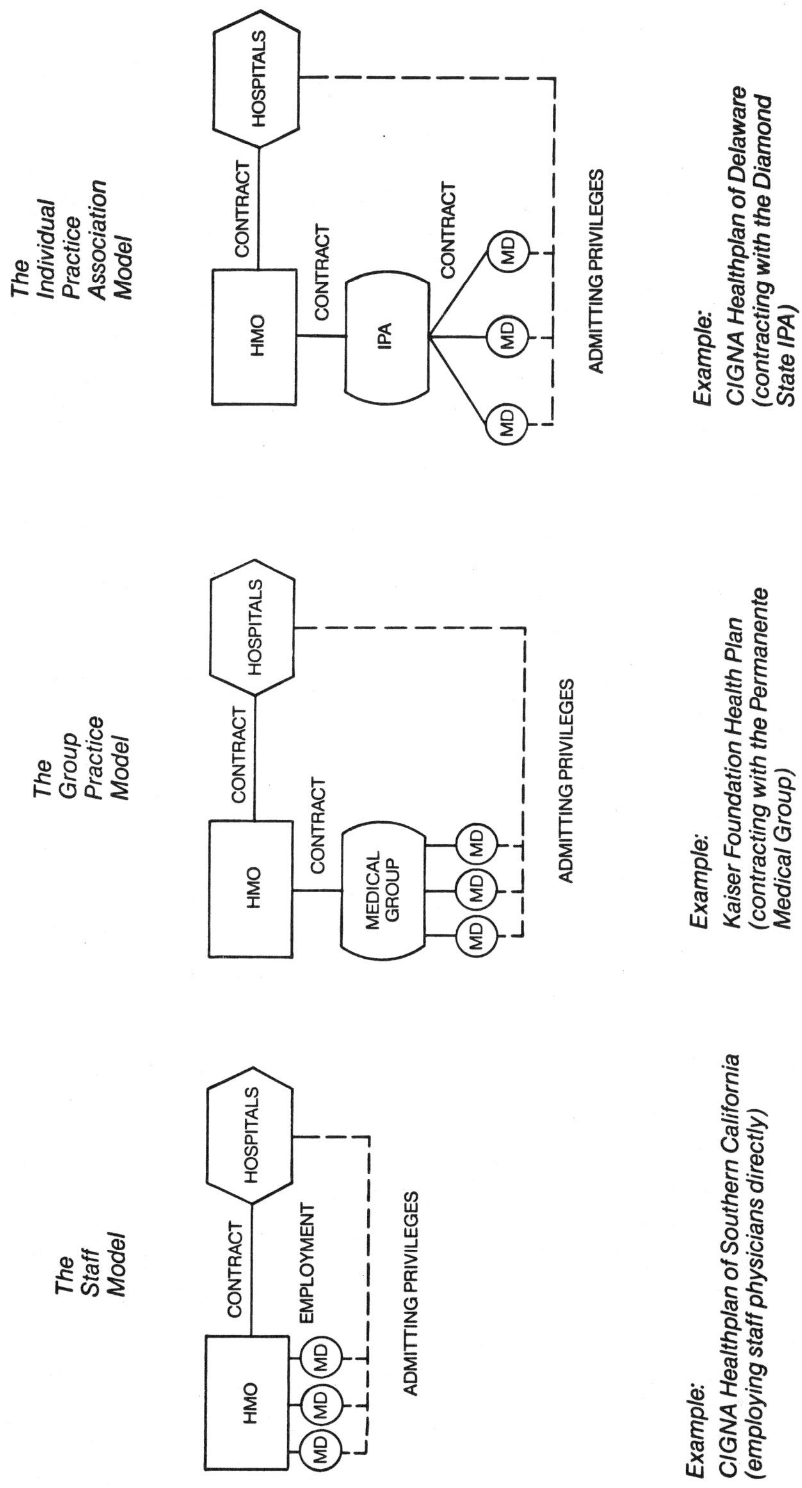

Figure 1. Alternative HMO configurations.

when appropriate. A checklist of key developmental steps has been included in the boxed material, "IPA Development Checklist."

The basic structure of the IPA model HMO in Figure 2 requires that employers pay a monthly premium to the HMO for health services for those employees and their eligible dependents who have voluntarily enrolled. The HMO then pays the IPA a monthly fee per member called a capitation, based on actuarial estimates of the cost of the medical services to be provided. Finally, the IPA most often reimburses the physician on a fee-for-service or individual capitation basis. An alternative form of IPA arrangement is an HMO that contracts directly with individual physician providers without the involvement of a second umbrella organization, the IPA. (This arrangement is still classified as an IPA model because the HMO does not employ physicians or contract with an existing medical group.)

IPA Development Checklist

- Assess market conditions and competition
- Evaluate feasibility for market entry and development options
- Quantify goals and objectives
- Determine availability of financial resources
- Establish IPA legal entity
- Identify optimal HMO partner or sponsor
- Secure key management personnel
- Formalize board committee structure and work process
- Negotiate terms of HMO/IPA service agreement
- Initiate development of provider group
    - Specify service area parameters
    - Select key provider targets
    - Formulate preferred risk-sharing approach
    - Identify utilization management strategy
    - Prepare budget guidelines and estimates
    - Draft reimbursement policy specifics
- Review benefit plan design and actuarial assumptions
- Design plan for compliance with regulatory requirements
- Formalize terms and conditions for physician agreements
- Commence physician recruitment activities
- Determine nomenclature, coding, and claims processing conventions
- Implement physician credentialing process
- Collaborate with HMO on hospital and ancillary facilities contracting
- Formulate medical policy development process
- Specify utilization control, quality assessment, and related program protocols and particulars
- Finalize the parameters for financial and risk management systems
- Design, test, and implement management information systems
- Prepare all forms, provider manuals, notices, and related materials for operations
- Establish provider orientation, training, and professional relations programs
- Conclude business development details and activate program

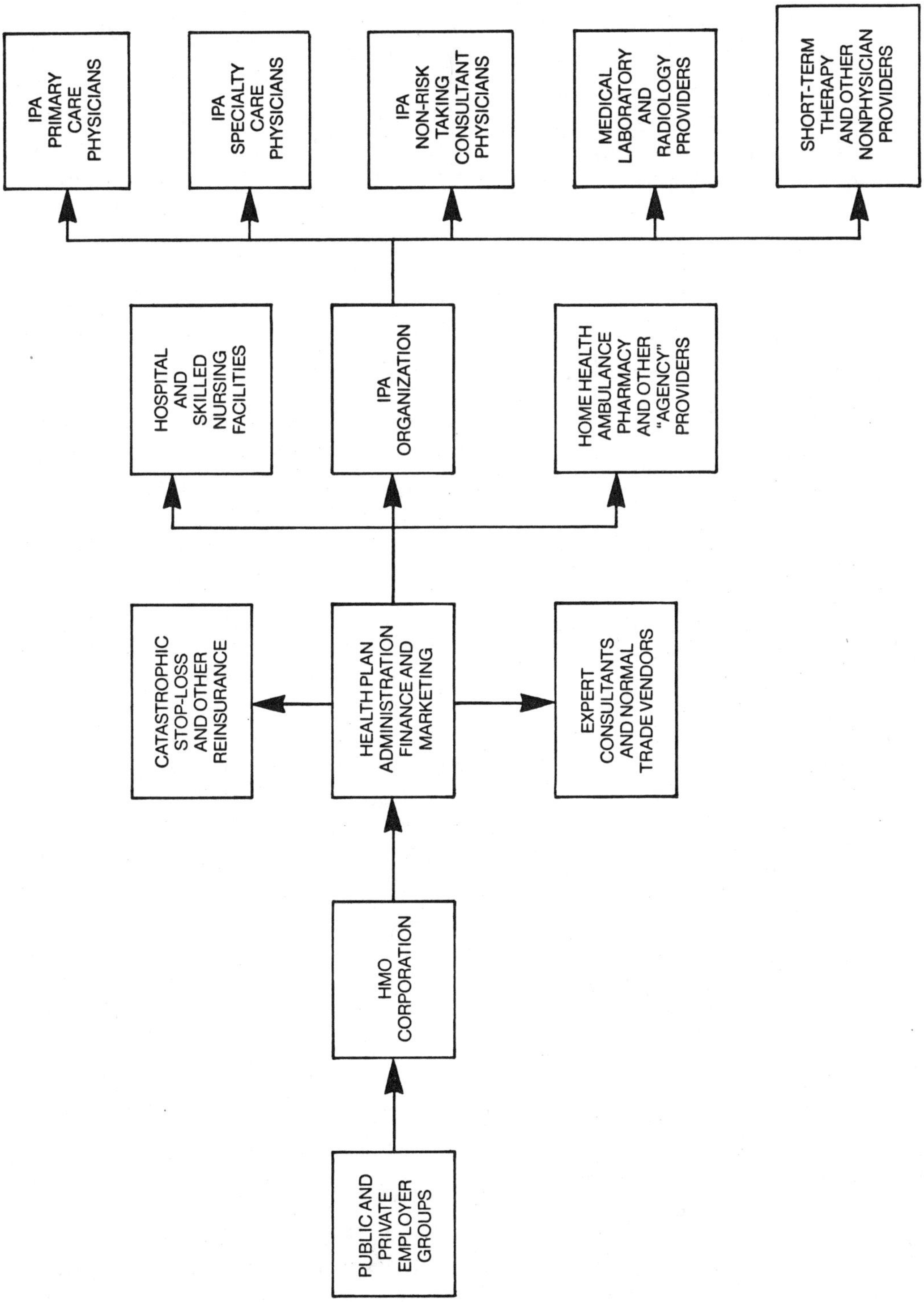

Figure 2. Cash flow of premium dollars.

IPA model differentiation

The traditional form of HMO is a staff or group practice model with a closed panel of practitioners. The physicians usually work in the same centralized facilities or in clinics provided by the medical group or HMO and share medical equipment, personnel, and records. An IPA, on the other hand, is an open panel with the physicians practicing in their own private offices. They work in a much looser affiliation and have weaker ties to the organization. The practice of physicians in an IPA model HMO is predominantly on a fee-for-service basis. Generally, at the outset, only 5% to 10% of the patients are from the IPA or prepaid. In a group model, federal HMO regulations require that not less than 35% of the group physicians' practice be prepaid[3] and in a staff model the physician's practice is almost entirely prepaid.

HMO and IPA roles

The IPA is responsible for organizing and providing the professional medical services within the plan. The HMO is responsible for marketing and collecting premiums. Depending on the particular IPA/HMO arrangements negotiated or local circumstances, various services can be administered either by the IPA or the HMO. Contracts with facilities such as hospitals, home health care agencies, ambulance services, and pharmacies are usually provided by the HMO. Utilization review and contracting with nonphysician providers often are handled by the IPA.

The IPA is responsible for organizing and providing the professional medical services within the plan. The HMO is responsible for marketing and collecting premiums.

A look at the flow of the money indicates that for an individual who joined the HMO and whose employer pays a monthly premium of $100, that $100 is paid to the HMO. The HMO might set aside approximately $35–$40 for hospitalization and about $40–$45 for medical expenses, including outpatient visits, hospital visits, diagnostic procedures, and medication. These are generally classified as variable expenses because they vary directly proportional to membership growth. The remaining $15 or so is for the generally fixed HMO administrative and marketing costs and for such other minimal expenses as costs incurred by members when medical emergencies occur outside the IPA service area.

Naturally, when the health plan initiates operations and membership volume is low, there will not be sufficient revenues to cover the fixed overhead costs. Therefore, there must be an availability of enough capital to sustain the operating plan until the financial breakeven point is reached. Typically, in a well-managed IPA this occurs after the plan has enrolled about 15,000 members.

Physician compensation and risk

In an IPA the physician must bear some financial risk, either as an individual provider or as part of a larger contract group.[4] This risk-sharing requirement can be as minimal as fee-for-service reimbursement with a small amount of withhold (10%–20%) or as great as full per patient capitation. IPA reimbursements fall into two main categories; one in which the IPA organization of physicians is capitated and the other in which the individual physician is capitated. Individual capitation models vary from one where the primary care physician may be capitated for all primary care physician services whereas specialists have no risk and are paid on a contracted fee-for-service basis to one where all physicians are capitated. The HMO's premiums and the capitation payments to the IPA, as well as the fee-for-service reimbursement levels to the IPA physician panel or the individual physician capitation, are based on the benefit plan design shown in Table 1. Payments are predicated on an actuarial analysis of expected frequency and unit costs of covered services that would then be negotiated between the HMO and the IPA.

IPA ORGANIZATION CAPITATION

The IPA organization capitation includes the cost of all professional services that are controlled by the physicians. These include outpatient and inpatient physician, specialists, and ancillary provider fees as well as outpatient laboratory and radiology. This amount is generally computed on a per-member-per-month basis prospectively, and a monthly payment is tendered from the HMO to the IPA for the provision of such services.[5] Therefore, the IPA organization is operated on a prepaid capitated basis. In turn, usually with this model, the IPA provides compensation on a fee-for-service basis to each participating provider for professional services rendered. The agreed to compensation can be based on the physician's usual and customary charge with a maximum allowable IPA fee or a set fee from a relative value scale with appropriate conversion factors. This scheme could include a discount or a maximum percentile calculation. There is usually a withhold provision. The amounts withheld from fee-for-service reimbursements are placed into a risk pool, which is used in case actual costs exceed budget expectations. One such withhold variation might be 12% of the reimbursement amount for outpatient physician services rendered and 25% for physicians' inpatient services. Services outside the realm of local physician or IPA control are risks usually retained by the HMO. These include out-of-area emergency care for both the emergency department and physicians' offices. Ambulance services, home health agency services, and durable medical equipment (DME) might be included within the IPA capitation. The HMO generally also secures reinsurance protection for individual catastrophic cases, which may incur exceedingly high expenses.

The other medical expense portion of the premium constitutes in-area hospital and emergency department ser-

Table 1. Benefit plan design (Responsibility of the HMO)

- Review service area benefit plan offerings
  - Prevalent employer group purchasing practices
  - Prepaid market products and options
- Analyze local current cost data
  - Professional fee schedules
  - Hospital costs and utilization trends
  - HMO benefit levels, copays, and premium rates
- Develop reasonable budget targets
  - Medical, hospital costs
  - Premium estimates
  - Pricing strategies
- Determine optimal benefit package parameters
  - Federal qualification requirements
  - State mandated benefit requirements
  - Local standards and customs
  - Competitive market shares
- Specify covered services
  - Copayments
  - Limitations and exclusions
- Estimate inflation factors
- Select provider compensation system and payment parameters to be employed
  - Hospitals, skilled nursing facilities
  - IPA
  - Ancillary (nonphysician) providers
  - Other contractors
- Estimate by plan type ("high option," "low option," etc.)
  - Medical service unit costs
  - Use frequencies
- Estimate total per member/per month premium requirements
  - Medical costs
  - General administrative costs
  - Profits, reserves, premium tax, etc.
  - Inflation factors
- Estimate contract mix (single, couple, family)
  - Average family size
  - Average contract size
  - Premium standard weighting ratios
- Establish schedule of supplemental packages and premiums
  - Prescription drug plan
  - Mental health
  - Vision care
  - Durable medical equipment
  - Dental care
  - Long-term rehabilitation
- Develop group service agreement
  - Low-option plan
  - High-option plan
  - Final premium
  - Individual "conversion" contracts
  - Supplemental riders

vices. An annual budget is agreed on by the HMO and the IPA at the beginning of the year. The budget specifies an expected utilization of services in terms of day per 1,000 members per year and an associated expense in terms of average hospital per diem costs. The per diem hospital costs derive from the hospital contracts negotiated by the HMO. Although these inpatient hospitalization expenses are usually the responsibility of the HMO, there is most often implemented a risk-sharing and incentive compensation arrangement between the HMO and the IPA with respect to actual outcomes. If the actual hospitalization expenses at the end of the year are less than the budgeted amounts, then the HMO and the IPA share in the surplus amount. On the other hand, if actual hospital costs exceed budget, then the IPA covers the same percentage of the resulting deficit up to the limit of the amount of funds in the physicians' shared risk pool. In other words, assume that the hospital budget was $1 million for the year, and the actual hospital expenses ran $1,100,000, then the IPA in a 50–50 hospital risk-sharing agreement would recompense the HMO one-half of the loss, or $50,000. On the other hand, if the actual hospital expenses only amounted to $850,000, then the HMO would pay the IPA $75,000 as its share of the surplus and these funds would be placed into the physicians' risk pool. Therefore, at the end of the year, the physicians' risk pool might have more funds available than the amounts withheld from the fee-for-service reimbursements. The IPA determines how the risk pool amounts are distributed to the participating physicians. Any additional compensation could be distributed based on the individual IPA physician's pattern of utilization or in any other way that the IPA determines to be reasonable. In short, on the down side, the physicians could lose their percentage withholds; on the up side, they could receive all the amounts withheld plus an additional bonus that might be based on performance. Because they have control of the utilization, both outpatient and hospital, physicians can earn additional remuneration if they practice cost effectively. It should be remembered that the purpose of the withhold and risk sharing is to get the physicians to recognize and act on the importance of careful utilization. For the plan to succeed, the utilization patterns should be cost effective enough to allow the withhold to be returned. When the experience of the plan lowers the reimbursement rate, the morale and effectiveness of the physician panel is impaired.

PRIMARY CARE PHYSICIAN INDIVIDUAL CAPITATION MODEL

In another IPA model variation, each primary care physician is capitated individually. In this situation the IPA contracts with primary care physicians who become the financial managers for the cost of care of their patients. The primary care physician is paid a monthly capitated fee for each patient, which includes all nonhospitalization expenses except the costs of administration of the plan and out-of-area emergency care. (There is yet an additional IPA model variation that includes hospitalization costs within each primary care physician capitation.) The primary care physician provides for all of the required services. The amount paid is expected to cover the total costs of medical care, which are actuarially calculated on the basis of the age and sex of the patients. A separate account is held for each primary care physician; from that account is taken all the consultants' fees and any non-office-based procedures, including outside laboratory work, emergency department care, and radiology services. In essence, the cost of all medical services performed by anyone other than the primary care physician is charged to his or her account. Specialists are usually reimbursed on a contracted fee-for-service basis. At the beginning of the month the HMO credits each primary physician's account with the negotiated and contracted capitated amount. At the end of the month the physician receives a statement itemizing the cost of each patient service incurred on the physician's referral. That amount is deducted from the total amount initially placed into the account. To protect the physician against extraordinary financial losses, there is generally a stop-loss provision afforded for each patient. The hospitals are paid by the HMO on a per diem or capitation basis.

There are some important differences between the two IPA models. When funds are taken directly from an individual account, the physician more clearly understands the high costs of high-technology procedures and the need for cost-effective referrals. There is the possibility of underutilization, which may lower the quality of medical care and is difficult to determine. In these cases, very sophisticated and intrusive monitoring for quality assurance is essential. Such careful monitoring can interfere with the physician–patient relationship and may not detect some underutilization. With the IPA organization capitated, the concern becomes one of overutilization. Very deliberate utilization controls become necessary—controls through which there is again careful and sometimes intrusive monitoring. In the early stages of an HMO, when there are few patients, it is impossible to distribute the risk safely over the small number of patients that each individually capitated primary care physician has been assigned. The system, to be fair, depends on each capitated physician having a sufficiently large number of patients, probably a minimum of 50, so that there is reasonable predictability to the patient utilization patterns. Otherwise, a single hospitalization or severe illness can absorb the entire risk fund. Without the requisite patient volume, the individual physician capitation method becomes an untenable gamble and not a situation in which good medical practice determines the outcome. In comparison, when the group in the aggregate is capitated, the physicians are forced to be actively involved so that the medical care is carefully scrutinized across the board by physicians who are concerned participants in utilization management. The involvement of colleagues tends to make each physician keenly aware of the quality and cost-effectiveness of the care being provided. In the individual capitation mode the physician is in a competitive, high-risk situation with the possibility of high income; in the IPA capitation alternative he or she is a member of a group with the financial risk and income opportunities diluted. A middle position is the capitation of a small number of primary care physicians and specialists, such as a subset of a hospital's organized medical staff. The risk is shared, but the number of individuals sharing the risk is small and discrete enough so that everyone is involved in cost and quality monitoring. In addition, a smaller IPA economic unit as suggested would benefit the desired goal of shared values and better promote group cohesiveness.

PHYSICIAN PANEL

The development of the provider network is probably the most difficult and time-consuming part of the process. What should be the base for the provider organization? Contacting the major hospitals, group practices, and physician organizations can be a way of starting. In an urban location, hospitals that geographically cover the intended service area can be approached. Working with the help of hospital administration and physician leaders, a panel can be organized. The nature of the hospital's medical staff organization is to provide due process for its members. It is easy for a few members who are dissident to the formation of an IPA organization to impede the effectiveness of the rest of the medical staff. Also, it may be politically impossible to have a meaningful selection process in an organization that often has multiple factions with different objectives. Maintaining the numbers of physician participants at the appropriate level means keeping out some people who want to join and are qualified. This kind of decision making may not be possible for the medical staff. It is pragmatic to separate the IPA from the medical staff organization.

Frequently there will be an already established physician panel acting as an IPA or preferred provider organization (PPO). An experienced organization has probably developed working policies and leadership and should be able to negotiate more quickly. Even if the organization is only in an early stage of formation and still amorphous in structure, it can become the focus for development. Time will be saved if potential leaders have emerged and have had experience working together as managers. If there is a PPO, it is a natural base for an IPA. A PPO has very much the same structure as the IPA portion of an IPA model HMO. The

A smoothly functioning provider organization with operational experience, good utilization patterns, and cooperative physicians is invaluable in forming an IPA.

utilization, quality controls, and leadership are essential elements of both structures. A smoothly functioning provider organization with operational experience, good utilization patterns, and cooperative physicians is invaluable in forming an IPA.

Participation in any alternative delivery system demands changes in practice patterns from physicians. Although an IPA presupposes less alteration of a physician's practice than any other alternative prepaid delivery system, it does take time for physicians to accept even moderate change and to alter the way they practice. Probably the most valuable aspect of an already operational group is that the physicians will have been educated in working together in an organized and effective manner. They will be more comfortable with the new structure to their practices, scrutiny of other physicians, withhold or other risk-sharing arrangement, and serious utilization review. If there is no preexisting acceptable organization, an IPA can be started by knocking on doors. A few strategically located group practices can be the base for an IPA. Finding a few physicians who are acknowledged and respected leaders in the community and allowing them to be the nucleus is another acceptable approach.

ORGANIZATION OF THE IPA

In creating the IPA, it is generally advisable to establish the organization as a legal entity. A suitable name has to be selected, bylaws must be drawn up, and the members of the board of directors chosen. Although physicians are comfortable with medical staff organizations and medical societies, these entities are generally not appropriate models to be used because they are not sufficiently entrepreneurial or market oriented. The IPA will be part of a complex business enterprise and must be able to make important decisions in a timely manner. A small board usually works more effectively. The members should be selected for their ability to work together and for what they can contribute to the organization. Committee chairpersons should be appointed for credentials, quality assurance, peer review, utilization review, medical policy, and grievance. During an early phase, the board of directors may act as a committee of the whole and administer these functional requirements.

HMO–IPA relationship

In developing the formal relationship and contract agreement between the HMO and the IPA, as shown in the box, "HMO/IPA Service Agreement," the first issues that will be raised will be compensation for the physicians and the amount of risk that they will accept. If the physician panel is newly organized and it is the first time that they have been involved with prepayment and risk sharing, there will be apprehension and hesitation. To begin with a lower level of risk sharing than is ideal may be pragmatic. As the group gains experience and confidence in working together, there will probably

HMO/IPA Service Agreement

- Contractual relationship and provision of services
  - Obligations of IPA
  - Obligations of HMO
- Definition of terms
- Capitation compensation arrangements
- Payment and timing provisions
- Proscription against member surcharges
- Hospital risk/incentive sharing formulae
- Claims administration and adjudication
- Physician coverage criteria
- IPA physician agreement terms and conditions
- Role of the medical director
- Gatekeeper protocol and physician–patient relationships
- Quality assurance and monitoring responsibility
- Utilization management controls
- Professional selection, credentialing, and peer review processes
- Frequency and content of provider listings
- Description of benefit services, limitations, and exclusions
- Advance review of marketing materials
- Grievances and disputes resolution
- Administrative and reporting responsibilities
- Compliance with state statutes
- Records sharing and confidentiality
- Term of agreement and termination provisions
- Agreement modification and notification protocols
- Records retention requirements

be a willingness to accept greater risk sharing. Physicians in individual practice no doubt have been involved in an entrepreneurial enterprise that has considerable risk, although of a different nature. The concern that occurs at this stage may come from a sense of not being in control because the organization is new and may appear large and threatening.

Physicians in the IPA may perceive the administrators in the HMO as businesspersons who have different ethical standards. Physicians may think such businesspersons are too interested in money or possibly have little sensitivity for the welfare of the patients. Administrators may believe that physicians are a necessary evil, who "should be seen and not heard." Neither position is helpful. A partnership must be pursued. Clear and openly candid discussions of all the factors involved, especially financial issues, should occur. Attempting to diminish the risks or skirting the difficult issues does not lead to trust. Ultimately, the organization must be seen as a joint venture of the HMO and the IPA that is market-driven and dependent on the confidence and good will of all parties concerned.

At some point a letter of intent may be drafted so that there is clarification of the agreement and the responsibilities of the parties on the major points. From this framework the service agreement between the HMO and the IPA will be developed. An initial budget, both for the HMO and the IPA, must be prepared. A rational timetable for completing the final service agreements and for a date of operations should be planned. Some aspects of the development process will necessarily depend on a previous phase. Physicians who have not had related business experience or who are involved with busy practices tend to slow the pace. Typically, regulatory approval by the appropriate state agency takes longer than anticipated. IPA sponsors should allow many months or a year to complete the total start-up process, unless the group has already been developed and is well organized or operational.

IPA management

The next major step is the recruitment and employment of key personnel by the IPA. Expertise is needed in several critical areas. These include administration, marketing, finance, medical direction, utilization management, and legal. Most frequently, administration, marketing, and finance are provided by the HMO. Only a part-time accountant may be necessary if the major financial work is done by the HMO. In the absence of HMO assistance, an administrator will be required to do the planning, set strategies, and develop the necessary procedures and policies. Legal counsel is needed to handle the drafting of contracts, sort out the complex business arrangements, and assist with statutory and regulatory requirements.

In an IPA, the interventions of the medical director bring about physician cooperation and help educate physicians in quality, cost-effective medical care. Often the position is filled for political reasons or as a nonthreatening sinecure. The medical director should be well trained medically to gain the respect of physicians, have management skills, a political sense, an ability to communicate easily, and an understanding of the present health care environment. He or she is responsible for utilization management and quality of care, and must be "tough" enough to enforce compliance and take the "heat" when necessary. The medical director must have the ability to work with administrators because this individual will be the interface between the HMO administration and the physicians. In terms of management, an IPA is a decentralized structure. It does not hire people but rather secures contracts for an individual's services. Both the administrator and the medical director must be flexible enough to negotiate and react to the changing market environment. The key managers should avoid being authoritarian and attempting to control people. The IPA management should engender cooperation and not competition. In this delicate contractual situation, power comes from respect and not from specific authority. Hierarchical management does not appear to work well in this type of complex business structure.

An IPA budget must be established that provides for general administration, quality and utilization management, committee expenses, personnel salaries and benefits, and the costs of recruiting staff and providers. A management information system (MIS) capability should be carefully developed. Selecting appropriate hardware and software components and determining the appropriate operating fees and costs of this hardware and software is critical. This equipment must be installed and tested and then information entered in terms of nomenclature and coding elements and conventions. Ground rules for billing, standardized forms, and data to be accumulated must be established and a decision must be made as to the nomenclature to be used, presumably Current Procedural Terminology (CPT–4) and International Classification of Diseases (ICD–9). Information reporting will be essential in the areas of finance, membership, claims, and utilization. These activities are best completed in close cooperation with HMO management.

Physician recruitment

When physician providers are to be recruited, the fee structure and the IPA physician contract, as delineated in the boxed list, "IPA/Physician Agreement," should be complete. In developing the provider panel there must be the right mix of physicians by primary care, specialty, and geographic distri-

IPA/Physician Agreement

- Compliance with IPA articles, bylaws, and rules
- Term of agreement and termination provisions
- Physician services to be provided
- Compensation arrangements
- Collection of member copayments
- Proscription against member surcharges
- Risk/incentive sharing particulars
- Billing procedures, coding conventions, and reporting times
- Case load minimums
- Quality assurance, peer review, and claims adjudication
- Utilization management and monitoring
- Gatekeeper and controlled referrals protocol
- Availability of coverage and continuity of care requirements
- Sanctions and expulsion process
- Professional liability (malpractice) insurance
- Sharing of medical records and confidentiality
- Access to business and finance records
- Permission for use of name in marketing materials
- Compliance with health plan grievance procedures
- Description of benefit plan services, exclusions, and limitations
- Notices and agreement modification protocols
- Binding arbitration for contract disputes

bution. If there is a good geographic spread and a large number of providers, the plan will be easier to market. However, too large a panel will leave the physicians with little involvement in the program because they have too few patients. Contracting with hospitals early can facilitate using the hospitals to help recruit physicians from their staffs. Sometimes, it is necessary to recruit physicians by directly contacting physicians in the specific areas that are desired. Starting with politically important physicians or those who are referral sources may help to speed the recruitment of others. Some specialties that are not directly involved in utilization decisions may not be appropriate candidates for risk. A contract system for these physicians may be preferable.

Credentialing

In an IPA it is possible that the more marginal, problematic providers will want to join because they have a great need for patients. While recruitment of the physicians occurs, begin the credentialing process. The IPA participation criteria should be more strict and selective than for hospital privileges. There is a variety of useful criteria, including board certification, adequate malpractice coverage, longevity in the community, and hospital privileges. In addition, a physician's utilization pattern or complete malpractice history may be available. It is necessary to get a signed release for professional information concerning the physician applicant to obtain previous practice history and hospital information. Physicians usually know which of their colleagues have a poor reputation. Information from these local sources can help to select out inappropriate applicants. Selecting only the "best" may be difficult; avoiding the individuals who are either inappropriate utilizers or provide poor or questionable quality medical care should be the minimal standard.

Hopefully, the credentialing process will select out those who are not able to provide the kind of care the group expects because it will be considerably more difficult under the provisions of "due process" to remove them later. It is very important to develop a panel of physicians that can provide quality medical care in a cost-effective manner. Over a period of time an exceptional physician organization can develop. When this happens, the cost of the health benefit plan can be more accurately predicted, allowing more risk taking, lower-cost premiums, and more competitiveness in the marketplace. Some employer group purchasers of health plans now require a performance appraisal of the provider organization.

Medical policy and quality assurance

Medical policy should be developed in accordance with local norms to provide medical standards and guidelines for the IPA to follow. These can spell out specific limits to benefits, reasonable frequency of treatment rules for the "gatekeeper," and standards for physician reviewers. There should be lists of procedures approved for ambulatory surgery and a clear policy on second opinions. Ensuring the maintenance of a consistent level of high-quality medical care is also essential to an organized delivery system. The quality assurance committee should be chaired by the medical director, given authority and staffed by individuals who have the ability and interest to do useful analyses. In addition, quality assurance should be an integral part of all operations—especially utilization review, where there should be a constant search for indicators of underutilization or deviance from standard practice. The development of practice pattern information and norms is most helpful. Regulatory agencies and our present consumer orientation demand a structured quality assurance program.

UTILIZATION MANAGEMENT

If there are enough patients, the success of the plan will depend more on utilization management than on anything else. Utilization management, the components of which are listed in the box, "Components of Utilization

Components of Utilization Management

- Carefully credentialed physician panel
- Risk incentive (or capitation) for physicians
- Sanctions for noncompliance
- Structured quality assurance program
- Provider education and notification/feedback system
- Patient education and wellness orientation program
- Gatekeeper and controlled referrals policy
- Mandatory day-of-surgery admission
- Preadmission outpatient laboratory testing
- Preadmission authorization protocol
- Surgical second opinion program
- Clear documentation by physician
- Admission certification process
- Mandated ambulatory surgery list
- Regular concurrent review on-site
- Early discharge planning
- Alternative to inpatient care
  - Ambulatory surgery center
  - Home health care
  - Skilled nursing facility
- Capitated mental health services
- Ambulatory chemical dependency programs
- Urgent care centers benefit coverage
- Retrospective review—inpatient and outpatient (management information system [MIS])
- Patterns of care norms for community
- All-inclusive hospital per diem by bed type contract (or capitation)
- Capitated pharmacy program
- Capitated outpatient laboratory

Management," works well when all the elements are properly orchestrated. It begins with a carefully selected panel of physicians and a tightly written IPA physician agreement that includes sufficient risk and incentives, strong sanctions to enforce utilization policy, and a strict gatekeeper protocol. As a principle, the process should involve the most conscientious individuals in the organization. At the beginning of the program, the main focus will be on hospitalization, the most cost-intensive aspect of health care. This function should not be delegated to the hospitals, but their involvement and expertise should be sought. Utilization management will best succeed when it is a cooperative effort of the physicians, hospitals, and utilization review staff. Utilization management depends on the ready availability of lower-cost alternatives to inpatient care: ambulatory surgery, home health care, and skilled nursing facilities. Discharge planning for maximum effectiveness should begin before admission. When a hospital admission is anticipated, the patient's support system and post-hospital needs should be evaluated. Knowing what care will be required in advance will avoid the delays that occur when some unexpected service must be found. Close ties with home health care providers and skilled nursing facilities expedite the referral process.

Because of the increased focus on review, physicians should be educated to provide, in the admission notes, clear documentation of the reasons for hospital admission, the need for an acute care facility, complications, multiple diagnoses, the initial treatment plan, and preliminary discharge planning. Progress notes with hard data should reflect the continuing need for acute hospitalization. Any denial must be based on the carefully documented decision of a physician reviewer. Procedures for appeal must be explicit and fair. For all elective hospitalizations, preadmission authorization should be required. Admission should not be determined on the basis of diagnosis alone because frequently admission diagnoses are inaccurate. Criteria for admission should depend on the severity of the patient's illness and the need for services that can only be provided in an acute care facility. Specific findings from the patient's history, physical examinations, and laboratory work should substantiate the severity of the illness and the need for inpatient care. All admissions should be concurrently reviewed, even those that have had preadmission certification. The review should be on-site from the chart within 24 hours. There should be continuing concurrent review to determine whether the acute hospitalization is necessary or, if the patient is in a special care unit, whether that specific level of care is justified.

Control of utilization and the ability to regulate physician behavior in an IPA is more difficult because of the looseness of the structure. Organizational values and culture are not easily maintained. The information system accumulates charge and service information, including hospital data to determine a physician's pattern of care and to develop norms for the provider group. The average cost of all the care that has been provided by physicians to their patients is determined, including hospitalization, laboratory, other diagnostic procedures, pharmacy, consultant costs, and the physician's own charges. Reports are generated comparing each provider to others in his or her specialty; these reports in a coded form should be sent regularly to every physician.

Physicians do not provide a standard medical product. There are no established scientific criteria to structure medical care. Practice patterns vary within the same community and between comparable communities. The incidence rates of some surgical procedures and of hospitalization are not consistent. The IPA should attempt to control the variations so that outlier providers will modify their practice patterns. The norms of medical care of the organization should be compared to regional or national norms.

It will be necessary to develop a system that impels each physician to provide quality, cost-effective care. The risk sharing and withhold are one part of it. All utilization data and reports of patterns of care should be part of the feedback provided to each physician. Warnings and probation are useful; however, if serious sanctions are not in place, the physician may not pay attention. Sanctions can include increasing an individual's withhold, requiring payback of unjustified costs, or assigning no new patients. If a noncompliant provider has been given feedback, there have been frank discussions, there has been a warning issued, probation has occurred, and there has been little or no change, then the only practical solution is expulsion. Unless an organization is willing to go the entire route in the rare cases when this is indicated, utilization management will not work.

THE GATEKEEPER CONCEPT

When the member enrolls, a physician is selected from a list of participating primary care physicians. The patient then obtains all care from that individual or from specialists or facilities to whom that physician refers. The primary care physician approves all consultations, emergency department use, and hospitalization. If a patient self-refers to a facility or a specialist, the service is considered a noncovered benefit and billed charges may not be paid. The primary care physician has control of all the consultations, hospital admissions, diagnostic tests, and prescriptions. In essence, the gatekeeper process establishes and legitimizes the primary care physician's role as the case manager. To the extent that primary care physicians are likely to use less costly medical procedures, fewer high-technology procedures, and less surgical treatment for initial management of common problems, the costs are generally lower. Moreover, the continuity of care provided by the gatekeeper is likely to reduce unnecessary duplication of diagnostic tests and therapeutic trials and reduce "doctor shopping" by patients. But most important, coordination of care and appropriate utilization enhances the quality of care.

HOSPITALS AND AGENCY CONTRACTS

Usually the HMO negotiates and executes the hospital contracts. Although sometimes that is completed late in the process, it is preferable for the purposes of recruiting physicians and marketing to select the hospitals early. As soon as location and practice patterns of the physicians are known, this information can be used to select the hospitals. For ease of access and marketing, contracting with many hospitals may seem appealing. However, an increase in market share and an increased volume of patients is essential to make a substantial cost reduction rate realistic and the hospital a valid partner. The capability of the facilities, their reputation, costs, and location should be carefully and critically evaluated. The reimbursement mechanism for the hospitals should be determined: an all-inclusive per diem by type of service, capitation with case mix adjustment, a sliding scale discount for volume (for a new IPA this may be demanded), discounted fee-for-service, and diagnostic related groups (DRGs). The contract should always specifically state what services are to be included for the fixed rate of payment. Providing some risk sharing can reward cost-efficient hospitals.

HMO contracts should be negotiated with skilled nursing facilities, laboratories, home health care providers, and pharmacies. The plan must also obtain the specific insurance protection needed to conduct business.[6] Provider relations personnel must train the office staff and physicians in all the requirements of the new system. Forms for enrollment, change of physician, notification of referral, and request for authorization of procedures and hospitalization all have to be available before members are enrolled.

• • •

The medical care literature is replete with both postmortem analysis of failures and laudatory reports of successful IPA programs. As suggested by the title, the authors had in mind the presentation of some notes regarding the subject that could be taken as food for thought for any potential sponsor attempting to digest the notion of IPA development. Due to the immense variability of options and tremendous range of local circumstances, it is not possible for the reader to be overexposed to some of the key principles and concepts inherent in the IPA prepayment approach.

NOTES

1. According to figures cited by *Health Market Survey*, as of September 30, 1985, there were 308 federally qualified HMOs; 177 were IPA models, and 131 were staff or group practice models (Vol. II, No. 17, October 16, 1985). Other HMO "census takers" place the *total* number of HMOs (i.e., qualified and nonqualified) at over 390, with approximately the same proportional

share of IPA models. Clearly, during the course of the last 10 years, the trend line has demonstrated an ever-increasing share of plans to be classified as IPA model HMOs.

2. The federal Office of Health Maintenance Organizations (OHMO) recently reported the following utilization data for selected federally qualified HMOs:

	Annualized incurred patient days per 1000 members	Average length of stay under 65	Annual encounters per member
Total plans (N = 143)	355	4.2	4.4
Group model (42)	343	4.2	4.2
IPA model (83)	362	4.0	4.6
Staff model (17)	356	4.7	4.3

(Source: *OHMO Statistical Data,* "Table 3: Utilization and Ambulatory Encounter Statistics for Non-Medicare and Non-Medicaid Membership by Type A Federally Qualified HMO by Model for the Quarter Ending March 31, 1985," OHMO; Rockville, Maryland [September, 1985].)

3. Actually, this requirement for the HMO medical group's patients to meet the "35% rule" may be phased in during a 4-year period. The period begins with the month following the month in which the HMO becomes federally qualified. Under special conditions that warrant compliance to be unreasonable or impractical, the HMO may secure a waiver. Waivers may be granted for HMOs that (a) serve nonmetropolitan or rural areas, (b) contract with multispecialty medical groups that provide consultation on a regional or national basis, or (c) know there will be an insufficient number of HMO members because the majority of residents in the service area are not eligible for employee health benefit plans. In such an instance, the HMO will not be able to require utilization of at least 35% of the entity's services (42 CFR Part 110, Section 110.104(a)(3), Subpart A, *Federal Regulations: Requirements for a Health Maintenance Organization*).

4. Federal regulations require that HMOs include in their contracts with IPAs, ". . . a description of mechanisms, such as risk sharing, financial incentives, or other incentives, to be applied to monitor utilization and to control costs of basic and supplemental health services and to achieve utilization goals. . ." (*Ibid.,* Section 110.104 (c)(iv)).

5. An alternative methodology employed for tendering risk payments to the IPA is based on a "percent of premium" (as opposed to a "per-member-per month" dollar figure) computation. Although this scheme is also predicated on the actuarial estimates of the cost of care, it more easily accommodates the pricing strategies of plans that are nonfederally qualified. These plans generally use "experience-rating" techniques whereby premiums vary from one subscriber group to another. This aspect makes pm/pm payments difficult to administer. Federally qualified plans, on the other hand, are required to use "community rating," which may not be dependent on the enrolled group's claims or utilization experience.

6. In addition to the "standard" business insurance policies affording protection against fire, theft, fraud, public liability, property damage, and other casualty risks, an HMO will need to carefully consider additional types of indemnified protection. These coverages, which may or may not name the IPA as an "additional insured" based on local need or circumstances, would include directors' and officers' liability, corporate professional liability ("malpractice"), antitrust and restraint of trade, individual catastrophic stop loss, insolvency and out-of-area reinsurance, fidelity bonding (for "money-handlers"), and possibly "key man" insurance (indemnifying against the loss or incapacity of the chief executive officer).

The private delivery of Medicaid services: lessons for administrators, providers, and policymakers

Deborah A. Freund, PhD
Associate Professor
Department of Health Policy and Administration
School of Public Health
University of North Carolina
Chapel Hill, North Carolina

THE MEDICAID program has not been sheltered from the cost crisis that has hit all other public and private health and medical care programs over the last 20 years. In response to statistics, state officials have looked for new solutions to check the rise in health care costs; however, the sentiment over the appropriate means of cost containment has changed. Public policymakers, who initially instituted a series of regulatory measures and eligibility cuts, have now turned to initiatives and demonstrations that attempt to alter provider and consumer behavior through competitive inducements such as prepaid capitation arrange-

---

Preparation of this paper was partially supported by contract HCFA 500-83-0050. The opinions expressed are those of the author and should not be construed as representing the policy of the Health Care Financing Administration or the Department of Health and Human Services. The author also acknowledges the assistance of her colleagues at Research Triangle Institute; University of North Carolina; Medical College of Virginia; Lewin and Associates; American Enterprise Institute; and Tillinghast, Nelson and Warren.

ments and primary care case management—hereafter referred to as alternative delivery systems (ADSs).

The focus of this article is on Medicaid's use of these ADSs and on a selected list of the key issues that administrators, policymakers, and providers must confront in extending ADSs to the Medicaid population. Medicaid may represent either a new line of business for existing ADSs that have marketed previously to the private sector or the sole enrollee group for a newly-formed plan.

This article explores two generic issues that affect all the new forms of health care delivery systems serving the poor in the 50s Medicaid programs—those that concern county/state or plan/state relations and those issues involved in internal implementation decisions that new ADSs, formed to provide services to welfare patients, must make in order to survive.

ADS TYPES—IMPLEMENTATION EXPERIENCE

Prior to the passage of the Omnibus Reconciliation Act (OMBRA) of 1981, several provisions of Title XIX precluded states from implementing ADSs as we know them today. In 1981, states received authority to set state qualification standards; under health maintenance organizations (HMOs) that contracted with a state Medicaid program, up to 75% of plan enrollment can be Medicare and Medicaid beneficiaries. In addition, the Health Care Financing Administration (HCFA) granted waivers authorizing selective contracting with cost-effective providers and the development of case management programs for Medicaid beneficiaries. The notion of case management (CM)—sometimes called gatekeeping or managed care—is in essence a coordinating and rationing strategy designed to make the unique role of the primary care physician (PCP) the key to cost control. Under these programs, Medicaid recipients select a physician (available 24 hours a day) to deliver all primary care services and give prior authorization for referrals, consultations, and hospitalizations. CM programs vary in the way in which physicians receive reimbursement and share in financial risk, the aid categories covered, and organizational arrangements.

State initiatives or demonstrations can be characterized as one of three types:

1. competing health plan models;
2. health insuring organization (county at risk) models; and
3. partial capitation models.

A fourth model, which retains fee-for-service payment but requires beneficiaries to select a PCP as case manager, is discussed more fully elsewhere (Freund, 1984a). In the competing health plans model, competition is the presumed mechanism for reducing health care costs. The state contracts with two or more state or federally qualified HMOs in a given area. By obtaining federal waivers, states can require all Medicaid beneficiaries in an area to join one of the qualified HMOs, thus the HMOs must compete for enrollees.

In the health insuring organization (HIO) model, the state contracts with an intermediary that meets all state insurance requirements and is willing to contract with providers for all acute care on an at-risk basis. Although the intermediary can be a private organization, it is often a county government; for this reason, this type of ADS is often a county/plan (at-risk) model. The HIO usually institutes financial incentives and other administrative controls in an effort to make physicians provide cost-effective services.*

States also have used the new waiver authority to enter into prepaid arrangements that are only partially capitated. Typically, the state capitates the PCP only for his or her professional services and for CM and provides other financial incentives to reduce costs of referrals or patient care.

In a majority of ADSs, it is mandatory that a Medicaid beneficiary participate in the ADS by selecting a primary

Table 1. Status of Medicaid alternative delivery systems

State health-insuring organizations/county at risk	County area	Operational status	Voluntary/mandatory enrollment
California	Santa Barbara County	operational	mandatory
	Monterey County	terminated	mandatory
	San Mateo	under development	mandatory
Kentucky (Citicare)	Jefferson County	terminated	mandatory
Nebraska	Omaha, Lincoln	under development	mandatory
Pennsylvania	Philadelphia	under development	mandatory
Washington	Western counties	under development	mandatory
	Competition Among HMOs		
Arizona	Entire state	operational	mandatory
Missouri	Jackson County	operational	mandatory
New York	Monroe County	operational	mandatory
Minneapolis	Hennepin, Itaska counties	under development	voluntary (random assignment)
Wisconsin	Madison, Milwaukee	operational	mandatory
California	San Diego County	under development	mandatory
Ohio	Cleveland, Dayton	under development	mandatory
Illinois	Chicago	under development	mandatory
	Partial capitation		
New York	Suffolk County	operational	voluntary
New Jersey	statewide	operational	voluntary
Michigan	Kalamazoo, Detroit	operational	voluntary
North Carolina	Wilson County	under development	voluntary
Tennessee	Maury County	operational	voluntary

Recent federal legislation (PL 99-272) now prohibits HIOs from being established to serve exclusively the Medicaid population. Since most HIOs have been formed for this expressed purpose, it is questionable whether this organizational form can continue to play a significant role in case management programs.

care case manager, either a PCP or an HMO (that serves as a case manager). A beneficiary can choose any provider he or she wishes. If a beneficiary does not make a choice, he or she is randomly assigned to a plan or case manager. In a few cases, participation in the ADS is voluntary, and the beneficiary may choose to remain in fee-for-service Medicaid. Table 1 presents a list of the states that have started Medicaid ADSs and the status of these demonstrations.

MANAGEMENT ISSUES

County/state and plan/state relations

Whether the new program is an HIO organized around managed care concepts or a demonstration of effects of competition among several health plans, unique management issues confront physicians, plan administrators, and government policymakers.

Voluntary versus mandatory enrollment

The first issue involves whether enrollment in the demonstration should be voluntary or mandatory for all Medicaid beneficiaries living in the demonstration area. Mandatory enrollment is desirable from the point of view of state, county, and plan. Typically, a plan or county is paid a capitation equal to 95% of the fee-for-service cost for the service. Thus, the state is assured at least 5% savings and a lessened administrative burden (surveillance, utilization review, third party payment). For the plans (counties) mandatory enrollment provides a guaranteed flow of patients and a constant source of cash needed to defray early development costs. The record shows that voluntary programs attract between 5% and 15% of all eligible Medicaid beneficiaries in the first year or two of operation. Thus, voluntary programs designed to service a Medicaid population cannot be financially viable even in the most densely populated urban areas in the early years of operation.

Welfare rights groups and Medicaid beneficiaries often view mandatory enrollment as undesirable because of denial of freedom of choice of provider and the threat to established provider–patient relationships. In reality, however, provider relationships are rarely severed. Most physicians who treat a substantial number of Medicaid patients decide to continue and join the ADS demonstration.

Linking eligibility to enrollment

Another issue concerns how eligibility determination and enrollment processes are linked at the local level. Traditionally, eligibility is within the purview of a social services (welfare) department; the department of health is concerned with ADS enrollment. The two departments often use different computer systems. In a demonstration, separation of the information system

In a demonstration, separation of the information system into two departmental systems can mean the demise of the demonstration program.

into two departmental systems can mean the demise of the demonstration program. There are three critical problems connected with eligibility matters and enrollment processes. The first is whether the plan should enroll all Medicaid eligibles during a short period of time or should phase in enrollment over a longer period. A short enrollment period requires dispersed enrollment sites and a very productive staff to notify Medicaid beneficiaries of the demonstration, to make appointments by phone for choosing a health plan or primary care provider. Usually, beneficiaries are not easy to contact and many eligibles are automatically (computer) assigned to plan or provider.

The states choosing to phase in enrollment over a long period enroll individuals newly eligible for Medicaid first and then enroll the remaining beneficiaries as they are recertified. Thus, enrollment of the entire population can take 9 to 12 months. Although savings are not immediate, the long enrollment period makes administration much smoother and gives the staff time to find and remedy any "kinks" in the process. When enrollees are phased in slowly, a small cadre of well-informed staff can objectively counsel each enrollee and see that each makes a thoughtful choice of health plan or primary care provider. Frequently, welfare case workers often not familiar with the Medicaid program or new alternatives have provided enrollment counseling services. However, at least one state (Utah) has successfully trained a group of enrollment workers familiar with health education and the prepayment concepts. Utah places these counselors in the same location as welfare case workers. Eligibles seeking recertification are required to make an appointment for the same day with the plan enrollment counselor to learn about the plan and choice of provider (Freund, 1984a).

A second issue concerns a lock-in period and guaranteed eligibility. In the case of a lock-in, the eligibles must enroll for one year with the chosen health plan or primary care physician. Unless the beneficiary has a serious grievance, he or she may only switch plans at his or her 1-year anniversary or at an open enrollment period. This provision minimizes administrative burdens for the state. From the plan perspective, the lock-in is also desirable because it allows time for patient education and prevention.

Guaranteeing eligibility for 6 months (a waiver that can be obtained from HCFA) affords the same advantages as a year's lock-in to the state, county, or plan and also provides an incentive for an eligible to join an ADS in a voluntary demonstration. Because many individuals go on and off state Medicaid rolls monthly, administration becomes a nightmare, with individuals losing and regaining eligibility several times during a year.

The third issue concerns the necessity of linking eligibility and enrollment to minimize retroactive denials of claims or capitation payments. On average, eligibility files completed by the 25th of the month are used as a basis for enrollment. However, because eligibility is constantly updated and is not generally computer linked to plan enrollment dates, plans or PCPs frequently must find out if individuals enrolled at the first of the month are eligible for services at a later date. Plans may render care and then learn that they cannot be reimbursed for care that has been delivered. For this reason, plans need to link eligibility and enrollment files and have access to updated enrollment and/or eligibility files on a timely basis. Even a 1-day lag in responding to a query concerning eligibility status can be costly to the plan.

Linkage is particularly important for files on the medically needy population. Although many counties (plans) do not cover the medically needy population, those that offer coverage do have to negotiate with the state agencies to determine the limits of their financial responsibility. Individuals classified as medically needy frequently become eligible for Medicaid by "spending down" their assets during a hospital stay or an extended illness. If a new plan has enrollees who become Medicaid eligible by "spending down" during an illness, the plan could be driven to financial ruin. Thus, to ensure the long-run success of the demonstration, state agencies should agree to continue paying fee-for-service for medically needy patients through the illness episode.

Marketing

All the initiatives described are based on consumer choice of a primary care physician or plan. Thus, the question of how Medicaid beneficiaries choose among plans or physicians becomes critical. Yet, very little is known about the determinants of health plan (provider) choice among Medicaid beneficiaries. Among the facts known is that whether simple mailing or extensive multimedia advertising is used, somewhere between 30% and 50% of the eligible population never makes a choice of plan at the required time and therefore must be randomly assigned to a provider (health plan or physician) (Freund, 1984a). Frequently, the only time an eligible individual is willing to make a choice is when he or she becomes ill. At that time, the individual frequently finds out that the plan to which he or she has been assigned is not affiliated with his or her usual physician. This situation presents problems in continuity and quality of care, but the provider assignment stands, although the usual physician could have been chosen had the choice been made at the proper time. Plans use a variety of auto-assignment algorithms, including

- assigning all individuals to the lowest bidder (as in the Arizona Health Care Cost Containment System);
- assigning the individual to the plan or primary care physician located closest to the individual's home; and
- assigning the individual to a specialist according to the age of the patient (so that a 40-year-old is not assigned to a pediatrician).

Computer algorithm programs designed to auto-assign enrollees routinely have a high error rate initially.

States have been concerned about what type of plan marketing should or should not be encouraged and what the state regulatory function should be. Because little is known about marketing strategies to help Medicaid beneficiaries select a plan during an enrollment period, plans have tried a number of inducements—including presentations at community groups (including welfare rights organizations and churches); advertising by billboards, public transportation space, and radio and television spots; and mailing of detailed brochures. Some have even undertaken door-to-door canvassing. States have been especially concerned about controlling marketing efforts to prevent abuses. The majority of states have chosen to restrict marketing activities to mail brochures—the content of which must be approved in advance by the state (Freund, 1984b). In many states, state agencies design and distribute a brochure, objectively presenting the attributes of each plan. Because some plans have expressed concern that plans described first or second have an advantage, states have chosen to scramble the order in which plans are presented.

INTERNAL IMPLEMENTATION DECISIONS

Among the many issues managers of competing health plans or county-sponsored primary care networks must face, if they are to be successful, is how to design a management information system (MIS) to monitor provision of managed care and to monitor the financial "health" of the plan. Other critical issues concern how to pay physicians and how to create administrative controls to change physician behavior, how to manage all aspects of plan operations, and how and when to enter into management contracts.

Management information systems

Because ADSs operate under fixed revenue constraints, management and providers must be able to match revenues with expenses so that deficits can be readily identified. The tool for providing information on cost and utilization patterns is an MIS. At its best, an MIS provides utilization and cost data that can be broken down by patient, by physician, by type of physician (such as by specialty) or utilization category (ambulatory, hospital, pharmacy, durable medical equipment, etc.). Although most administrators and physicians understand the concept, the harsh reality is that many ADSs created for the sole purpose of serving Medicaid patients do not have access to an appropriately designed MIS, do not have funds to build an MIS, or do not implement the MIS quickly enough to put the ADS on a sound basis. An MIS is never easy to design. Plan administrators tend to greatly underestimate the time required to design an MIS "from scratch" or to adapt an already existing system. A common reason for bankruptcy of a new ADS is failure to implement an adequate MIS in a timely manner. The plan that cannot maintain accurate and up-to-date reporting of utilization and expenditure data cannot survive. Failure of the Monterey Health

Initiative and Health Care Providers, one of the participating plans under the Arizona Cost Containment System, is one example of the price of failure of an MIS.

An MIS for a Medicaid ADS differs from a purely private sector system in two ways: (a) it must maintain current data on the patient's Medicaid eligibility status, and (b) it must meet the detailed reporting requirements of the state for use in surveillance and utilization review systems (SURs). Utilization for individuals and detailed financial information must be reported on a quarterly to yearly basis. On the other hand, private sector systems generally provide information in aggregate utilization categories rather than by individual patient, and they are not designed to produce reports quickly. The private sector plan, undertaking Medicaid services, must build a system with these capabilities.

In implementing any MIS, the administrator must make a critical choice between two types of data collection mechanisms, each with its own distinct advantages and disadvantages. In the first, the ADS collects encounter data on (paper) encounter forms. Usually, the encounter form is given to the patient when he or she first registers for a visit. The patient then fills out the form with relevant demographic and eligibility status information. Information on content of the visit (diagnosis, procedure, and hospitalization) is filled out by the physician. Encounter forms are then batched and keypunched into the central computer for analysis at a later date.

In implementing any MIS, the administrator must make a critical choice between two types of data collection mechanisms, each with its own distinct advantages and disadvantages.

HIOs, individual practice associations (IPAs), and other types of decentralized ADSs often prefer use of computerized encounter forms. The computerized system allows the provider to call a central control site and give patient's name to verify eligibility, time of appointment, expected procedures, and approximate charges (if requested). The central control operator issues an authorization number for care the provider schedules. The authorization number must be listed on any claim for payment. The central operator immediately enters data acquired in the telephone call into a centralized computer data bank. Thus, the manager or medical director has immediate access to information on daily patterns of use and costs. The authorization number serves a dual purpose—as a prior approval mechanism and as a means to track utilization. This kind of MIS allows the plan to easily estimate expenses incurred but not reported; without timely and accurate information, management can develop a false sense of financial security. Access to constantly updated information on utilization and expenditure patterns gives the manager a sound basis for decision making.

On the other hand, the MIS that

relies on paper encounter forms to collect data must deal with problems of cumbersome administration—encounter forms may be lost; there may be lag time between receipt of data and delivery of service. Key punch and data processing prevents management access to timely data; management decisions and quality assurance activities reflect the inadequacies of the data base. Medicaid ADS programs started by hospitals, counties, health departments, or provider groups frequently find that the paper encounter form approach is cheaper because they can rely on existing staff to fulfill their information needs without buying a computer. The ADS that pays physicians by capitation rather than fee-for-service can survive while using paper-generated data systems because, under capitation, data on incurred but not reported expenditures are not as critical as in a fee-for-service-oriented plan.

Physician payment and administrative systems

A related issue concerns physician payment under case management programs serving Medicaid beneficiaries and issues of administrative controls. A variety of strategies are currently being used. Capitation methods have the advantages of placing strong cost containment incentives on PCPs and/or specialists, and of deflecting adverse risk from the plan county or state to the physician. However, capitation has been traditionally hard to sell to physicians not accustomed to it, particularly specialists who feel that malpractice exposure is significantly increased (Freund, 1984a). Many plans have chosen to combine fee-for-service and capitation reimbursement. The most common way is to pay PCPs on a capitation basis, specialists on fee-for-service, and hospitals per diem. Under this arrangement, about 80% of the capitation funds are allocated directly to participating PCPs and 20% are held in escrow to serve as a trust fund for overruns on specialty care and hospital care authorized by PCPs. If a PCP authorizes more specialty and hospital care than has been budgeted and thus generates a deficit, the 20% hold-back pool from primary care capitation is used to offset all or part of the deficit generated. If there is a surplus in the specialty or hospital account, because the physician authorizes less care than budgeted, the PCP generally shares in the savings with the plan at the end of the year when the entire 20% trust fund account, including interest earned, is returned. The advantage of such a system is that it blends financial incentives for delivery of cost-effective primary care with incentives to authorize specialty and hospital care in an equally cost-effective manner. The disadvantages of such an approach, however, include complex problems in administration and communication with physicians.

Plans that cannot convince PCPs to accept capitation often pay physicians a case management fee (usually \$1 to \$3 per enrollee per month) in addition to fee-for-service to compensate for the administrative burden of case management. Evidence across plans, however, suggests that even the strongest financial incentives in current capitated plans are not successful in reducing health care costs in the absence of strong administrative controls like extensive utilization review, prior authorization, and concurrent review of hospital stay (Gibson-Kern, 1984). Thus, it is important for new plans to institute utilization review and other types of administrative cost control policies immediately, even when the response from the provider community is hostile. One approach for combatting such hostility is to choose as medical director a well-respected member of the physician community or to establish a quality assurance committee made up of such individuals.

Contract management

The final internal management issue concerns whether the plan should contract for any or all administrative services. Many new plans choose to contract for all administrative services with a national HMO firm because of the firm's expertise in the areas of provider relations, utilization review, and quality assurance. Examples include Citicare (Freund, 1984a), Maricopa and Pima County Health Plans (Freund, 1984b), the Santa Barbara Health Initiative (Freund, 1984a; Gibson-Kern, 1984), and the Hartford Health Network (Pollack, 1985). Other plans have chosen to contract only for specialized services such as the management information system or third party reimbursement. Three features appear to be related to the success of contract management:

1. All aspects of the plan design must be formalized before any request for proposal (RFP) seeking potential contractors is let out for bid to allow the RFP to be specific about what potential contractors are to do and to allow precise evaluation of proposals. If plans are still in the design stage, contractors cannot know what to propose and contracts that can be enforced cannot be written.
2. Plans must hire the management contractor well before the plan implementation date—at least 6 to 9 months in advance—especially if one of the specified duties is to design an MIS that will be functioning on the first day of plan operation. Plans that have not allowed adequate lead time have found that the implementation of MIS and quality assurance systems is deferred until well after the plan starts operating.
3. A potential contractor should be evaluated on understanding of the needs of the Medicaid population. Companies accustomed to managing HMOs for the private population may not be competent for one that is public. For example, contract management must understand the necessity of locating their office close to the target population, and the necessity of being open after hours in order to be responsive to questions and problems.

• • •

Many states and localities look to new Medicaid ADSs to bring rising health care costs under control. The hope is that new systems will develop cost-effective behavior without diminishing quality of care. Several intensive studies are currently underway to investigate the cost-saving potential of such plans (Research Triangle Institute, 1984). Preliminary results suggest that there is promise of a good performance. For example, results from Citicare and the Michigan Primary Sponsor Plan show substantial savings in hospital use and emergency department use (Freund, 1984a; Spitz, 1985). In addition, at the end of the first year, the Santa Barbara Health Initiative shows county-wide savings of approximately $1,000,000 (Gibson-Kern, 1984). However, ADSs are not easy to implement for the Medicaid population and many issues must be confronted and solved for plans to be successful.

Plans (counties) must be able to recruit a large volume of patients. Because the most appropriate marketing strategies are not clear, mandatory enrollment, rather than voluntary enrollment, is a distinct advantage. In addition, because the Medicaid population is very changeable, large swings in enrollment can lead to the success or the demise of a plan. Plans must implement effective mechanisms for communicating about patient eligibility status to minimize retroactive denials of capitation payments. Managers and providers must make several critical decisions on how to pay physicians, what type of MIS to employ, and who should manage the plan itself. There is evidence that only plans that provide physicians with strong incentives to economize and implement strong administrative controls are successful; however, because combining capitation methods of reimbursement with administrative controls can cause significant underutilization, management must establish effective information systems to monitor quality of care.

Medicaid capitation programs provide cost-saving potential and provide creative experiences for managers. The key to success, however, is careful planning, something that has been lacking. Programs are admittedly complex. Funds are often not available for planning; when they are, planning funds can never be used to run a pilot test of the program. Granters need to fund planning and pilot programs to allow testing of all key program elements.

REFERENCES

1. Freund, D. (1984a). *Medicaid reform: Four studies of case management.* Washington, DC: American Enterprise Institution.
2. Freund, D. (1984b, December). Description of the plans. *In Evaluation of the Arizona Health Care Cost Containment System.* Menlo Park, CA: SRI International.
3. Gibson-Kern, R. (1984). *Evaluation of Medicaid competition demonstrations: The Santa Barbara County Health Initiative* (Contract HCFA 500–83–0050). Research Triangle Park, NC: Research Triangle Institute for the Health Care Financing Administration.
4. Pollack, R. (1985, October). *Profile: The Hartford*

Health Network. Paper presented at a meeting of the Group Health Association of America, St. Louis, MO.

5. Research Triangle Institute. (1984, May). *Preliminary evaluation design for the Medicaid competition demonstration evaluation,* submitted to the Health Care Financing Administration. Research Triangle Park, NC: Author.
6. Spitz, B. (1985). Medicaid lessons for business. *Business and Health, 2*(8), 16–21.

Second opinion programs and their impact on alternative forms of health care delivery

Eugene McCarthy, MD, MPH
Director
Health Benefits Research Center

Lisa Astor, MPH
Administrator
Health Benefits Research Center
New York Hospital Cornell Medical Center
New York, New York

THE COST OF health care in the United States is estimated at $310 billion annually. Of this, $85 to $95 billion, or about 30%, is directly attributable to surgical and surgery-related expenditures (Moore, Martin, & Richardson, 1985). Many companies are now taking action to reduce health care costs, especially in the area of this high ticket item—surgery. One of the most promising programs to save money in the short run as well as in the long run is the use of a second opinion program. It is reported by Freeland (1984) that 76% of insurance companies have some form of a second opinion program.

Surgery rates have increased 93% from 1971 to 1982 in short-term care hospitals (National Center for Health Statistics, 1982). Several theories have been put forth to explain the sudden increase in rates. The most prevalent theory is that "surplus" physicians create demand for surgery. The Graduate Medical Education National Advisory

Committee (GEMNAC, 1980) study revealed that by 1990 there will be a surplus of up to 92,000 physicians.

COST REDUCTION

Second opinion programs seek to reduce costs in three ways. First, they attempt to prevent unnecessary surgery by having a board certified surgeon render his or her opinion of the necessity of the surgery. It has been shown that 85% of those patients not confirmed for surgery do not go on to have the surgery within 6 months (McCarthy, 1985). Secondly, second opinion programs attempt to ward off unnecessary surgery from even being suggested to the patient in the first place. This has been labeled the "sentinel effect." Namely, when a physician knows that his or her patient will have to undergo a second opinion, the primary physician will be more prudent in his or her recommendation (McCarthy, 1979). The third cost reduction is that obtained by having the surgery performed on an outpatient basis. At the time of the consultation the second opinion physician is also requested to determine the appropriate setting for surgery. The physician, living in the same geographical area, is aware of the facilities available to the patient.

There are two cost reductions associated with shifting surgery to an outpatient basis. The first is the monetary difference between inpatient and outpatient care. Berk and Chalmers (1981), in an extensive review of 109 papers, determined that 75 showed there was a lower cost associated with an ambulatory setting. A shortcoming in the studies, the authors noted, was that they often did not take into account earnings lost by the patient and his or her family.

The authors also noted that the source of savings is often not indicated. The majority of the studies reviewed indicated that the quality of care was not sacrificed by the ambulatory setting. Marks et al, in their study of the Kaiser-Permanente Medical Care Program in Oregon (Platt, 1983), concluded that a nationwide program aimed at shifting surgery to an ambulatory setting would save over $750 million annually.

Several studies have raised the question of whether a shift to ambulatory care will reduce the quality of care of the patient (Levin, 1983). Second opinion consultations offer the advantage of a direct "laying-on-of-hand" medical examination rather than a recommendation based on a list of procedures developed by a precertification group. The second opinion program may also intervene to assist in arrangements, if requested by the patient or by the primary physician.

METHOD FOR PROVIDING SECOND OPINIONS

The Health Benefits Research Center of the New York Hospital-Cornell Medical Center provides second opinion consultations for the members and employees of over 2,000 companies, insurance companies, and welfare funds. The patient, when suggested for surgery on the focus list of procedures given below, would contact the center on a toll-free telephone line. The center gives the patient a choice of three board-certified surgeons in a location convenient for the patient. After the patient selects a physician, an appointment is scheduled.

The second opinion physician examines the patient and reviews any tests. At this time the physician indicates to the patient whether the proposed surgery is necessary. If the surgery is necessary, the physician will indicate the appropriate level of care: inpatient, outpatient, or office.

This study examines the results of 5,265 consultations for which a second opinion was rendered. The focus list of procedures for which these companies required second surgical opinion consultations includes

- tonsillectomy/adenoidectomy;
- back surgery;
- breast surgery;
- cataract surgery;
- coronary surgery;
- deviated septum repair;
- foot surgery;
- gall bladder removal;
- hemorrhoidectomy;
- hernia repair;
- hysterectomy;
- knee surgery;
- laparoscopy/D & C; and
- prostatectomy.

RESULTS

The distribution of the procedures for which a second opinion consultation was rendered is displayed in Figure

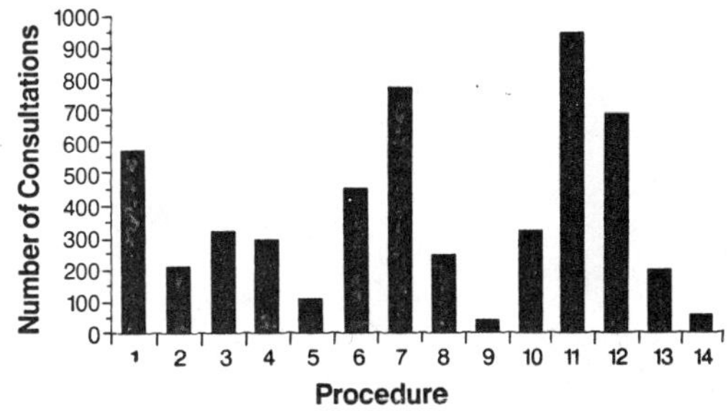

Figure 1. The distribution of procedures for which second opinion consultations were rendered in this study (see Table 1 for list of procedures, numbered 1 to 14).

1. Second opinions were most frequently requested for hysterectomies (951 cases). Knee surgeries (687 cases) and foot surgeries (767 cases) were the second and third most frequently arranged consultations.

Table 1 displays the number of cases for which a second opinion was rendered for each procedure and the number of cases for each procedure that could be performed as outpatient.

Twenty-one percent of the surgical cases confirmed for surgery could, in the opinion of the second opinion physician, be safely shifted to ambulatory care.

The highest shift to ambulatory care was for laparoscopy/D & C (55%). Cataract surgery, with a 43% shift rate, closely followed. Tonsillectomy/adenoidectomy, 20% shift rate, deviated septum, 30% shift rate, knee surgery, 28% shift rate, and hernia surgery 21%, also closely follow. Not surprisingly, several procedures were never suggested for ambulatory care: coronary surgery, gall bladder removal, and hemorrhoidectomy. The other procedures infrequently suggested for ambu-

Table 1. Summary chart showing the confirmed rate and the shift rate to outpatient

	A Procedure	B Confirmed	C Not confirmed	D Total	E Outpatient	F % Not confirmed	G % Outpatient
1	tonsillectomy/adenoidectomy	519	53	572	102	9	20
2	back surgery	169	44	213	3	21	2
3	breast surgery	293	30	323	77	9	10
4	cataract	276	27	303	120	9	43
5	coronary surgery	98	16	114	0	14	0
6	deviated septum	415	42	457	126	9	30
7	foot surgery	620	147	767	204	19	33
8	gall bladder	227	18	245	0	7	0
9	hemorrhoidectomy	39	3	42	0	7	0
10	hernia	312	17	329	64	5	21
11	hysterectomy	852	99	951	25	10	3
12	knee surgery	619	68	687	171	10	28
13	laparoscopy/d & c	177	26	203	97	13	55
14	prostatectomy	53	6	59	1	10	2

latory surgery include: back surgery (2%), breast surgery (10%), hysterectomy (3%), and prostatectomy (2%). The percentage for each procedure of cases that can be performed in an ambulatory surgery is displayed in Figure 2.

DISCUSSION

In an attempt to contain costs and provide improved employee health care, many employers are looking toward second surgical opinion programs. In addition to determining the necessity of the suggested surgery, the second opinion physician can determine the appropriate setting.

Companies often provide a list to their employees of procedures that should be performed on an outpatient basis, such as cataract surgery and D & C. Precertification programs claim that they prescreen patients in order to render an appropriate level of care. The second opinion consultations, however, offer an advantage over a list or telephone screening in that they are

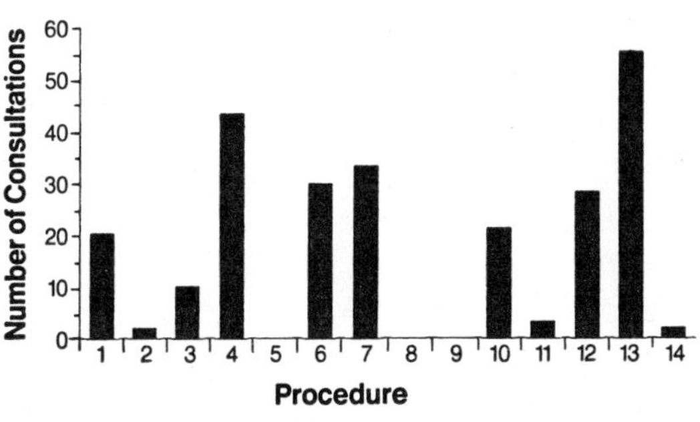

Figure 2. The percentage for each procedure of cases that can be performed on an ambulatory surgery (see Table 1 for list of procedures, numbered 1 to 14).

based on direct patient evaluation. During the course of an examination the physician may evaluate whether there are any complicating conditions that would require that the procedure be performed as inpatient. The physician is also aware of the availability of services in the area, such as outpatient clinics and surgicenters. If the patient is unaware of the availability of ambulatory facilities, the second opinion physician as well as the second opinion program can intercede and provide this information.

The authors' study clearly indicates that 21% of the surgeries covered by the second opinion program could safely be performed as outpatient. If the procedures that are never performed as outpatient are removed (such as coronary surgery), the percentage of cases increases to 23%. The main thrust of the second opinion programs is to reduce unnecessary surgery. In the center's experience in rendering over 250,000 consultations, there has been a 14% nonconfirmed rate for surgery. Further savings are realized through the sentinel effect—physicians will be more hesitant about suggesting surgery if they know that the patient will have to undergo a second opinion consultation.

The use of the second opinion surgeon to determine the level of care has not been previously examined. It appears from this study that this aspect of second opinion consultation should be further pursued and emphasized. Future studies may examine second opinion programs that take this into consideration.

REFERENCES

Berk, A. A., & Chalmers, T. C. (1981). Cost and efficacy of the substitution of ambulatory for inpatient care. *New England Journal of Medicine, 304*(7), 393–397.

Freeland, M. S., & Schendler, C. E. (1984). Health spending in the 1980s: integration of clinical practice patterns in management. *Health Care Financing Review, 5*(3)1–68.

Graduate Medical Education National Advisory Committee. 1980. Summary report to the Secretary, Department of Health and Human Services (DHHS Publication No. HRA 81-651). Washington, DC: Department of Health and Human Services.

Levin, J. M. (1983). Effect of utilization review on surgical training with reference to the increasing importance of the ward service in this changing environment (editorial). *American Journal of Surgery, 145*(2), 191–192.

Marks, S. D., Greenlis, M. R., Hurtado, A. V., Johnson, J. D., & Henderson, J. (1980). Ambulatory surgery in an HMO: a study of costs, quality of care, and satisfaction. *Medical Care, 18*(2) 127–146.

McCarthy, E., Finkel, M., & Ruchlin, H. (1979). Second opinion elective surgery. Boston: Auburn House Publishing Co.

McCarthy, E. (1985). [Analysis of compliance with second opinion consultants recommendation]. Unpublished data.

Moore, S. H., Martin, D. P., & Richardson, W. C. (1983). Does the primary care gatekeeper control the costs of health care? Lessons from the SAFECO experience. *New England Journal of Medicine, 309*(22), 1200–1204.

National Center for Health Statistics, 1982. Discharge summary (DHHS Series 13, No. 78, PHS84–1739). Washington, DC: Department of Health and Human Services.

Platt, R. (1983). Cost containment—another view. *New England Journal of Medicine, 309*(12), 726–730.

Health maintenance organizations: the future of the for-profit plan

Dan Ermann, MPH, MBA
Economist
National Center for Health Services Research
and Health Care Technology Assessment
Public Health Service
Department of Health and Human Services
Rockville, MD

HEALTH MAINTENANCE organizations (HMOs) are not a new phenomenon. The oldest HMO still in existence, the Ross-Loos Health Plan, was organized in 1929 to provide care to employees of the Los Angeles Water Department (Office of Health Maintenance Organizations [HMOs], 1982). Despite their long history, it is only recently that HMOs have become a major force within the health care delivery system and viewed as a potential restraining wall to the ever-rising crest of health expenditures. The for-profit HMO sector is growing rapidly and may well become a dominant factor in the health care delivery system. This article examines for-profit HMOs,

The views expressed in this article are those of the author. No official endorsement by the National Center for Health Services Research and Health Care Technology Assessment is intended or should be inferred. The author wishes to thank Tina Boez, Jon Gabel, Fred Hellinger, Ira Raskin, and Linda Siegenthaler for their helpful comments on earlier drafts of the article.

within the context of the total HMO industry, to assess their future growth and potential impact.

By the late 1970s the focus in health delivery shifted from regulation to competition. The Tax Equity and Fiscal Responsibility Act of 1982 (TEFRA, P.L. 97–248), together with the Social Security Amendments of 1983 established the Medicare Prospective Payment System that, although regulatory in structure, established a payment system with strong hospital cost containment incentives. For the first time hospitals were reimbursed prospectively on a per case basis and not by a cost-plus system. TEFRA also provided for Medicare beneficiaries to obtain their care from prepaid health plans (mainly HMOs). Private industry was also awakening to the health cost dilemma during the late 1970s and early 1980s. Corporations shifted their health care premium structure and coverage of services, and increased deductibles and copayments. Simultaneously, there was a dramatic increase in the use of self-insurance by larger companies (Hart & Luecke, 1984). Interest in HMOs was growing, with more than 50,000 employers offering an HMO to their workers in 1982 (Gardner, Kyzr-Sheeley, & Sabatino, 1985). A survey of the Fortune 500 companies found that the percentage of these major corporations offering an HMO option increased from 76% in 1982 to 82% in 1983 (National Industry Council [NIC] for HMO Development, 1983).

The health care delivery system changed dramatically during this period. New forms of alternative delivery providers (e.g., freestanding ambulatory and surgery centers [Gardner et al., 1983]) expanded geographically, and their numbers flourished. Multihospital systems (both for-profit and nonprofit) became a dominant factor in the hospital field and diversified into many other health delivery arenas, for example, HMOs and preferred provider organizations (PPOs) (Ermann & Gabel, 1984). In this competitive marketplace entrepreneurial firms have appeared and many nonprofit organizations have converted to for-profit corporations. The debate over the role of profit in health care has been heated. Proponents of for-profit providers have argued that their expansion will lead to a more efficient delivery system (Sloan & Becker, 1984). Opponents counter that the profit motive does not belong in health care and that it will lead to a lower quality health care, especially for the poor and disadvantaged (Relman, 1980). The literature and empirical findings are inconclusive, although some industry-specific findings may be made, for example, for-profit multihospital systems are more expensive than comparable independent hospitals (Ermann & Gabel, 1984).

In order to examine the for-profit HMO sector the following questions will be addressed:

- What has been the growth pattern for HMOs? How has the for-profit HMO sector grown, and what are the major factors leading to this growth?
- What has been the effect of for-profit HMOs on cost, quality, and access to care?

- What can we expect the future HMO industry to look like, vis-à-vis the profit status of the organizations? Are there unanswered questions requiring further research of this issue?

Analyses presented in this article rely extensively on data from the Office of Health Maintenance Organizations (OHMO), Department of Health and Human Services (DHHS). OHMO data are supplemented with data from various private and trade association sources. OHMO data may be considered representative of the total HMO industry. Federally qualified HMOs, which comprise this data set, represent approximately 60% of the total number of HMO plans. However, federally qualified HMOs are generally larger than average, and encompass almost 80% of HMO enrollment (Office of Health Maintenance Organizations [HMOs], 1985).

WHAT IS AN HMO?

An HMO is an organization that delivers a stated range of services to a defined enrolled population for a fixed monthly or annual premium. In addition, the HMO must assume at least part of the financial risk and/or gain from providing the services.

What does the "typical" HMO look like? We address this question by examining three characteristics: size, organizational model, and for-profit or not-for-profit ownership.

The first characteristic we will use to describe HMOs is their size. The largest HMO, the Kaiser Foundation Health Plan, Inc., served 4.6 million enrollees in 1984 (Office of HMOs, 1985). Kaiser revenues exceeded $1.7 billion in 1980 with assets valued at over $1.1 billion, including 30 hospitals. Kaiser is one of the largest not-for-profit companies in the world and would rank among the Fortune 250 if it were an industrial company (*Dun's Business Monthly,* 1983). Blue Cross and Blue Shield Association ranks second with two million enrollees; Health Insurance Plan of Greater New York is third with 900,000 enrollees (Tatge, 1985). Although thirteen plans had enrollments exceeding 100,000 in 1980 (Tatge, 1985), by 1984 28 plans had entered this size category. During this period the percentage of total HMO enrollment in plans with more than 100,000 members remained stable at about 60% (National HMO Census of Prepaid Plans, 1980).

There are three organizational models for HMOs: staff, group, and individual practice association (IPA). Under the staff model the HMO employs physicians and provides them with a central office facility and administrative support. Physicians in staff HMOs usually receive a salary plus a bonus based on the HMO's cost performance. Group model HMOs contract with a multispecialty medical group practice and sometimes provide a central medical facility. The medical group receives a monthly capitation fee for each HMO member—regardless of services provided—and reimburses its individual physicians according to its own established practices. Individual practice association HMOs either contract with a physicians' association, which in turn contracts with the individual physician, or contract directly with individual physicians. Physicians provide care in their own offices, usually receiving a percentage of their usual and customary fee. The remaining portion of the fee is often retained by the HMO and paid to the physician later if agreed on cost and utilization targets are met (Office of HMOs, 1982). The dominant organizational form among the 60 largest HMOs is the group model. The IPA model is most common among the rest of the industry (Office of HMOs, 1985), and the dominant for-profit model (Office of HMOs, 1985).

HMOs may be either for-profit or nonprofit entities. For-profit HMOs fall into two general categories: partnerships and corporations. Many for-profits are operated by holding companies. This allows the HMO to incorporate in a state such as Nevada, which levies no general income tax on corporations. Nonprofit HMOs may also be organized in a variety of ways. They may be a cooperative (where profits can be passed through to its members), or a nonprofit nonstock entity such as Kaiser (where income and assets cannot inure to the benefit of private individuals). Nonprofit HMOs need not satisfy demands of equity holders and have greater access to tax-exempt bond issues and donations, however, they are excluded from the equity and venture capital markets and have a more difficult time competing in the debt market (Group Health Foundation [GHF] and National Health Lawyers Association [NHLA], 1982).

HMO GROWTH AND LOCATIONAL PATTERNS

There were 33 HMOs serving about three million enrollees in 1970 (less than 2% of the population) (National Industry Council [NIC] for HMO Development, 1983). By the end of 1984, 366 HMOs (both federally qualified and not) were serving 16.7 million people (over 6% of the population) (Office of HMOs, [SMSA], 1985). Several factors have contributed to the dramatic growth of HMOs. The passage of the Health

The passage of the Health Maintenance Act of 1973 made federal funds available for HMO operating grants and loans. By 1983, OHMO had loaned $364 million. This support helped 115 HMOs, or over 40% of HMOs operating at that time.

Maintenance Act of 1973 made federal funds available for HMO operating grants and loans. By 1983, OHMO had loaned $364 million. This support helped 115 HMOs, or over 40% of HMOs operating at that time (NIC for HMO Development, 1983). In addition, this act requires employers who are subject to minimum wage laws, have 25 or more employees, and offer health care benefits to include local federally qualified HMOs as "dual choice" options in addition to traditional health benefits. This marketing incentive has encouraged many HMOs to apply to be federally qualified. As of August 30, 1985, 204 HMOs had been federally qualified. Since the inception of the program in 1976, only 25 federally qualified HMOs had gone out of business, with none in 1983 and 1984 (Office of HMOs, (Database), 1985).

By the end of 1983, HMOs were operating in 42 states, the District of Columbia, and Guam (NIC for HMO Development, 1983). Although HMO market penetration has historically been highest in the west and upper midwest, eastern and southern states have had the highest growth rates in recent years. Between 1977 and 1982, 25 states had an HMO enrollment growth rate of more than 10%. HMO growth has been concentrated in urban areas. More than 90% of HMO enrollment, and 71% of operational plans, are located in areas with populations of 500,000 or more (Iglehart, 1984). Market penetration varies dramatically between states and regions, as well as between urban and rural areas. California led the nation with an overall market penetration of 19% in 1982, followed by Minnesota with 14%. During this time, market penetration in all standard metropolitan statistical areas (SMSAs) with populations over one million was about 9.7%. However, HMO market penetration for the United States as a whole was only 5.0% (Office of HMOs, 1983). Projections of future HMO growth are high. Frost and Sullivan, a market research firm, predicts HMO enrollment will grow to more than 40 million by 1990. The Congressional Budget Office estimates that enrollment will reach 47 million by 1990 (Tatge, 1985). HMO growth has resulted from increasing enrollment of existing plans, expansion of established plans into new areas (e.g., Kaiser acquired struggling plans in Hartford, Dallas, and Washington, D.C.), and the development of new plans. New plans have been sponsored by a variety of entities, including venture capitalists, nonprofit organizations, corporations (Ford, R. J. Reynolds, and John Deere), and insurance companies (Dun's Business Monthly, 1983). In addition, business coalitions are now more heavily involved in promoting health care cost containment. Some coalitions (e.g., Southeast Louisiana Health Cost Management, Inc.) are attempting to create a competitive atmosphere by encouraging the use of alternate delivery systems (e.g., HMOs [Powills, 1985]).

Figure 1 indicates that for-profit HMOs grew dramatically in 1983. This expansion followed the best year financially for the HMO industry. An OHMO study (based on a sample of the 60 largest HMOs) found 90% of HMOs were operating profitably in 1982, as opposed to only 50% in 1979 (Office of HMOs, 1983). For-profit HMOs are increasingly entering the equity markets in order to obtain needed capital. The first for-profit HMO to trade stock publicly was U.S. Health Care Systems, which converted to for-profit status in September 1981. The stock was offered in February 1983 at $20 a share and its value tripled over the next few months. Six months later U.S. Health Care made a second stock offering, which also sold well (Iglehart, 1984). A number of other for-profits have followed this path to the Wall Street market.

The federal government has actively

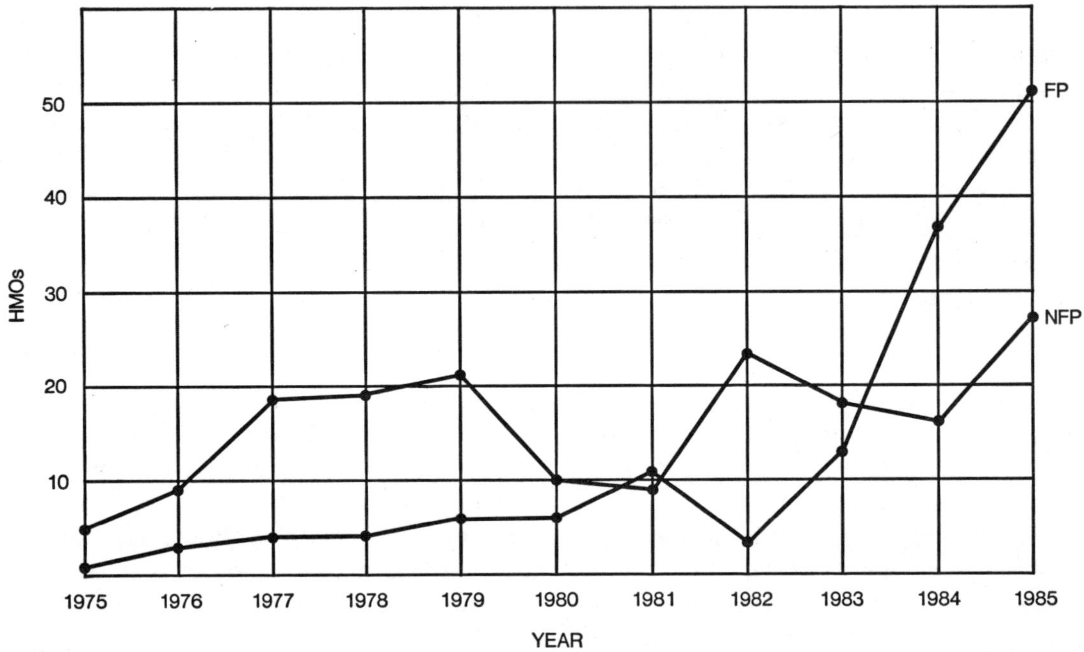

Figure 1. New federally qualified HMOs. FP—For-profit; NFP—nonprofit. Source: Office of Health Maintenance Organizations Data Base, August 1985.

supported the for-profit HMO sector. First, the Tax Equity and Fiscal Responsibility Act of 1982 enabled Medicare and Medicaid beneficiaries to enroll in an HMO. The HMO may be either for-profit or nonprofit, but must be federally qualified. Second, the 1982 change in the federal HMO regulations allows the secretary of the Department of Health and Human Services (DHHS) to "waive all or part of the amount of funds repayable to the secretary" when an HMO converts to for-profit (Code of Federal Regulations, 1983). Third, the DHHS has been supportive of this activity through official press releases and documents (Schweiker, 1982). States have also begun to eliminate their long-standing bans on for-profit health care organizations. New York, for instance, now allows for-profit HMOs (IPAs and nonstaff models) to operate in the state. For-profit publicly traded chains, however, are still prohibited ("New York to Permit," 1985).

As Table 1 shows, 28% of enrollees were in for-profit HMOs in 1984. During 1984, federally qualified HMOs grew at the rate of 196,000 new enrollees per month. Fully half of the growth was attributable to for-profit plans (Office of HMOs, 1985). Of the 14 largest federally qualified HMOs in 1984 (with enrollments exceeding 100,000), 7 were for-profit and 6 were multiplan organizations (see Table 2). There does not appear to be a relationship between for-profit status and the likelihood of being a multiplan organization. It must

Table 1. 1984 federally qualified HMOs (One million enrollees)

Plan	For-profit	Nonprofit	Total
Multiplan system	1.71	4.85	6.56
Single plan	1.59	3.40	4.99
Total	3.30	8.25	11.55

Source: 10th Annual Report to Congress, Fiscal Year 1984, OHMO, DHHS, June 1985.

be noted that this list does not include some of the largest plans (e.g., Blue Cross/Blue Shield and Health Insurance Plan of Greater New York) that are not federally qualified.

A unique database compiled by Mark Schlessinger at Harvard University (1983), provides information on the size and growth of HMOs (Schlessinger, 1983). This database includes all federally qualified, and the largest state qualified, HMOs in 1983 (63 for-profits and 222 nonprofits). It depicts the HMO industry in 1983 and will not reflect changes that have occurred since 1983. This is an especially important limitation when analyzing for-profit HMOs.

In 1983, for-profit HMOs had 50% fewer enrollees than nonprofit HMOs (30,000 vs. 46,000) and were more homogeneous in size. This may be a function of plan age (4.7 years old for for-profits and 7.3 for nonprofits) and the existence of a few very large nonprofits (e.g., Kaiser). Kaiser, with a

Table 2. Fourteen largest federally qualified HMOs–1984

Organization	Enrollment	For-profit/ not-for-profit	Multiplan organization
Kaiser	4,500,000	NFP	MP
Cigna	486,000	FP	MP
Maxicare	396,000	FP	MP
Prudential	356,000	FP	MP
Health Maintenance Network of Southern California	285,000	NFP	
HMO of PA (Pennsylvania)	194,000	FP	
Harvard Community Health Plan	178,000	FP	
Family Health Program	165,000	NFP	MP
MedCenters Health Care, Inc.	164,000	NFP	
Health Alliance Plan of Michigan	139,000	NFP	
International Medical Centers, Inc.	136,000	FP	
Physicians Health Plan of Minnesota	133,000	NFP	
Group Health Association	115,000	NFP	
HMO Illinois	109,000	FP	MP

Source: 10th Annual Report to Congress, Fiscal Year 1984, OHMO, DHHS, June 1985.

1984 enrollment of 4.5 million (38% of federally qualified HMO enrollment and 29% of total enrollment), dwarfs all other plans and significantly influences all industry averages. The for-profits, however, enrolled more new members in 1983 than did nonprofits (Schlessinger, 1983).

In terms of market characteristics (average hospital length of stay, occupancy, days per 1,000 population, admissions per 1,000 population, and average hospital cost per capita), for-profits appear to locate in areas similar to nonprofits. For-profits locate in more populous areas with, surprisingly, a lower local cost of living ($24,459 vs. $25,430). Similar to the hospital industry, the recent trend is toward larger, multistate organizations. Multistate plans are usually networks of HMOs affiliated by ownership or management. These plans, often operated by a holding company, are both for-profit (e.g., HealthAmerica Corporation with 37 plans in 1984) and nonprofit (e.g., Kaiser Health Plans with 11 plans in 1984) (Tatge, 1985). In mid-1982, 69% of total HMO enrollment was accounted for by multistate plans. By mid-1983, these plans accounted for 83% of total HMO enrollment (NIC for HMO Development, 1983). HMOs owned by multihospital systems reported the largest percentage increase in enrollment, up 26.7% to 1.68 million enrollees in 1984 (Tatge, 1985). This may reflect the multihospital systems' desire to develop total health care delivery systems. This synergistic relationship affords the system greater control over their patient flow while assisting the HMO with subsidized rates.

WHY FOR-PROFIT HMOs GROW

There are a number of claims proffered as justification in favor of for-profit HMOs. First, as mentioned earlier, it is asserted that for-profits instill greater cost consciousness and operate in a more cost-effective manner. The factors that may lead to cost savings include: increased efficiency, greater access to less expensive capital, and economies of scale. Although the literature dealing with HMOs is voluminous, there is little empirical analysis. There is no conceptual reason to believe that for-profits should achieve greater economies of scale than nonprofits. However, corporately organized (for-profit status) HMOs are purportedly able to "generate otherwise unavailable capital through equity financing, [able] to offer more attractive employee incentives, and [operate with] a simpler corporate and administrative structure (Dunn & Shields, 1984). For-profit HMOs are in a good position to reward management for outstanding achievement through financial incentives. They are not faced with the prohibitions faced by the nonprofits and may establish profit-sharing plans and incentive stock option plans (GHF and NHLA, 1982).

The most compelling force driving nonprofit HMOs to convert to for-profit is their need to acquire capital to maintain operations and expand into new locations. It has been estimated that capital needs for the HMO industry will be as high as $8.4 billion for the decade of the 80s (S. Sheingold, personal communication, April 20, 1981). The substantial capital needs result from start-up costs associated with establishment of new HMOs and capital required by mature plans that are growing and acquiring more sophisticated plant (e.g., laboratories) and expanded facilities (e.g., owned hospitals). As Leonard Schaeffer, president of Group Health (a large nonprofit HMO) said, "Capital markets are only interested in for-profit entities. It is not our desire to become for-profit that drives us in this direction. It is our determination to compete" (GHF and NHLA, 1982). This move toward the debt market appears to be increasing. It was reported in mid-1984 that "at least 38 HMOs with a minimum of 50,000 members will be able to obtain financing from the capital markets" (Group Health Association of America, Inc., 1984). Although nonprofit HMOs have obtained capital from the sale of tax-exempt state bonds, this source has been limited because many state bonding authority enabling statutes do not include nonprofit HMOs as eligible participants.

The search for new capital has been spurred by the elimination of federal grants and loans. No federal loan or grant has been awarded to an HMO since 1982. Prior to 1982 the private sector was supplying substantial amounts of capital. Between 1974 and 1980, 83% of total HMO investment was funded by the private sector (Private Sector Investment, 1981). However, when one excludes plans operated by national HMO firms, or sponsored by Blue Cross/Blue Shield, the federal government accounted for 70% of funding for independent HMOs (Private Sector Investment in HMOs: A Case Study, 1982). Although it does appear that for-profits and multistate plans have greater access to capital, there is no evidence of the impact of these organizational forms on the "cost" of capital.

Multistate HMOs, because of their larger size, are in a better bargaining position for negotiating hospital discounts, obtaining needed capital, and growing. These large systems will undoubtedly strive for economies of scale and improved management through shared purchasing and data systems, capital development, and national account marketing (NIC for HMO Development, 1983). There is, however, no evidence of this yet.

Multistate HMOs, because of their larger size, are in a better bargaining position for negotiating hospital discounts, obtaining needed capital, and growing.

Numerous studies have probed HMOs to discern the reasons for their lower health care costs. Although there is limited research examining the efficiency of HMOs, there is no evidence that HMOs are more efficient in their delivery of specific services. In terms of the mix of services HMOs produce, HMOs are more efficient. The consensus is that HMOs' lower costs are primarily attributable to lower hospital utilization (Luft & Trauner, 1981). No studies have assessed the efficiency of for-profits vis-à-vis nonprofits.

COST, QUALITY, AND ACCESS

Future growth of the for-profit sector will depend on its ability to compete on both cost and quality. The database compiled by Schlessinger provides some insights into the cost comparisons between for-profits and nonprofits (Schlessinger, 1983). These data show for-profits to be more costly. For-profits had a higher cost per inpatient day ($538 vs. $492), higher average total ambulatory cost ($364 vs. $330), and higher average inpatient cost per enrollee ($214 vs. $196). In addition, for-profits averaged higher revenues per enrollee ($696 vs. $654). It is impossible to discern from these data the causes for the higher costs (e.g., higher utilization; higher capital costs; newer, more expensive facilities; different patient mix; greater use of ancillary services; or inefficient operations). However, this does force a careful evaluation of the consequences of the profit motive in HMOs and the significance for the payers of health care (government, employers, and consumers).

Surprisingly, the Schlessinger data show for-profits to have a negative average margin per member ($.81), whereas nonprofits show a positive margin ($1.20). Again, this could be due to a variety of factors, including the inclusion of a few very large, successful nonprofits (e.g., Kaiser), which could bias the data; the significant difference in age between for-profits and nonprofits; or even accounting variations.

There is an ongoing controversy concerning the quality of care provided in prepaid plans. This concern surfaced as a result of the change in use of hospital services, with the emphasis on outpatient care, distrust by the medical profession, and possible lack of knowledge by the general public. Luft, in his exhaustive review of the HMO literature, states, "One commonly held assumption is that HMOs achieve lower costs by underserving and skimping on quality. There is very little evidence to support this notion. The quality of care in HMOs seems comparable to or somewhat better than the community average (Luft & Trauner, 1981, p. 57). There is no research examining the quality of care delivered in for-profit HMOs. However, the Schlessinger data do provide us with one structural measure of quality. For-profits had a much higher ratio of physicians to members than did nonprofits (2.77 physicians per 1,000 members vs. 1.94 physicians per 1,000) (Schlessinger, 1983). This information, while useful, is too limited for arriving at any conclusions.

A last question is the willingness of HMOs to serve the disadvantaged. There is little information on this. Recent changes in federal and state laws now allow HMOs to serve the poor (Medicaid) and the elderly (Medicare). The Schlessinger data show nonprofits serving a greater percentage of Medicare eligibles (5.04% vs. 2.98%), although neither percentage is very high. Nonprofit plans cover more Medicaid beneficiaries (198,000) than do for-profits (138,000) (Schlessinger, 1983). Again, neither type of HMO enrolls many Medicaid beneficiaries, and a few plans account for the majority of Medicaid patients.

• • •

HMOs are playing an increasingly important part in the health care delivery system. The HMO industry has grown in terms of number of plans, enrollment, and market share. Many of the forces that are expected to facilitate HMO growth will undoubtedly assist for-profits in particular. Some of the major factors responsible for HMO growth include (a) the abundant oversupply of physicians and hospitals, (b) increased acceptance of HMO practice by physicians (Louis Harris and Associates, 1984), (c) high levels of satisfaction with HMO care by enrollees (Louis Harris and Associates, 1984), (d) the continuing search for an efficient, less-expensive mode of care by insurers, employers, government, and consumers and their acknowledgment of the potential of the HMO delivery approach, and (e) changes in federal and state laws encouraging HMO growth. These forces appear to be culminating in a world of increased price competition in health care.

Against this backdrop of continuing HMO growth, what does the future portend for the for-profit organization? There is every reason to believe that for-profit HMOs will play a major role in this industry. As in the past, this growth will probably result from the development of new for-profit entities as well as the conversion of nonprofits to for-profit. "Conversions are seen by health care officials as a trend toward more fierce competition among health care insurers as a means of survival, a way of raising capital and a response to pressures from the government, business, and labor to hold down health care costs" (Renech, 1984). The termination of federal support for HMOs has had the same effect as in the hospital field. HMOs in need of capital have found the private capital markets attractive and are assuming a for-profit status in order to compete for available funds.

Although some data reported on above suggest that some for-profits may not be financially strong (with negative margins), the investor market has continued to support this sector with needed capital. What we may be observing are the financial strains faced by young organizations in their formative stage. Some of these pressures may be a result of recent growth and acquisition of financially weak HMOs. It should be emphasized that no federally qualified HMO has gone out of business since 1983, an indication of the industry's financial strength (Office of HMOs, 1985).

There also exists the move toward larger, organizationally diversified HMOs. These larger organizations will unquestionably strive for economies of scale and a better position in the financial markets. There is also some evidence that they are attempting to diversify into such areas as contract management (Millenson, 1982). This emulates the strategy employed by the multihospital systems that have been very successful in recent years.

Although this article concludes with an optimistic appraisal of the for-profit HMO sector, there are possible impediments to their growth. The competitive market for health care that has fostered HMO growth may also be a factor in constraining future expansion. For example, there is evidence that many PPOs, which are growing at a phenomenal rate, are competing directly with HMOs (Rice, de Lissovoy, Gabel, Ermann, 1985). In addition, "competitive medical plans," defined under TEFRA to combine many HMO characteristics with experience-rated premiums and deductibles, may in the future provide serious competition for the HMO industry.

This review has highlighted the need for further research. A few of the more important issues include

- Are there organizational and structural differences between for-profit and nonprofit HMOs that affect their delivery of care and use of resources?
- Are there differences in the cost of care delivered at HMOs depending on their tax status?
- Does the profit orientation of the plan influence the quality of care?
- Do for-profit and nonprofit HMOs employ different marketing strategies? What are the implications for various segments of the disadvantaged population (e.g., the elderly or the poor)?
- Do for-profit HMOs use different criteria for selecting areas in which to locate?

REFERENCES

Code of Federal Regulations, United States Public Health Service Act 42 U.S.C. Section 110, January 12, 1983.

Dunn, K., & Shields, G. (1984). For-profit status creates new financing opportunities. *Healthcare Financial Management, 14*(12), 36–46.

Ermann, D., & Gabel, J. (1984). Multihospital systems: Issues and empirical findings. *Health Affairs, 3*(1), 50–64.

Ermann, D., & Gabel, J. (1985). The changing face of American health care: Multihospital systems, emergency centers and surgery centers. *Medical Care, 23*(5), 401–420.

Gardner, S., Kyzr-Sheeley, B., & Sabatino, F. (1985). Big business embraces alternative delivery. *Hospitals, 59*(6), 84.

The Group Health Foundation and The National Health Lawyers Association. (1982). *HMOs and the law: Legal issues for HMO lawyers and managers.* pp. 8–11.

Group Health Association of America, Inc. (1984, April). *Group Health News,* p. 2.

Hart, J., & Luecke, R. (1984). Corporate health care costs: A strategy for containment. *Corporate Accounting, 2*(4), 12–19.

Iglehart, J. (1984). Health policy report: HMOs (for-profit and not-for-profit) on the move. *New England Journal of Medicine, 310*(18), 1204.

Louis Harris and Associates, Inc. (1984). *A Report Card on HMOs: 1980–1984.* New York, NY: Author.

Luft, H., & Trauner, J. (1981). *The operations and performance of health maintenance organizations: A synthesis of findings from health services research.* San Francisco: University of California School of Medicine, Institute for Health Policy Studies.

Millenson, M. "Investors Eye HMOs As A Way To Remain Financially Healthy," *Chicago Tribune,* Chicago, Illinois, May 18, 1982.

National HMO Census: 1984. (1984). Interstudy, Excelsior, MN: Author.

National HMO Census of Prepaid Plans: June 1980. (1980). Interstudy, Excelsior, MN: Author.

National Industry Council for HMO Development. Group Health Association. (1983). *The Health*

Maintenance Organization Industry Ten-Year Report: 1973–1983, Washington, DC: Author.

New funding for health care. (1983, March). *Dun's Business Monthly,* p. 140.

New York to permit for-profit IPA HMOs. (1985, September). *Washington Report on Medicine and Health, 39*(36), 2.

Office of Health Maintenance Organizations. (1982). *Investor's Guide to Health Maintenance Organizations* (DHHS p. 9). Washington, DC: U.S. Government Printing Office.

Office of Health Maintenance Organizations. (1982). *Private Sector Investment in Health Maintenance Organizations: A Case Study of Debt Financing.* Washington, DC: Department of Health and Human Services.

Office of Health Maintenance Organizations. (1983). *The 1983 Investor's Guide to Health Maintenance Organizations* (DHHS 83-50202). Washington, DC: Department of Health and Human Services.

Office of Health Maintenance Organizations. (1985). number of HMOs, enrollment, and penetration by standard metropolitan statistical area (SMSA). Department of Health and Human Services, Washington, DC: Author.

Office of Health Maintenance Organizations. (1985). *OHMO Data Base.* Department of Health and Human Services, Washington, D.C.: Author.

Office of Health Maintenance Organizations. (1985). *10th Annual Report to the Congress, Fiscal Year 1984.* Washington, DC: Department of Health and Human Services.

Powills, S. (1985). Business needs spur HMO, PPA growth. *Hospitals, 59*(18), 98–99.

Private Sector Investment in HMOs: 1974–1980. (1981, June). Interstudy, Excelsior, MN: Author.

Relman, A. (1980). The new medical-industrial complex. *New England Journal of Medicine, 303*(17), 963–970.

Renech, D. (1984, February 11). Plan for profit-making HMO draws fire from some in area health establishment. *Journal.*

Rice, T., de Lissovoy, G., Gabel, J., & Ermann, D. (in press). The state of PPOs: Results from a national survey. *Health Affairs.*

Schlessinger, M. (1983). *HM database.* Center for Health Policy and Management, Harvard University. Harvard, MA.

Schweiker, R. (1982). HMOs: a healthy investment. *National Journal, 14*(48), 2052–2053.

Sloan, F., & Becker, E. (1984). For-profits vs. non-profits: A phantom issue. *Technology Review, 87*(3), 11–15.

Tatge, B. M. (1985). HMO enrollment up 26.7% to 1.68 million. *Modern Healthcare, 15*(12), 140.

Index

O

P

Q

R